The Mosaic Tradition

NEAR AND MIDDLE EAST SERIES

1. The Mosaic Tradition. *By F. V. Winnett*

וַיֹּאמֶר יְהוָה אֶל־מֹשֶׁה וַיֹּאמֶר יְהוָה אֶל־מֹשֶׁה

The Mosaic Tradition

BY

FREDERICK VICTOR WINNETT

Associate Professor of Semitic Languages
University College
University of Toronto

Toronto, 1949
UNIVERSITY OF TORONTO PRESS

וַיֹּאמֶר יְהוָה אֶל־מֹשֶׁה וַיֹּאמֶר יְהוָה אֶל־מֹשֶׁה

Copyright, Canada, 1949
University of Toronto Press
Printed in Canada
London: Geoffrey Cumberlege
Oxford University Press

Reprinted in 2018
ISBN 978-1-4875-7322-5 (paper)

To my beloved Teacher

Dr. W. R. Taylor
Principal of University College
and
Head of the Department of Oriental Languages

Preface

FOR WELLNIGH SEVENTY YEARS OLD TESTAMENT SCHOLARSHIP has been under the spell of the Wellhausen Hypothesis according to which the Hexateuch is a combination of four literary sources, namely J, E, D, and P (this being their chronological order), with numerous additions and retouchings by editors denoted by the symbols Rje, Rd, and Rp. It is true that some scholars of a conservative bent of mind have refused to adopt this hypothesis but the majority have accepted it as providing the most satisfactory solution of the numerous problems which the Hexateuch presents, and any modifications proposed have been largely in the nature of attempts to show that the four major documents are themselves a compound of diverse elements. Thus Eissfeldt has attempted to demonstrate the existence of an L (lay) Document,[1] Pfeiffer an S (Seirite, Edomite) Document,[2] Morgenstern a K (Kenite) Document.[3] Others speak of J_1, J_2, J_3, E_1, E_2, E_3, and of P_g, P_s, and P_z.[4] The plain truth is, the documentary analysis of the Hexateuch has become an exceedingly complex affair, as reference to the most recent *Introduction to the Old Testament*, that by Pfeiffer, will show. A student approaching the subject for the first time may well feel that the Hexateuch is such a hodge-podge that no reliable reconstruction of Hebrew history and religion can ever be built upon it.

In recent years there have been signs of a reaction against the absurdities of the position to which this fragmentary hypothesis has led us. Dr. Edward Robertson remarks: "When you can subdivide your main documents into two, three, four or more 'hands' the disintegration of the theory

---

[1] *Hexateuch-Synopse* (Leipzig, 1922).

[2] Cf. the references in his *Introduction to the Old Testament* (New York, 1941), pp. 159-67.

[3] "The Oldest Document of the Hexateuch," *HUCA*, IV (1927), 1-138.

[4] Cf. Eissfeldt, "The Literature of Israel: Modern Criticism" in *Record and Revelation*, ed. H. Wheeler Robinson (Oxford, 1938), chap. II.

comes perilously near."¹ H. M. and N. K. Chadwick also declare that "it is indeed difficult for a student of early Western literature to resist the suspicion that this analysis has been carried too far."² The reaction has taken the form, first, of an attack on the generally accepted date for Deuteronomy and second, of a denial of the existence of an E Document. Welch³ has led the attack on Deuteronomy but his views have not met with general acceptance.⁴ Volz and Rudolph⁵ have led the attack on E but their views have not found favour either. I am convinced, however, that the basic contention of Volz and Rudolph is correct, although I cannot always agree with the manner in which they have worked their thesis out.

My own view, in so far as the Books of Exodus and Numbers are concerned, is that they constitute one primary source, the Mosaic Tradition, which has been supplemented and touched up and rearranged here and there by P. To apply to it either of the traditional symbols, J or E, is apt to be misleading. But if a choice must be made between them, then I would employ J, though only on condition that J be recognized as a product of the Northern Kingdom. For there is no doubt in my own mind that the national tradition of the Israelite people took shape in the Northern Kingdom.⁶

[1]"The Pentateuchal Problem: Some New Aspects," *Bulletin of the John Rylands Library*, XXIX (1945), 141. See also his "Temple and Torah: Suggesting an Alternative to the Graf-Wellhausen Hypothesis" in the same *Bulletin*, XXVI (1942), 183-205. For other reactions against the Wellhausen theory, see J. Coppens, *The Old Testament and the Critics* (Eng. trans.; Paterson, N.J., 1942); W. F. Albright, "Archaeology Confronts Biblical Criticism," *American Scholar*, VII (1938), 176-88; and W. C. Graham, "Higher Criticism Survives Archaeology," *ibid.*, 409-27.

[2]*The Growth of Literature* (Cambridge, 1936), II, 630.

[3]*The Code of Deuteronomy: A New Theory of Its Origin* (London, 1924) and *Deuteronomy: The Framework of the Code* (London, 1932).

[4]Cf. *JBL*, XLVII (1928), 305-79.

[5]Volz, *Grundsätzliches zur Elohistischen Frage: Untersuchung von Genesis 15-36*, Beiheft *ZAW*, LXIII (Berlin, 1933); Rudolph, *Der "Elohist" von Exodus bis Josua*, Beiheft *ZAW*, LXVIII (Berlin, 1938). The covering title for both works is *Der Elohist als Erzähler—ein Irrweg der Pentateuchkritik?* The view of both scholars is that the materials assigned to E either belong to J or are a miscellaneous mass of supplements to J from various hands and periods. See the review by R. E. Wolfe in *JBL*, LX (1941), 417ff.

[6]This is also the view of the Chadwicks, *The Growth of Literature*, II, 701f.

Preface

However, evidence will be presented below to show that shortly after the fall of the Northern Kingdom in 722 B.C., the Southern Kingdom under Hezekiah (c. 715-687 B.C.) took advantage of the extinction of its rival to issue a revised version of the national tradition, one which was definitely biased in favour of Judaean prejudices and claims. As time went on the Southerners grew bolder, until in the seventh century B.C. they dared to put out a completely recast version of the Mosaic Tradition which took the form of the Book of Deuteronomy. In the post-exilic period an attempt was made by P (the Jerusalemite priesthood) to harmonize the original tradition with the Deuteronomic version of it but the result was only "confusion worse confounded." The key to the Pentateuchal problem lies in a recognition of the fact that the tradition in its present form reflects the claim of the Jerusalem sanctuary and priesthood to primacy over the Northern, "Samaritan," priesthood and sanctuary, a claim which was without historical foundation.

If it be objected that in the following pages not enough attention has been paid to the reading of the Versions, let it be said that our first duty is to try and explain the Hebrew text that we have. The problem of Pentateuchal interpretation is primarily an historical problem, not a textual problem. Once we have solved the historical problem, the remarkable trustworthiness of the Massoretic text will become apparent. The variations of the Versions seem to be largely due to a failure to interpret the historical evidence correctly.

I wish to acknowledge my indebtedness to my colleagues, Professors T. J. Meek and W. S. McCullough, and to Professor W. A. Irwin of the Oriental Institute, University of Chicago, for reading my manuscript and making numerous suggestions for its correction and improvement. They are not, however, to be held in any way responsible for the views expressed. I also wish to thank Mr. S. Campbell, B.A., who drew the map which appears at the end of the volume, and Miss F. G. Halpenny, M.A., whose painstaking editorial labours improved the MS at many points.

F. V. W.

Abbreviations

AASOR	*Annual of the American Schools of Oriental Research*
AJSL	*American Journal of Semitic Languages*
BASOR	*Bulletin of the American Schools of Oriental Research*
HTR	*Harvard Theological Review*
HUCA	*Hebrew Union College Annual*
JAOS	*Journal of the American Oriental Society*
JBL	*Journal of Biblical Literature*
JEA	*Journal of Egyptian Archaeology*
JPOS	*Journal of the Palestine Oriental Society*
PEF Annual	*Palestine Exploration Fund Annual*
ZAW	*Zeitschrift für die alttestamentliche Wissenschaft*

Contents

Preface		vii
I	The Story of the Plagues	3
II	The Tradition of the Oppression and of the Raising-up of a Deliverer	16
III	The Tradition of the Law-Giving	30
IV	The Tradition of the Tent of Meeting and of Moses' Father-in-Law	57
V	The Tradition of the Wilderness Itinerary	70
VI	The Tradition of the Ten Murmurings or Testings	121
VII	The Corruption of the Mosaic Tradition by the Jerusalem Priests	155
Appendix: The Original Form of the Mosaic Tradition		173
Map: The Problem of the Exodus and Wilderness Journey		facing 206
Index of Subjects		207
Index of Authors		213
Index of Scriptural Passages		214

The Mosaic Tradition

"He it is who hath sent down to thee the Book; in it are clearly formulated verses; these are the mother of the Book..." (Koran 3:5).

I The Story of the Plagues[1]

IT IS EASIER TO DEMONSTRATE THE INADEQUACY OF THE current theory of the composition of the Hexateuch by a close study of one portion of the field than by a survey of the whole. Therefore, I have chosen to confine my investigation to that part of the Hexateuch dealing with the life of Moses, which will be referred to hereafter as the Mosaic Tradition.

In approaching the study of this tradition I shall not begin with the earlier chapters of the Book of Exodus but with the Story of the Plagues in Ex. 7-12 because this story possesses such unmistakable evidences of unity of design that it lends itself admirably to an exposure of the weaknesses inherent in the accepted theory of documentary admixture. Smend[2] has drawn attention to the presence in the narrative of an "artistic rhythm" and recognizes that this implies unity of authorship; but he confines this observation to the seven plague stories which he regards as the work of J_2 (viz., Scenes I, II, IV, V, VII, VIII, X). I believe it can be shown that not only these seven but all ten plague stories conform to a definite literary pattern and that this pattern presupposes unity of authorship.

The various plague stories, like the stories of the *shôfetîm* in the Book of Judges, can be broken up into three parts: an Introductory Formula, a Central Core, and a Concluding Formula. Let us examine each of these elements separately.

THE INTRODUCTORY FORMULAE

A review of the Introductory Formulae will show that the setting of the ten scenes is arranged as follows:

---

[1]The substance of this chapter was presented as a paper at the seventh annual meeting of the Canadian section of the Society of Biblical Literature and Exegesis, 1944.

[2]*Die Erzählung des Hexateuch* (Berlin, 1912), pp. 126ff.

4   *The Mosaic Tradition*

⎧ I   The interview with Pharaoh occurs *outside* (7:14-17).
⎪ II   "   "   "   "   "   *inside* (7:26f.,
⎨   EV 8:1f.).
⎪ III   The place of the interview is not stated (8:12,
⎩   EV 8:16).

⎧ IV   The interview with Pharaoh occurs *outside* (8:16f.,
⎪   EV 8:20f.).
⎨ V   "   "   "   "   "   *inside* (9:1-3).
⎩ VI   The place of the interview is not stated (9:8).

⎧ VII   The interview with Pharaoh occurs *outside* (9:13f.).
⎨ VIII "   "   "   "   "   *inside* (10:1-4).
⎩ IX   The place of the interview is not stated (10:21).

   X   The place of the interview is not stated (11:1a).

A thrice-repeated pattern is apparent in Scenes I-IX; Scene X manifestly stands outside the schematic arrangement. This arrangement can scarcely be accidental; nor is it probable that the process of documentary admixture presupposed by most scholars would produce such a result. It is surely more reasonable to see in this pattern the work of a single mind striving after stylistic arrangement.[1]

Modern analysis of the Introductory Formulae rests primarily on the observation that in some Aaron wields the rod at the bidding of Moses while in others Moses himself is the wielder. All references to Aaron are regarded as later insertions by P or Rp. But scholars have failed to perceive that the placing of the rod in the hand of Aaron can be regarded as further evidence of the original author's striving after schematic arrangement and artistic effect. In the first three scenes he places the rod in the hand of Aaron (7:19; 8:1, EV 8:5; 8:12, EV 8:16), in the next three the rod is not mentioned (cf. 8:26, EV 8:30; 9:6; 9:10), in the following three the rod is placed in Moses' hand (9:22f.; 10:12f.; 10:21f.[2]). Surely this arrangement is not the chance result of

[1] The schematic arrangement of the plague stories was noticed by W. H. Green; cf. H. M. Wiener, *Essays in Pentateuchal Criticism* (Oberlin, Ohio, 1909), pp. 72f.

[2] The rod is not actually mentioned in 10:21f. but it would seem to be implied. Cf. 14:21, 26f. with 14:16.

haphazard literary growth, nor can it be due to later "doctoring-up" by the hand of P editors. It has all the earmarks of being part of the design borne by the drama from the beginning.

Indeed, the assumption that Aaron is a late importation into the narrative rests on a very shaky foundation. The theory has been buttressed by three arguments: (i) The employment of a singular verb before the mention of Moses and Aaron in 8:8 (EV 8:12) and 10:3 indicates that only one subject was mentioned originally. (ii) In several instances where Moses and Aaron are represented as going in to interview Pharaoh, only Moses comes out (cf. 8:21 and 8:26, EV 8:25 and 8:30; 9:27 and 9:33; 10:3 and 10:6; 10:16 and 10:18). (iii) According to 3:18 Moses *and the elders* are to interview the king of Egypt. Therefore the present form of 5:1 which states that Moses *and Aaron* interviewed Pharaoh must be due to a later redactor.[1] Moreover, it is clear from 7:8—11:10, where Moses is constantly the speaker, that Aaron did not figure as Moses' prophet in all the narratives of the Exodus.[2]

In reply to the first argument it may be noted that the employment of a singular verb before a compound subject is quite normal in Hebrew.[3] In reply to the second argument it may be urged that it was both more convenient and more effective from the dramatic point of view to have the action following the exit from Pharaoh's presence centred in one figure. In reply to the third argument it may be pointed out that the author could not very well mention Aaron in 3:18 without spoiling his story of Moses' hesitancy about undertaking the role of deliverer and the appointment of Aaron as his assistant.

Moreover, an acceptance of the theory that the references to Aaron are not original but secondary involves a denial of the whole present form of the tradition which asserts unequivocally that Aaron acted as Moses' spokesman in the nego-

---

[1] Cf. W. Rudolph, *Der "Elohist" von Exodus bis Josua*, Beih. ZAW, LXVIII (Berlin, 1938), 15.
[2] Cf. A. Kuenen, *The Hexateuch* (Eng. trans.; London, 1886), p. 150.
[3] Cf. Gesenius-Kautzsch, *Hebrew Grammar* (2nd Eng. ed.), § 146 f, g.

tiations leading up to the Exodus. Thus scholars have been forced to get rid of 4: 13-16—where Yahweh promises to send Aaron to meet Moses and to make him Moses' mouthpiece—by assigning it to Rje. But they have been unable to dispose of 4: 27-30 which relates how this promise was carried out. Verses 27 and 28 have been assigned to E and 29-31 to J. Aaron's name is excised at the beginning of v. 29, but v. 30 still remains which states that "Aaron spoke all the words which Yahweh had spoken to Moses and performed the signs in the sight of the people."[1] The attempt to do away with Aaron must thus be pronounced a failure.[2] It is quite possible that in an earlier *oral* form of the Exodus tradition Aaron played a less conspicuous role. The fact that Joshua rather than Aaron was Moses' earliest assistant in the Tent of Meeting suggests that the tradition which makes Aaron Moses' spokesman from the beginning is not historical. All that I am concerned to urge here is that in the written form of the tradition as it now appears in the Book of Exodus (even after the P portions are excised) the figure of Aaron is an integral part. The historicity of the account is another matter.[3] Let us turn now to an examination of the Concluding Formulae.

THE CONCLUDING FORMULAE

SCENE I (7: 22b)
    And the heart of Pharaoh became stubborn (*wa-yeḥezaq*)
    And he did not listen to them, just as Yahweh had said.

SCENE II (8: 11b, EV 8: 15b)
    And he hardened (*we-hakbed*, Sam. *wa-yakbed*) his heart
    And he did not listen to them, just as Yahweh had said.

SCENE III (8: 15b, EV 8: 19b)
    And the heart of Pharaoh became stubborn (*wa-yeḥezaq*)
    And he did not listen to them, just as Yahweh had said.

---

[1] Rudolph would alter "Aaron" to "he" and "Moses" to "him."
[2] This is also the opinion of R. E. Wolfe, *JBL*, LX (1941), 419, and Wiener, *Essays in Pentateuchal Criticism*, pp. 64ff.
[3] That there was even a written tradition in which the figure of Aaron was less conspicuous will be shown below, p. 27.

The Story of the Plagues

SCENE IV (8:28, EV 8:32)
> And Pharaoh hardened (*wa-yakbed*) his heart this time also
> And he did not let the people go.

SCENE V (9:7*b*)
> And the heart of Pharaoh became hard (*wa-yikbad*)
> And he did not let the people go.

SCENE VI (9:12)
> And Yahweh made the heart of Pharaoh stubborn (*wa-yeḥazzeq*)
> And he did not listen to them, just as Yahweh had said to Moses.

SCENE VII (9:35)
> And the heart of Pharaoh became stubborn (*wa-yeḥezaq*)
> And he did not let the Israelites go, just as Yahweh had said through (LXX, unto) Moses.

SCENE VIII (10:20)
> And Yahweh made the heart of Pharaoh stubborn (*wa-yeḥazzeq*)
> And he did not let the Israelites go.

SCENE IX (10:27)
> And Yahweh made the heart of Pharaoh stubborn (*wa-yeḥazzeq*)
> And he was not willing to let them go.

The Concluding Formula in 11:10*b*, "And Yahweh made the heart of Pharaoh stubborn [*wa-yeḥazzeq*] and he did not let the Israelites go from his land," comes before the narration of the tenth plague and is probably not a part of the original narrative but the work of P.[1]

The stylistic arrangement of these Concluding Formulae might be presented in tabular form thus (the capital letter denoting the first line of the formula, the small letter denoting the second line):

$$\text{I} \quad K + a$$
$$\text{II} \quad L + a$$

---

[1] For a further discussion of 11:10*b*, see pp. 11f.

III $K + a$
IV $L + b$
V $M + b$
VI $N + c$
VII $K + d \ldots$
VIII $N + d$
IX $N +$ variant of d

It will be observed that in I to IV there is an alternation between clause K and clause L in the first line; in VI to IX clause N prevails, except in VII where it is quite possible that the Massoretic text is at fault in pointing the verb as a *Qal* rather than a *Pi'el* which, with the insertion of *Yahweh*, would give us a clause of the N type. In the second line of these Concluding Formulae we note evidence of a striving after schematic arrangement also. The fact that the number nine cannot be divided evenly perhaps accounts for the presence of a different type of clause at the beginning of V and at the end of VI.

Reference to the Hebrew original strengthens the impression that these Concluding Formulae proceed from the hand of a single author, for we find an alternation in the first four formulae between *wa-yeḥezaq* and *wa-yakbed*,[1] a different form *wa-yikbad* in V which is the middle scene of the series, and the form *wa-yeḥazzeq* in the last four formulae except in Scene VII where, as has been indicated, there is a deviation which probably crept in during the oral transmission of the story.

The ordinary documentary analysis[2] of these Concluding Formulae has assigned types $K + a$ (Scenes I and III) and $N + c$ (Scene VI) to P. The formula of Scene II ($L + a$) is broken up, the L part being assigned to J, the a part to P.

[1] Adopting the reading of the Samaritan Version in Scene II.
[2] Here and elsewhere in this volume, I have given the documentary analysis as presented in A. H. McNeile's *Exodus* and L. E. Binns' *Numbers* (Westminster Commentaries). A catalogue of all the variations proposed in the different commentaries would only becloud the main issue. Convenient summaries of these will be found in E. S. Brightman, *The Sources of the Hexateuch* (New York, 1918) and Rudolph, *op. cit.* Cf. also the foot-notes to R. Kittel, *Geschichte des Volkes Israel*, I (5th and 6th eds.; Gotha, 1923), 306-94.

The Story of the Plagues

J is made responsible for types $L + b$ (Scene IV) and $M + b$ (Scene V), while to E are assigned types $K + d$ (Scene VII), $N + d$ (Scene VIII), and $N +$ variant of d (Scene IX). It will be observed that the lines drawn by this documentary analysis do not fall according to the stylistic arrangement noted above. Nor is it without significance that in Scenes VII, VIII, and IX the Concluding Formulae are assigned to a source different from that to which the verses immediately preceding are assigned.

All these evidences of conscious literary artistry in the design of the Plague Narrative point strongly to unity of authorship. Certainly they justify us in approaching the study of the Central Cores of the plague stories with the *a priori* assumption that each is a literary whole, not a jig-saw puzzle of pieces drawn from three different sources.

THE CENTRAL CORES

The accepted documentary analysis of the Central Cores rests primarily on a hypercriticism induced by the results obtained from the analysis of the Introductory and Concluding Formulae, and also on the belief that since more than one document is to be discerned elsewhere in the Book of Exodus, therefore it is to be expected that more than one strand is present in the Plague Narrative.

The Core of Scene I (7: 14-22) is usually divided among all three sources, J, E, and P. To E goes the mention of the rod in vv. 17*b* and 20*b*, to J the prediction in v. 18 that the fish in the Nile will die and the river stink, to P the prediction in vv. 19 and 20*a* that not only the Nile but all the water in Egypt will become blood, with its fulfilment in v. 21*b*, and also the reference to the magicians in v. 22. But there is no real basis for assigning vv. 17*b* and 20*b* to a separate source, E. It is implied that Aaron wields the rod and this, as pointed out above, is part of the author's dramatic arrangement of the actors in the play. Nor does the heightening of the miracle noted in vv. 19, 20*a*, and 21*b* imply a different hand. The author has simply developed the plague in three ever more intensive stages: (i) the waters in the Nile are turned to blood; (ii) the fish die and the river stinks; (iii) then, since the

Nile is Egypt's sole source of water-supply, all the water in Egypt is represented as becoming blood. If it had not been for the three-document theory the unity of the narrative would never have been called in question. As for the magicians, they appear in the first three scenes, which are constructed according to a carefully worked out pattern, as we have seen, and also in Scene VI where they are held up to ridicule and then disappear for good. The way in which they are fitted into the drama shows that they are an integral part of the narrative and there is not the slightest evidence that they are a later importation by P. In the introduction which P later prefaced to the Plague Story, viz., 7:1-13, the magicians do appear but it is manifest that the word *ḥarṭummîm*, used in the earlier narrative for "magicians," was obsolete in his day for he feels it necessary to refer to them first (v. 11) by the more common terms *ḥakamîm* and *mekashshephîm* ("wise men and sorcerers").

If the magicians are an original part of the narrative, then the Cores of Scenes II and III are a unity also, for it is only the belief that the reference to the magicians is the work of P which has led to the splitting-up of these Cores between two documents.

The Cores of Scenes IV and V are recognized to be a literary unity and are usually assigned to J. The unity of the Core of Scene VI is also recognized, but it is assigned to P because of the mention of the magicians, although none of the customary marks of P authorship are present. Moreover, Aaron plays little part in the narrative, and its Concluding Formula does not correspond to the kind of formula elsewhere assigned to P.

An examination of the documentary analysis of the Cores of Scenes VII, VIII, and IX will reveal that it rests primarily on the assumption that the wielding of the rod by Moses rather than by Aaron points to a different source. But if the placing of the rod in the hand of Moses be merely one aspect of the author's dramatic scheme, as suggested above, then the whole documentary analysis of these scenes collapses like a house of cards. In Scene VII (9:13-35) the attempt to split the narrative on the basis of the mention of both hail and

The Story of the Plagues

fire in vv. 23a and 24a and the mention of only hail in v. 23b can scarcely be called convincing. It has also been maintained that Scenes VI and VII must be from a different source than Scene V because in Scene V "all the cattle of Egypt" are represented as having died as the result of a pestilence (9:6) whereas Scenes VI and VII have them in existence again, being smitten by boils and hail (9:9f., 22, 25). But the word used in Scene V is *miqneh*, "livestock," whereas the word used in Scenes VI and VII (except in 9:19-21[1]) is *behemah*, and it is used as the opposite of *'adam*, i.e., it denotes animals generally as opposed to human beings.[2]

Chapter 11 which introduces the story of the tenth and final plague is analysed by McNeile as follows: E, vv. 1-3; J, vv. 4-8; Rje, vv. 9f. The chief argument for assigning vv. 1-3 to a different source is that they are said to interrupt the connection between 10:28f. and 11:4-8. But it is by no means certain that 11:4-8 is the natural sequel to 10:28f. In the latter verses Moses is represented as declaring that he will never again see Pharaoh's face and the only natural sequel would be to have him stalk out. Furthermore, there can be no denying the fact that 10:28f. would find its most appropriate place after the announcement of the final plague, i.e., after 11:8a and before the words "and he departed from Pharaoh's presence in a rage." Now it has long been noticed that 11:9f. creates a difficulty in that it mentions the failure of the tenth plague before it has actually occurred. Further, it uses the term *môphēth*, found elsewhere in Exodus only in P passages, viz., 4:21 and 7:9.[3] It becomes fairly certain that this conclusion to the Story of the Plagues is the work of P whose hand is apparent in 12:1-20 immediately following. P wanted the Plague Story proper to end with the ninth plague in order that he might use the tenth plague as an introduction to his account of the institution of the Passover, and so he composed a summary conclusion to the Plague Narrative which he inserted after 11:8. He did not, however, destroy the bit of narrative which he was displacing. He

---
[1]For the exception in 9:19-21, see p. 13f.
[2]Cf. the similar use of *behemah* and *'ish* in Ex. 19:13.
[3]See p. 19.

simply transferred it to the conclusion of the ninth plague where it appears as 10: 28f. That it is out of place there is evident from the fact that it comes after the Concluding Formula of the ninth plague (10: 27). Thus the original form of the tenth plague story is to be found in 11: 1-8a; 10: 28f.; 11: 8b; 12: 29-36.[1]

This examination of the accepted documentary analysis of the Plague Narrative indicates that it rests on false assumptions and that the literary phenomena presented by the narrative can be explained better by a theory of stylistic arrangement than by a theory of documentary admixture, by a theory of single rather than composite authorship. The threefold pattern adopted by the biblical author, although sensed only imperfectly by the analysts, gives some support to their triple-document theory. But, as shown above, the documentary lines drawn by the analysts correspond very imperfectly to the stylistic divisions which seem to have been intended by the author.[2]

It may be argued by some that while the narrative does possess a stylistic arrangement, this arrangement is due to the last editor, P or Rp. It may be maintained that it was he who added the third and sixth plagues to bring the total number up to ten and arranged the scenes with their Introductory and Concluding Formulae according to their present sequence. But P is said to have found J and E already combined so that it would be necessary to assume that the affixing of E conclusions to three J stories (Scenes VII-IX) was the work of Rje and that it was he who began this stylistic arrangement. But what arrangement was he aiming at if, after putting E conclusions to *three* J stories, he allowed J conclusions to remain in *four* scenes (I, II, IV, V)? We would also have to assume that P came along and added two new scenes (III and VI) and for some reason made alterations

[1] For the character of 12: 21-7, see pp. 155f., 159-61.
[2] That there is something wrong with the usual documentary approach is evident from the absurd results obtained by C. A. Simpson in his analysis of the Plague Story in *The Early Traditions of Israel* (Oxford, 1948), pp. 170-81, 433, 542-5, 617-19.

to the conclusion of Scene II. Such a complicated literary process leading to such a highly artistic result makes too great a demand upon our credulity. Did such a process ever lead to the creation of a great work of literature, which the Story of the Plagues undoubtedly is? Great literature simply does not arise in that way. It is the creation of a single imaginative mind, not the mechanical fitting together of pieces drawn from various sources, two verses from J, a half-verse from E, a touch of P. It is true that even a literary masterpiece is full of pre-existing materials in the form of vocabulary, metaphors, ideas, literary patterns, and so on, but what makes it great literature is the transforming power of some gifted mind which fuses and transforms these diverse elements into an ordered and organic whole. Now it may be that some late priestly writer took materials already existing and created out of them the wonderfully dramatic narrative that we possess; but all that we know of the priestly writers is strongly against any such assumption.

While the existence of a stylistic arrangement in the Plague Narrative has, I believe, been demonstrated, there are three passages which do not conform well to the pattern, viz., 7: 23-5, 9: 19-21, and 9: 34. Let us examine these in turn.

1. The Concluding Formula in 7: 22 is not the end of the story of the first plague as we should expect in view of the fact that the same or a similar formula marks the end of every other plague story except the tenth. It is followed by three verses which point out that the plague lasted for only seven days. This answers the very natural question how the Egyptians survived when all the water of Egypt had been turned to blood, but the fact that these verses stand outside the schematic arrangement suggests that they are of later origin than the Concluding Formula.

2. The story related in 9: 19-21 raises a difficulty since it represents the *miqneh* of the Egyptians as still in existence, whereas according to 9: 6 they were all destroyed by the fifth plague.[1] The passage has been very generally regarded as a later expansion by Rje, since Moses' advice to the servants of Pharaoh tends to weaken the effect of the plague.

[1]See p. 11.

3. The Concluding Formula of the seventh plague story (9:35) is preceded by a statement (v. 34) that Pharaoh "hardened his heart, he and his servants." Either this statement or the Concluding Formula is superfluous. There can be little doubt that the formula is the later in origin. Verse 34 belongs to a period before the stories had been provided with their present Introductory and Concluding Formulae. It may even have suggested the pattern of the Concluding Formulae.

In considering the problem presented by these three "nonconformist" passages we need to bear in mind that the written story which we possess passed through a long period of oral transmission. Whatever the original nucleus of the Plague Story may have been, it doubtless grew with the passing of time. There would be added to it other plagues to which Egypt is subject, and attempts would be made to impress the whole with an artistic character. But once the story was written down I believe the process of growth came to an end. The assumption of modern biblical scholars that extensive liberties were taken with the written traditions and that a long series of redactors tampered with the text, adding remarks of their own, is to my mind quite unwarranted and inherently improbable. Whatever growth there was took place when the tradition was in the oral stage.[1] The three passages discussed above reveal three different stages in the development of the Plague Story. In the first stage, revealed by 9:34, the story lacked the Concluding Formulae which it now possesses. In the second stage, revealed by 9:35, these formulae were added. In the third stage came the addition of bits like 7:23-5 which are of later origin than the Concluding Formulae. This particular bit, as well as 9:19-21, and possibly 9:31f., may very well be from the hand of the author who finally reduced the story to writing.

The admission of the literary unity of the Plague Narrative has revolutionary implications. For one thing it exposes the absurd extremes to which the documentary theory has been carried. The question of the existence of a P element is not affected, although it is evident that scholars have tended to

[1] Of course at a late date the written form was subjected to a revision by P.

assign material to P without adequate warrant. But the theory of two early documents, J and E, is seriously called in question. The fact that the literary phenomena presented by the narrative can be explained more naturally by a theory of stylistic arrangement than by a theory of documentary admixture raises doubts as to whether two such documents ever existed. In the chapters which follow I shall endeavour to utilize the freedom from the traditional viewpoint engendered by our examination of the Plague Story to approach the other parts of the Mosaic Tradition unencumbered by the JE hypothesis.

II *The Tradition of the Oppression and of the Raising-up of a Deliverer*

OUR RE-EXAMINATION OF THE TRIPLE-DOCUMENT THEORY AS applied to other parts of the Mosaic Tradition will begin with the chapters which precede the Plague Narrative, those dealing with the oppression in Egypt and the raising-up of a deliverer in the person of Moses (Ex. 1: 1—4: 31).

That 1: 1-5 is the work of P is generally recognized. The genealogy of which this section consists serves as a link between the individual biographies in Genesis and the national history which begins in Exodus. The hand of P is also to be discerned in 1: 7 in the words *parû wa-yishreṣû ... bime'odh me'odh*, "were fruitful and multiplied ... exceedingly." P obviously has Gen. 1: 22 in mind; he regards this new multiplying as marking the birth, the "creation," of the Israelite people. It is very doubtful, however, if the whole verse should be assigned to P for, as Rudolph points out, v. 9 presupposes a prior mention in the original narrative of the multiplying of the Israelites. P's hand has also been detected in 1: 13 and 14*b* on the ground that v. 13 is a doublet of 14*a* and because the word *perek*, "rigour, compulsion," is found elsewhere only in Leviticus and Ezekiel. This argument may be sound, but we shall see that it was not P's practice to insert remarks into documents which he utilized unless some important end was to be served thereby.

What about the remaining material in chapter 1, viz., vv. 6, most of 7, 8-22? Does it represent one document or two? The accepted theory maintains that there are two: J and E.[1]

---

[1]Rudolph and Jülicher, however, maintain the unity of the narrative, apart from the P additions, though Jülicher assigns it to E and Rudolph assigns it to J; cf. W. Rudolph, *Der "Elohist" von Exodus bis Josua*, Beih. *ZAW*, LXVIII (Berlin, 1938), 3.

The Tradition of the Oppression

The principal argument advanced in support of this contention is that in vv. 8-12, 14a, 20b, 22 (assigned to J) the Hebrews are represented as a community which has become so numerous that Pharaoh is alarmed and takes measures to reduce their growing numbers by enslaving them and putting them to hard labour, whereas in vv. 15-20a, 21 (assigned to E) the Hebrews are represented as a small group for whom the services of two midwives are sufficient, and these midwives are ordered by Pharaoh to dispose of all Hebrew male children at birth.

But are not these two stories interdependent parts of the same narrative? It is when the first measure, hard labour, fails that Pharaoh has recourse to the second, the murder of the male babies. Moreover, the very fact that Pharaoh gives an order for the murder of the children implies that in the assumed separate source also the Hebrews were regarded as a numerous community. To argue from the mention of only two midwives that the Hebrews must have been few in number is fallacious, for manifestly a group whose maternity needs could be met by only two midwives could not possibly give the Pharaoh of Egypt cause for alarm. Thus the narrative does not contain two different points of view as to the size of the Hebrew community. The mention of the two midwives was in all probability intended to impart a touch of historicity to a legend which can have had no basis in fact. The legend of the Massacre of the Hebrew Innocents in 1:15-22 grew out of the application to Moses in 2:1-10 of the ancient Semitic legend of the Hero Cast Away in Infancy.[1] It provided the necessary prelude, the answer to the question, How did Moses come to be cast away in infancy? Only a very tragic happening could have separated a mother from her child. And so a tragic setting was invented.

Chapter 2 consists of three sections: (i) the legend of Moses' birth and upbringing, vv. 1-10; (ii) the cause of his flight to Midian, vv. 11-15; (iii) the flight to Midian, vv. 16-22. The accepted analysis recognizes that sections (ii) and (iii) form interdependent parts of the same narrative and assigns them to J. The literary unity of section (i) has been

[1] Cf. A. J. Toynbee, *A Study of History*, III (London, 1934), 259ff.

called in question on the ground that in vv. 1f. Moses is presented as the first-born, whereas in vv. 4, 7ff. an older sister appears. This has led Gressmann,[1] followed by Rudolph, to regard vv. 4, 7-10a as a later stratum of J. But the purpose of vv. 1f. is merely to point out the tribe to which Moses belonged, and while the way in which the author has expressed himself undoubtedly lends itself to the interpretation that Moses was the first-born, it is by no means certain that he intended us to draw that inference. Certainly the theory that vv. 4, 7-10a represent a late J stratum has little to commend it.

The usual documentary analysis assigns vv. 1-10 to E on the ground that they contain the word *'amah*, "maidservant" (v. 5) for which J is said to use *shiphḥah*, and because the Israelites are represented as living, not in the land of Goshen, but in the immediate vicinity of the capital. Actually the argument from *'amah* and *shiphḥah* is worthless, as Rudolph[2] has seen, for these words are used interchangeably in Hebrew (cf. I Sam. 1: 16, 18; 25: 24f., 27, 41; II Sam. 14: 15-17; Ruth 2: 13; 3:9). The supposed inconsistency as to the dwelling-place of the Israelites is a figment of the imagination. In chapters 1 and 2 there is only one point of view: the Israelites are regarded as dwelling in the immediate vicinity of the capital. It is quite true that there is an inconsistency of view in the remaining chapters, but that is another problem which will be dealt with in the appropriate place.[3] Thus there are no grounds whatsoever for denying that vv. 1-10 are part of the same narrative as vv. 11-22.

With regard to the end of chapter 2, it has long been recognized (even by the LXX translators) that v. $23a^\alpha$[4] finds its natural continuation in 4: 19f. Hence 2: $23a^\beta$-25 must be assigned to another source, and it is universally recognized that this source is P. These verses are manifestly designed to

[1] *Moses und seine Zeit* (Göttingen, 1913), p. 1, n. 1.
[2] *Op. cit.*, p. 4, n. 4. A. H. McNeile, *Exodus*, p. viii, admits that *shiphḥah* occurs in E as well as in J, yet cf. R. H. Pfeiffer, *Introduction to the Old Testament* (New York, 1941), p. 172, n. 4.
[3] pp. 77-9.
[4] The word "many" in v. 23a is probably an addition by P, designed to make the story conform to his chronology according to which Moses was eighty years old at the time of the Exodus (cf. Ex. 7: 7).

smooth the transition to the Story of Moses' Call beginning in chapter 3, and to provide the necessary background for it. The situation is dark but God is moving behind the shadows and about to raise up a deliverer.

In 3: 1—4: 18 we have the Story of Moses' Call, which will be discussed below.[1] Then come 4: 19f. which, as just stated, constitute the continuation of 2: 23a^a. It is very probable that, in 4: 20, P changed an original "his son" to "his sons" to conform to the tradition in 18: 3f. that Moses had two sons, and that he added the phrase "and Moses took the staff of God in his hand," for this particular source has not yet made any mention of the rod. Verses 21-3 are regarded as later additions because they interrupt the natural connection between vv. 19f. and 24-6. They are usually assigned to Rje but are almost certainly the work of P. Note the use of the word *môphēth* in v. 21[2] and the reference to Israel as Yahweh's first-born son.

Some scholars deny that vv. 24-6, which relate how Yahweh tried to kill Moses while he was on his way back to Egypt, have any connection with vv. 19f. In fact, this denial is the cornerstone on which Eissfeldt erected his theory of an L Document, separate from J and E. Rudolph also regards the passage as an addition to J from an older source, while Morgenstern[3] would assign it to his K Document. But the transition from v. 20 (in its pre-P form) to v. 24 is so natural that I feel the two passages must come from the same narrative. Moreover, the mention of Zipporah and her son suggests a connection with 2: 21f., which belongs to the same source as 4: 19f. As for 4: 27-31, it forms the natural sequel to 4: 18. The weakness of the argument for dividing this passage into J and E elements has been pointed out above.[4]

Let us turn now to the Story of Moses' Call in 3: 1—4: 18. This story is analysed by McNeile as follows: to J are assigned 3: 2-4a, 5, 7, 8a, 16-18; 4: 1-12; to E 3: 1, 4b, 6, 9-14, 21f.; 4: 17f.; to Rje 3:15, 19f.; 4:13-16; while Rd expansions in the

[1] pp. 24-6.
[2] See p. 11.
[3] "The Oldest Document of the Hexateuch," *HUCA*, IV (1927), 51-4.
[4] p. 6.

form of lists of the pre-Israelite inhabitants of Canaan are thought to occur in 3: 8b, 17b.[1]

The analysis of the narrative into two primary strands, J and E, rests primarily on the appearance of two different names for the deity, *Yahweh* and *Elohim* or *ha-'elohim*. But an examination of the Book of Exodus as a whole (minus the P elements and chapters 1 and 2, on which see below) will disclose the fact that the employment of *Elohim* or *ha-'elohim* is dictated by logical reasoning and dramatic feeling and has nothing to do with the presence in the narrative of another literary strand. I have no intention of disputing the validity of using the divine names as a criterion for differentiating the component elements of the Book of Genesis but I do emphatically deny that this criterion holds good for the Book of Exodus. The extension of the criterion beyond Genesis has led to endless confusion and, in my opinion, to an entirely wrong view of the composition of the Hexateuch. In view of this challenge to the accepted theory it will be necessary to devote a brief excursus to the divine names in the Book of Exodus.

The Divine Names in Exodus

The first fact which stands out is that the name *Yahweh* predominates in the narrative. The problem therefore resolves itself into an examination of those instances in which the normal nomenclature is abandoned in favour of *Elohim* or *ha-'elohim*. Is their presence to be explained by the assumption of a hypothetical E Document embedded in the narrative, or can it be accounted for in some other way?

It is obvious that those instances in which *'elohim* occurs as a common noun, "god" (e.g., "a god," "gods," "the god of my (your) fathers," "the god of the Hebrews," etc.), can be ignored for purposes of the present discussion. As for the proper name *Elohim*, "God," and *ha-'elohim*, "the Deity," no appreciable difference in usage can be discerned; the writer uses now one, now the other (cf. 18: 19, where both occur in the same sentence, and the law quoted in 22: 8). The problem,

---

[1] For the supposed Rd expansions, see the discussion on pp. 155-62.

therefore, is why either *Elohim* or *ha-'elohim* occasionally occurs in place of *Yahweh*.

I believe that the key to the solution of the problem is to be found, not in the theory of a separate document, but in the fact that, with the exception of four passages, all the occurrences of *Elohim* or *ha-'elohim* are found in connection with events which took place at "the mountain of *ha-'elohim*." The author's phraseology is coloured by his constant remembrance that this mountain was *the mountain of ha-'elohim*. In describing the events which took place there he constantly pays deference to this term but at the same time he makes it quite clear that *ha-'elohim* is Yahweh. This undoubtedly accounts for the somewhat awkward alternation between *Elohim* (or *ha-'elohim*) and *Yahweh* which we find in 3:4, 18:1, and 19:3.[1] The LXX removed the awkwardness by boldly substituting *Yahweh* for *Elohim* in 3:4 and *ha-'elohim* for *Yahweh* in 19:3, but there can be scarcely any doubt that the Massoretic text preserves the original reading.

Let us now examine the various occurrences of *Elohim* or *ha-'elohim* in the narratives associated with the sacred mountain. First we may mention those cases in which *ha-'elohim* is used with what amounts to adjectival force, "the divine," or "sacred," viz., "the mountain of *ha-'elohim*" (3:1, 4:27, 18:5, 24:13) and "the rod of *ha-'elohim*" (4:20, 17:9). There is no necessary connection with Yahweh but only with the abstract conception of divinity and supernatural power. Then there are a number of seemingly stereotyped expressions like "fearers of God" (18:21), "to seek God" (18:15), to bring cases to "*ha-'elohim*" (18:19; cf. 21:6 and 22:8). The use of *ha-'elohim* in 3:6 to express the idea that no man can see God and live probably comes in the same category. There would seem to be every justification for a writer who normally used the divine name Yahweh to substitute *Elohim* or *ha-'elohim* when expressing any of the above ideas.

Turning to the occurrences in 3:11-15, it is surely obvious that the author employs *Elohim* or *ha-'elohim* because he is

[1]Even omitting 19:3b-8 as an expansion by P (see p. 163), *ha-'elohim* in v. 3a is followed by *Yahweh* in v. 9.

about to relate the revelation of the name *Yahweh* to Moses and the effect would be spoiled by using the name immediately before the account of its revelation. There is not the slightest need to posit the presence of two documents. In chapter 18 the author has been influenced in his employment of *Elohim* or *ha-'elohim* in vv. 1, 12, 19, and 23 by the fact that the scene is enacted at "the mountain of *ha-'elohim*" and that the principal actor, Jethro, is a foreigner. In chapter 19, dealing with the theophany on "the mountain of *ha-'elohim*," we find three occurrences of *ha-'elohim*, in vv. 3, 17, and 19. If there is anything to the suggestion made below[1] that the wording of v. 2 has been tampered with by P and that the original read as follows: "Then they journeyed from Rephidim and came to Horeb, the mountain of *ha-'elohim*, and Israel encamped there before the mountain," then the wording of v. 3*a*, "while Moses went up to *ha-'elohim*," forms a very natural continuation. In v. 3*b*, "and *Yahweh* called to him from the mountain," or, ignoring vv. 3*b*-8 as from P, in v. 9, "And *Yahweh* said to Moses," we have a sudden switch to the other divine name, a phenomenon discussed above. After making a concession to the *'elohim* of the mountain in v. 3*a*, the author reverts to his customary *Yahweh* and continues to employ it as far as v. 15. But when he comes to a description of the actual theophany in vv. 15-19 and its continuation in 20: 18-21 he again employs *Elohim* or *ha-'elohim*, except in 19: 18 where the LXX, however, reads *ha-'elohim*.

Ignoring the laws in 20: 2-17 and 20: 23—23: 19, which do not represent the original author's handiwork, we next meet with a divine name in chapter 24 which deals with the ascent of "the mountain of *ha-'elohim*" (v. 13) by Moses, accompanied by Aaron and his sons and seventy of the elders of Israel, to receive a written copy of the decalogue. In vv. 1f. it is *Yahweh* who issues the instructions regarding the ascent, but when the author comes to a description of the actual meeting with the Deity, he switches to "the god of Israel" (v. 10) and *ha-'elohim* (v. 11). Having created the proper mysterious atmosphere, the author reverts in v. 12 to the customary *Yahweh* who is represented (as in vv. 1f.) as issuing further orders.

[1] p. 92.

The Tradition of the Oppression 23

The impression one gets from a perusal of the narrative is that when the writer wishes to impart a feeling of awe and mystery he employs the vaguer, abstract term *ha-'elohim*. The name *Yahweh* had a more intimate and personal connotation and was ordinarily employed. It is *Yahweh* who delivers his people from the Egyptians, it is he who speaks to Moses and issues commands to his people. But when a more mysterious note is demanded, it is *ha-'elohim* which fulfils the requirements.

Let us look now at the few remaining cases of *Elohim* or *ha-'elohim*. In 8: 15 (EV 8: 19) the author very naturally has the Egyptian magicians exclaim "It is the finger of *Elohim*" rather than "It is the finger of *Yahweh*," and likewise has Pharaoh in 9: 28 use *Elohim* rather than *Yahweh* in reference to the thunder and hail.[1] The reason for the employment of *Elohim* in 13: 17-19 is undoubtedly to be found in the fact that in v. 19 the author is going to quote the prophecy of Joseph in Gen. 50: 25 where *Elohim* is used as the divine name. It is the same *Elohim* of whom Joseph spoke that now directs their steps out of the land of Egypt. Then there is the reference to "the angel of *ha-'elohim*" in 14: 19a, a reference which has been used as a prop for the JE hypothesis. It is said that the J Document represents the people as led by *Yahweh* in a pillar of cloud by day and in a pillar of fire by night, whereas the E Document represents them as led by "the angel of *ha-'elohim*." Morgenstern[2] has gone so far as to assert that the Pentateuch records five different, contradictory, and mutually exclusive accounts of the way in which Israel was guided through the desert: (i) according to K he was guided by Hobab; (ii) according to J he was guided by the pillar of cloud and fire; (iii) according to E he was guided by the angel or messenger of *Yahweh*; (iv) according to P he was guided by the *kebôd Yahweh*; (v) according to C he was guided by the ark. That this elaborate hypothesis has little to commend it will become apparent as we proceed. As far as the reference to "the angel of *ha-'elohim*" in 14: 19a is concerned, it cannot

---

[1] The employment of *Yahweh Elohim* in 9: 30 is obviously dictated by a desire to explain to Pharaoh who Yahweh is. The phrase should properly be translated "Yahweh, that is, God."

[2] *Op. cit.*, pp. 41f.

be an original part of the tradition for two reasons: (i) 19*b* is quite sufficient by itself; 19*a* only complicates the picture, and the angel plays no further part in the story of the crossing of the sea; (ii) while "the angel of *Yahweh*" acts as the medium of revelation at the burning bush (3:2), it is not until 23:20ff. that Yahweh promises to send his angel to guide the Israelites on their way—thus the reference to the angel in 14:19*a* comes too soon in the narrative. There can be little doubt that it is the work of P.[1] Finally there are the references in 31:18 and 32:16 to the stone tablets: "written by the finger of *Elohim*," "the work of *Elohim*," "and the writing was the writing of *Elohim*." The choice of the word *Elohim* rather than *Yahweh* serves to enhance the supernatural origin and character of the tablets.

Surely the cumulative evidence which has been adduced is sufficient to prove that the use of *Elohim* or *ha-'elohim* was dictated by the dramatic demands of the narrative and is not an indication of a separate literary source embedded in it.

After this rather extended excursus, the result of which is to deny the validity of using the divine names as a criterion for a division of the Exodus narrative between two documents, J and E, we revert to a study of the Story of Moses' Call and first examine other arguments which have been advanced in favour of the hypothesis that chapter 3 consists of two strands. Rudolph maintains that vv. $12a^{\beta}b$, 14*a*, and 15 are later additions, the argument being that 14*a* ("And God said to Moses, I am who I am") is an interruption between Moses' question in 13 (". . . they will say to me, What is his name? What shall I say to them?") and the reply to it in 14*b* ("He said, Thus shalt thou say to the Israelites, I AM has sent me unto you"); and that in 15 ("God said further to Moses, Thus shalt thou say to the Israelites, Yahweh the god of your fathers, the god of Abraham, the god of Isaac, and the god of Jacob, has sent me unto you. This is my name eternally, and

---

[1] Even 23:20ff. is a later expansion by P. See p. 46. P probably derived the idea that the people were accompanied by a guiding and guardian angel from Nu. 20:16 where, however, the "angel" (or rather "messenger") is Moses. P gave to the term *mal'ak* in this passage a religious interpretation.

this is my designation to all generations") we have another reply to Moses' question.¹ But actually there is no need to feel that the question in v. 13 can have had only one reply and that it is necessary to make a choice between 14*b* and 15. The author wishes to make two things clear: first, the significance of the name *Yahweh* (14*b*) and, second, that this Yahweh is the god of their forefathers, Abraham, Isaac, and Jacob (15). Both answers are essential to the story and the use of the word *'ôdh*, "further," at the beginning of v. 15 is perfectly natural.²

The customary splitting-up of the narrative between J and E, assigning vv. 13f. to E, 15 to Rje, and 16 to J, has given rise to the theory that according to E the name *Yahweh* was first revealed to Moses, whereas in J men had been calling God by the name of *Yahweh* from the time of Seth, the son of Adam (cf. Gen. 4:26). If the narrative in Ex. 3 be a literary unity, as I maintain, then this theory is a figment of the imagination. There can be no denying the fact that P interpreted the story to mean that the name *Yahweh* was first revealed to Moses (cf. Ex. 6:3), but was P right in his interpretation? Is it not more natural to interpret the story as follows: Moses was startled by the voice of an invisible, unknown god in a foreign land. It is true that this god soon announced himself as the god of Moses' father (Amram) and of Abraham, Isaac, and Jacob, which was equivalent to saying, "I am Yahweh." But it was not in accordance with the beliefs of the time that a god should reveal himself far beyond the limits of his native land; moreover, there were such things as deluding spirits. Moses naturally wished to assure himself that it was indeed the god of the Hebrews who was speaking to him and so he asked him his name. This gave the author an opportunity to suggest the significance of the name *Yahweh*. It is not an explanation which satisfies the modern philologist but it is

---

¹W. A. Irwin also holds that v. 15 is a doublet of v. 14 and maintains that in v. 14 we should translate "I-AM is who I am" (*AJSL*, LVI (1939), 297f.).

²Even though it may be conceded that only one of these verses is original, there is no need to assume that the other verse was added from a separate document. It may be more naturally regarded as a later expansion of the tradition while the latter was still in the oral stage.

eminently satisfying to the religious sense. There is an appropriate air of vagueness and mystery about it—"He is what he is," an ineffable Being.[1] The author has no sooner interpreted the name than he hastens to declare that this god is the god of their forefathers. In spite of this affirmation P interpreted the story to mean that the name *Yahweh* was now revealed for the first time; the same god had been worshipped by their forefathers but had been known by a different name, *El Shaddai*.[2] But P's interpretation is at variance with the testimony of the patriarchal narratives. It is explicitly stated in Gen. 28:13 that Yahweh revealed himself to Jacob at Bethel with the words, "I am Yahweh, the god of Abraham, thy father, and the god of Isaac." As this study proceeds it will become evident that this is not the only place where P has misinterpreted and falsified the earlier tradition.

In chapter 4, vv. 13-16 are assigned to Rje on the ground that Aaron is a late importation into the narrative—a mistaken theory, as pointed out above.[3] The assignment of vv. 17f. to E rests on another erroneous theory, that the wonder-working rod belongs to a separate source.[4] There is no reason for doubting that vv. 1-18 form a continuous literary piece.

From the fact that the Story of Moses' Call (3:1—4:18) breaks the natural connection between 2:23a^a and 4:19 scholars have usually regarded it as, in the main, an E insertion into a J narrative. But a perusal of the Call Story

---

[1] Cf. the remarks of A. Lods, *Israel* (Eng. trans.; London, 1932), pp. 322f., and his further statement, pp. 323f.: "Amidst all these uncertainties one thing at least seems sure, namely, that this name did not appear for the first time in the Mosaic epoch, as E and P suggest, representing it as having been revealed, for the first time, to Moses. If this were its true origin, it would have an intelligible meaning in Hebrew, the remembrance of which would have been preserved by the Israelites. It is apparently a much older name whose meaning the Israelites had already forgotten, and to which they attempted later to give a meaning conformable to their own religious conceptions." See also E. Naville, *The Higher Criticism in relation to the Pentateuch* (Edinburgh, 1923), pp. 45, 59ff.

[2] P obviously means that the patriarchs worshipped God under the name *El. Shaddai* is only an interpretative adjective, whose pattern is to be explained not in the light of modern philological rules but by P's curious ideas on what archaic forms should be. Cf. his *Sarai* for *Sarah*, *Hoshea* for *Joshua*, *Jeshurun* for *Israel*.

[3] pp. 4-6.

[4] See p. 4.

The Tradition of the Oppression

shows that it is an integral part of the main narrative. It relates all the incidents which are necessary for an understanding of the Plague Narrative: the plan to ask Pharaoh's permission to make a three days' journey into the desert to offer sacrifices to Yahweh (3: 18), and to ask the Egyptians for gifts of gold and silver and clothing before setting out (3: 21f.); the provision of the wonder-working rod (4: 1-4); Moses' reluctance to undertake the role of deliverer because of his inability to speak well, and the appointment of Aaron as his assistant (4: 10-16). These incidents constitute the indispensable introduction to the Plague Narrative and show that the Call Story in 3: 1—4: 18 is an integral part of the main body of the Book of Exodus.

Is the material comprising 1: 6, 7 (part), 8-22; 2: 1-23$a^α$; 4: 19f., 24-6 also an integral part of the original Book of Exodus? This seems unlikely for the following reasons:

1. It knows nothing of the Story of Moses' Call at the burning bush. Yahweh merely makes a brief announcement to Moses in Midian that all the men who had sought his life are dead (4: 19).

2. It makes no reference to Aaron accompanying Moses back to Egypt. Moses returns accompanied only by his wife and child (4: 20, 24-6). In the Book of Exodus proper, however, Aaron is represented as going to Midian to meet Moses and returning to Egypt with him; there is no mention of Moses' wife and child (4: 10-18, 27-31).

3. It calls Moses' father-in-law Reuel (2: 18), whereas in the rest of the Book of Exodus he is called *Jethro* (3: 1; 18: 1, etc.).[1]

The discrepancies with the main narrative of Exodus are so glaring as to suggest that we are dealing with a separate document.

In the light of this possibility, the fact that chapters 1 and 2 are marked off from the rest of the book by possessing a P introduction (1: 1-5 and a bit of 7) and a P conclusion (2: 23$a^β$-25) begins to take on significance. It looks as though

---

[1]It is probable, however, that the name *Reuel* is not original in 2: 18 but was inserted at a later date; see pp. 63f. For a discussion of the names of Moses' father-in-law, see pp. 62-8.

28   *The Mosaic Tradition*

P, finding the Book of Exodus without a story of Moses' birth, drew upon an old document which contained such a story and prefixed it to the book which contained the official account of Moses' life. To smooth the transition from the Book of Genesis, which it now followed, he composed 1: 1-5, 7*, and to smooth the transition to the Book of Exodus proper, beginning with chapter 3, he composed 2: $23a^\beta$-25.

P took from this old document not only the story of Moses' birth and upbringing and flight to Midian, but also a curious account of Yahweh attempting to kill Moses when the latter was on his way back to Egypt. P evidently wished to preserve this story because it gave the origin of the rite of circumcision, and so he inserted it at the first appropriate place, namely, after 4: 18. But P was rarely able to insert anything from another source without adding a few comments of his own in the immediate neighbourhood. In this case, he seems to be responsible for making some changes in 4: 20 and for adding vv. 21-3.[1]

It may be felt that if the first two chapters be regarded as a later addition to the Book of Exodus, it is still necessary to assume that another account of Moses' birth once stood there, which account for some reason displaced P and was replaced by the account from the other source. But the abrupt manner in which Abraham is introduced in Gen. 12 (for it is very doubtful if any of the preceding genealogy is part of the original written story) should be a warning against forming too hasty a judgment on the matter. It is evident that story-tellers did not always feel it necessary to incorporate into their narratives all of the facts which had been handed down by tradition, such as the names of the ancestors of the hero of the tale. Later on P felt it desirable to incorporate into the written tradition the more important of these supplementary facts. Thus it may well be that the Book of Exodus never contained any birth story but began with the Story of Moses' Call in chapter 3.

The original tradition in 4: 1-18, 27-31 finds its continuation in chapter 5. The literary unity of this chapter is recognized by scholars except that vv. 1, 2, and 4 have been

[1]See p. 19.

The Tradition of the Oppression

assigned to a separate source on the ground that they are superfluous doublets. Actually they are nothing of the sort and no one would ever have thought of assigning them to a separate source had it not been for the JE hypothesis. The sequence of the narrative is in every way natural and the argument from vocabulary worthless. It is obvious that the author of chapter 5 was acquainted with the tradition of the oppression as narrated in the old source preserved in chapter 1, which tells how the Hebrews were compelled to labour in brick-making and building. But this does not prove that chapters 5 and 1 come from the same hand. The request made to Pharaoh in 5: 1-3 to be allowed to go a three days' journey into the desert and the association of Aaron with Moses in vv. 1, 4, and 20 show that chapter 5 is part and parcel of the main body of the book.

As for 6: 2—7: 13, all scholars are agreed that this section represents the handiwork of P and/or Rp and it is unnecessary to recapitulate the arguments which have been advanced in support of this view. The status of 6: 1 is more uncertain; it is probably a part of the original narrative.

III The Tradition of the Law-Giving

THE AMOUNT OF SPACE DEVOTED TO THE REVELATION OF THE Law on Mt. Sinai (viz., one whole book and parts of two others, Ex. 19-40, Leviticus, Nu. 1-10) shows that to the framers of the final form of the national tradition this event was the crowning incident. Yet it is in the interpretation of this all-important incident that the JE hypothesis fails most lamentably to provide a satisfactory solution of the numerous problems involved. It has indeed led to the identification of several codes within the corpus of laws attributed to Moses, but its proponents have ended by denying that any of these codes can possibly be Mosaic or, at least, by being very uncertain which one can be regarded as the work of the great lawgiver.[1] In what follows I hope to demonstrate that the confusion and uncertainty in which we rest can be removed by an abandonment of the JE hypothesis and the adoption of the theory of a single document which has been modified by P.

The codes which have been identified are as follows:

    1. the Moral Decalogue (Ex. 20: 1-17).

    2. a Ritual Decalogue (Ex. 20: 23-6, 23: 10-19) enclosing a Miscellaneous Code (21: 1—23: 9), the whole being usually referred to as "the Code of the Covenant."

    3. a Ritual Decalogue (Ex. 34: 14-26).

    4. various priestly codes.

Under the spell of the JEDP theory scholars have distributed these codes among the documents as follows: the Moral Decalogue to D, the Code of the Covenant to E, the Ritual Decalogue in Ex. 34 to J,[2] the various priestly codes to P.

---

[1] Cf. T. J. Meek, *Hebrew Origins* (New York, 1936), p. 35: "Just what laws are to be attributed to Moses is impossible to say." A. Lods, *Israel* (Eng. trans.; London, 1932), p. 313, also declares that "Moses apparently promulgated no code, since Yahweh's abiding presence among his people, to be inquired of at all times, made such a proceeding unnecessary."

[2] J. Morgenstern, in "The Oldest Document of the Hexateuch," *HUCA*, IV (1927), 1-138, assigns the Ritual Decalogue to his K Document but allows that K was later incorporated in J.

The Tradition of the Law-Giving 31

This simple and seemingly satisfactory solution of the problem of the relationship of the legal to the narrative materials received a rude jolt in 1924 from Professor R. H. Pfeiffer of Harvard University who demonstrated, conclusively, I believe, that the Ritual Decalogue in Ex. 34 is later, much later, than its parallel in Ex. 20, 23 and therefore cannot be a part of the J Document.[1] Pfeiffer drew attention to the following facts:

(a) The early name for the harvest festival, *ḥagg ha-qasîr*, found in 23:16, is replaced in 34:22 by the later name, *ḥagg shabû'ôth*, used from the time of Deuteronomy on (cf. Dt. 16:10, 16).[2]

(b) In 34:22 the date of the harvest festival is fixed more precisely than in 23:16. One can understand a change from the vague to the precise, but not vice versa.

(c) In 23:16 the festival of ingathering (*ḥagg ha-'asîph*) is dated "at the exit [*ṣē'th*] of the year." Such a festival must obviously have been celebrated in the autumn, and therefore the law is dated according to a calendar in which the year ended in the autumn. But in 34:22 the feast is dated "at the revolution [*teqûphath*] of the year." The substitution of the rather vague term *teqûphah* for the precise *ṣē'th* must surely indicate that a different calendar was now in use in which the year no longer ended in the autumn. We know that after the exile the Jews employed the Babylonian calendar, in which the year ended in the spring, even for religious purposes. This suggests that Ex. 34 comes from the post-exilic period when the autumnal festival of the ingathering could no longer be said to occur "at the exit of the year."[3]

(d) In 34:25 is found the verb *shaḥaṭ*, regularly employed by P in Leviticus, whereas 23:18 uses *zabaḥ*.

(e) If the Ex. 20, 23 version be later than Ex. 34, how

[1] "The Oldest Decalogue," *JBL*, XLIII (1924), 294-310; "The Transmission of the Book of the Covenant," *HTR*, XXIII (1931), 102-5; *Introduction to the Old Testament* (New York, 1941), pp. 221ff.

[2] In order to preserve an early date for Ex. 34, Morgenstern is obliged to maintain that the name given to the festival in that chapter is due to a late Deuteronomic hand ("The Oldest Document of the Hexateuch," p. 78).

[3] The Babylonian calendar was used for *civil* purposes in Palestine as early as the seventh century B.C.; cf. W. F. Albright, "The Chronology of the Divided Monarchy of Israel," *BASOR*, No. 100 (1945), p. 20, n. 13.

can we account for the omission from the former of such a fundamental law as the prohibition of the worship of other gods found in 34: 14?

It must be admitted that the cumulative effect of Pfeiffer's arguments is impressive.[1] But if the Ex. 34 version of the Ritual Decalogue be indeed of late, possibly post-exilic, origin—and we shall find additional support for this contention from an examination of the internal structure of the code as well as from a study of its narrative framework—then the usual interpretation of the Tradition of the Law-Giving is completely undermined and a new hypothesis must be sought which will more adequately account for all of the facts. Pfeiffer[2] himself has suggested such a hypothesis but his "snowball" theory of an original Canaanite ritual decalogue which has passed through no less than four Israelite editions (dated roughly to 1000, 650, 550, and 450 B.C.), during which process it has accumulated numerous accretions, ending up as the present Code of the Covenant, does not commend itself. A re-examination of the Tradition of the Law-Giving is, therefore, in order. This tradition, as is well known, exists in two versions, an Exodus and a Deuteronomic.

THE REVELATION OF THE CODES

According to the present arrangement of the Exodus version the sequence of events in chapters 19-23 is as follows: (i) Yahweh descends upon Mt. Sinai and summons Moses to the top of the mountain, where he gives him instructions regarding the conduct of people and priests and then orders him to go down and come back up again, accompanied by Aaron. Thereupon Moses descends the mountain (19: 20-5). (ii) God reveals the Moral Decalogue (20: 1-17) in the hearing of the people. (iii) They become afraid and ask Moses to act

---

[1]Rudolph, *Der "Elohist" von Exodus bis Josua*, Beih. *ZAW*, LXVIII (Berlin, 1938), p. 59, also regards the Ex. 34 code as late, a conglomerate drawn from the Code of the Covenant, especially Ex. 23. B. Baentsch, *Das Bundesbuch*, p. 101, asserts that "in its original form ... the Decalogue in Ex. 34 is older than the Book of the Covenant: in its revised form, on the other hand, in which it now lies before us, it bears manifestly the stamp of a later time"; quoted from R. H. Charles, *The Decalogue* (2nd ed.; Edinburgh, 1926), pp. lx, lxiv.

[2]"The Transmission of the Book of the Covenant," pp. 99-109.

The Tradition of the Law-Giving

as their representative in any further negotiations with the Deity. (iv) The people depart while Moses remains and has further laws imparted to him privately, these laws being the so-called "Code of the Covenant" in 20: 23—23: 19.

But there are indications that the first two items in this sequence were not present in the original tradition: (i) Ex. 19: 19 finds a more natural sequel in 20: 18 than in 19: 20. (ii) The material in 19: 20-5 sounds secondary for it has Moses make another trip up the mountain to receive orders which have already been given in vv. 10-13. The section seems to be modelled on Ex. 24. There Aaron and others accompany Moses, part way at least, when he goes up to receive the tablets; here also Aaron is made to accompany him at the oral revelation of the decalogue. (iii) The wording of the Sabbath law in 20: 8-11 betrays an acquaintance with the P narrative in Gen. 2: 1-3. These facts justify the conclusion that 19: 20—20: 17 is a later intrusion into the Exodus tradition. And, in view of the third fact noted, it is practically certain that the person responsible for this intrusion was P.

Are we to conclude, then, that 19: 19 was originally followed by 20: 18? That is what most modern commentators assert. But such an assertion is inconsistent with the Deuteronomic version of the tradition which asserts that the revelation of a code of laws intervened. Of course, D may be improvising at this point but since his version of the law-giving seems to be based on the Exodus version it is very probable that D found a code of laws after Ex. 19: 19. But was it the Moral Decalogue, as D maintains? Against D's assertion is the fact that in the Exodus version the Moral Decalogue is embedded in a section, 19: 20—20: 17, which gives evidence of being a late P intrusion into the narrative, as pointed out above. As for the Deuteronomic version of the Moral Decalogue in Dt. 5: 6-21, its vocabulary, style, and emphasis stamp it as a product of the Deuteronomic age. There seems no escape from the conclusion that the priests of Jerusalem, who were undoubtedly the authors of the Book of Deuteronomy, corrupted the original tradition by substituting another decalogue, the Moral Decalogue, for the original one. Their very insistence in Dt. 5: 22 that *"these words* [the Moral Decalogue, Dt. 5: 6-21] *without any additions*" Yahweh revealed at the mountain to the assembled Israelites shows that they expected opposition to their assertion, and that there was another decalogue for which a Mosaic authorship was claimed.

What can this other decalogue have been? An answer to this question is suggested by a study of the laws in Ex. 20: 23—23: 19 which Moses is said to have received in private.

As already pointed out, and it is a fact which has long been recognized by scholars, these laws, the so-called "Code of the Covenant," actually form two codes: a code of miscellaneous character (21: 1—23: 9), framed at the beginning and end by a decalogue of ritualistic laws (20: 23-6, 23: 10-19).[1] Since it is inherently improbable that the original tradition represented Moses as having two codes communicated to him in private, it follows that one of these codes cannot be in its proper position. The suspicion arises that the ritualistic laws constitute the original Mosaic decalogue.

The Ritual Decalogue

Since the assumption that the group of ritualistic laws in 20: 23-6, 23: 10-19 forms a decalogue may be challenged, it is necessary to discuss this matter at some length.

Many scholars maintain that the so-called Ritual Decalogue contains thirteen, not ten, laws and this has led them to suspect certain parts as later additions. But their treatment of the code is dominated by the idea that all the Hebrew laws were originally concise in form, and that if a long law is met with, it represents a later expansion. Because in the Moral Decalogue Commandments I, VI, VII, VIII, and IX are formulated concisely, it has been commonly assumed that the other five commandments were originally quite brief also.[2]

---

[1]There is a tendency, however, to regard 22: 28f. (EV 29f.) as part of this framework code (cf. McNeile, *Exodus* (Westminster Commentaries), p. 124), thus concealing the decalogic character of the code. S. R. Driver, in *Exodus* (Cambridge Bible Series), p. 202, even takes all the material in 22: 18—23: 9 as part of this code.

[2]Cf. Lods, *Israel*, p. 315; Charles, *The Decalogue*, p. lv; E. Robertson, "The Riddle of the Torah: Suggesting a Solution," *Bulletin of the John Rylands Library*, XXVII (1943), 369f.

The Tradition of the Law-Giving

This has led to the theory of a pre-D Moral Decalogue dated to the reign of Hezekiah, about a century before the promulgation of Deuteronomy in 621 B.C.[1] But of the existence of such a briefer decalogue there is not the slightest evidence. The Moral Decalogue is permeated through and through by the same spirit as animates the Book of Deuteronomy and it is entirely probable that it is in its original form in Dt. 5. Morgenstern,[2] by a comparison of the form of the Ritual Decalogue in Ex. 20, 23 with its parallel in Ex. 34, believed it possible to demonstrate which elements represent later expansions, and by a deletion of these to arrive at the original brief form of the various laws. His results are interesting but not convincing—all the more unconvincing if Ex. 34 be a late version and not early as he assumes. Surely it should be self-evident that while some subjects can be legislated for in a few words, not all subjects lend themselves to brief treatment.

If the assumption, false in my opinion, that all the Hebrew laws were originally formulated briefly is abandoned, it will be found that the ritual code in Ex. 20, 23 falls naturally into ten divisions, as follows:

1. A law against making gold and silver images of Yahweh (20:23).

2. A law regarding the construction of altars (20:24-6).

3. A law regarding a sabbatical year for the land (23:10f.)

4. A law regarding Sabbath observance (23:12).

5. A law against mentioning the names of other gods (23:13).

6. A law regarding the three annual festivals (23:14-17).

7. A law against employing leaven with sacrifices (23:18a).

8. A law against leaving the fat of sacrifices unconsumed till morning (23:18b).

9. A law regarding first-fruits (23:19a).

10. A law against boiling a kid in its mother's milk (23:19b).

[1] Cf. Morgenstern, "Decalogue" in *Universal Jewish Encyclopedia* (New York, 1941).
[2] "The Oldest Document of the Hexateuch," pp. 54-98.

The greatest divergence between commentators is found in their attitude toward the law of the three annual festivals (No. 6). Some see in it a unity, but most break it up into two or three or even four elements, being influenced by the fact that in Ex. 34, which they regard as the earlier version, the law actually is broken up. But the form of the festival law in Ex. 23: 14-17 is one of the clearest proofs of both the priority of the Ex. 20, 23 version to the Ex. 34 version and the fact that Hebrew laws were not always formulated briefly. For the law possesses an undoubted literary pattern, with an introduction in v. 14 and a conclusion in v. 17. The usual statement that v. 17 is a doublet of v. 14 and that therefore one of them should be excised as not original[1] fails to recognize the fact that the early Hebrew laws were formulated according to definite literary patterns. Thus in the civil laws (*mishpaṭîm*) of Ex. 21-2 the general principle which is to be followed is introduced by the particle *kî* followed by the verb in the third masculine singular imperfect; modifications of it to suit particular circumstances are introduced by the particle *'im*. Criminal laws involving capital punishment begin with the active participle and end with the words *môth yûmath*. Morgenstern believes that the differences in literary pattern point to differences in date, but it is much more likely that different patterns were devised for different types of laws. A recognition of the fact that the laws were moulded in many instances with a feeling for literary style would have prevented any attempt to dismember the festival law in 23: 14-17.

The Mosaic authorship of the Ritual Decalogue has sometimes been denied on the ground that some of the laws, such as those regarding a sabbatical year for the land and the

[1] e.g., G. R. Berry, "The Ritual Decalogue," *JBL*, XLI (1925), 40, justifies his omission of vv. 18, 22a, 22b in Ex. 34 and the retention of only v. 23 as the festival law by saying: "From a literary standpoint this omission greatly simplifies matters, because the confusion in the arrangement of the material is found largely in these three regulations. From the standpoint of thought they are unnecessary, since No. 9 [i.e. v. 23] is a summary statement which covers them. It has seemed evident to most that either these three regulations or No. 9 should be omitted, and No. 9 has much appearance of originality, being found in a substantially identical form also in Ex. 23: 17 and Dt. 16: 16."

three annual festivals, presuppose settled conditions of life. But it is necessary to remember that the Israelites had lived a settled life in Egypt and were not, therefore, pure nomads. Moreover, their sojourn at Horeb, where the decalogue is said to have been formulated, may have involved some years of sedentary existence which made the promulgation of such laws desirable.

The original position of this code must have been immediately after Ex. 19:19. When the code was replaced by the Moral Decalogue it was shifted to its present position framing the Miscellaneous Code, which was the code revealed in private. The distribution of the original decalogue in this manner gave to the Miscellaneous Code in 21:1—23:9 the appearance of being a later insertion within the decalogue and this has led scholars astray.[1]

But what can possibly have been the motive for treating Moses' decalogue in this curious way? Why was a different decalogue substituted for it? And why, when the substitution was made, was the earlier decalogue not discarded but merely shifted to another position in the narrative, although in broken form? Before a satisfactory answer can be given to these questions it is necessary to examine Moses' other code, the Miscellaneous Code (hereafter referred to as the Supplementary Code), found in Ex. 21:1—23:9.[2]

The Supplementary Code

This code presupposes a much more settled and developed state of society than that envisaged by the Ritual Decalogue. The time which the Israelites spent at Kadesh does not seem to have been of sufficient duration to allow for the social development implied by the code. Hence there is some justification for questioning its Mosaic authorship. It is almost certain that the code comes from the period after the

[1] e.g., Morgenstern, in his stimulating study entitled "The Book of the Covenant," maintains that it was the Ritual Decalogue (derived here from Ex. 34) which was split wide open and groups of other laws inserted at various times, even after the exile (*HUCA*, V (1928), 1-151; VII (1930), 19-258; VIII-IX (1931-2), 1-150).

[2] It is a serious weakness of the JE hypothesis that it makes no provision for the existence of a Supplementary Code in J.

Israelites settled in Canaan. Some light on the problem is to be found in the last chapter of the Book of Joshua. There it is stated that shortly before his death Joshua convened an assembly of the Israelite leaders at Shechem and won their assent to the promulgation of some new laws, the precise character of which is not given. "He made laws and statutes [*ḥoq û-mishpaṭ*] for them at Shechem, and Joshua wrote these words in the book of the law of God ..." (24: 25f.). This statement can scarcely mean that Joshua added a supplement to an already existing book of Mosaic laws, for in that case Joshua's laws should be found at the end of the Supplementary Code, whereas it is actually the first part of the code (21: 2—22: 19, EV 22: 20) which presupposes the most highly developed state of society and which can most naturally be attributed to him. Moreover, the careful formulation of these *mishpaṭîm*, a feature which has long impressed scholars, finds no parallel in the other set of laws which we have attributed to Moses (the Ritual Decalogue) and would seem to imply a difference of authorship. It is likely, therefore, that Josh. 24: 25f. is to be understood as implying that Joshua instituted a law-book. The fact that this book is called "the book of the law of God" rather than "the book of the law of Moses" is probably not without significance.[1]

Must the whole of the Supplementary Code be attributed to Joshua? Is the tradition that a Supplementary Code was revealed to Moses at Horeb pure fiction? The answer to this question is to be found, I believe, in a recognition of the fact that 21: 1—23: 9 falls into two parts: (i) a group of carefully formulated *mishpaṭîm* in 21: 1—22: 19 (EV 22: 20); (ii) a collection of ethical and humanitarian precepts in 22: 20 (EV 22: 21)—23: 9. Morgenstern[2] breaks up even this latter collection into two groups, both of which he dates to the post-

[1] Josh. 8: 31 refers to "the book of the law of Moses" which contained the altar-law of Ex. 20: 24-6 and, by implication, the whole of the Ritual Decalogue of which the altar-law forms a part. But this only tells us that at the time when Josh. 8: 31 was written the Mosaic laws existed in book form. No inference can be drawn from the statement regarding the situation in Joshua's day.

[2] "The Book of the Covenant," *HUCA*, VIII-IX (1931-2), 150. We shall await with interest his detailed treatment of these laws, to appear as "The Book of the Covenant, Part IV." Pfeiffer (*Introduction to the Old Testament*, pp. 223f.) believes they are slightly pre-Deuteronomic.

The Tradition of the Law-Giving

exilic period, but the fact that the collection ends with the same injunction with which it begins suggests that it possesses some sort of unity and may once have had an independent existence. This impression is strengthened by the fact that the injunctions of which it is composed fall naturally into ten groups, thus:

1. Ill-treatment of a *ger* (22: 20, EV 22: 21).
2. Wronging a widow or orphan (vv. 21-3, EV 22-4).
3. Loans and security (vv. 24-6, EV 25-7).
4. Cursing God or a ruler (v. 27, EV 28).
5. Offerings (vv. 28f., EV 29f.).
6. Forbidden food (v. 30, EV 31).
7. Charge to witnesses (23: 1-3).
8. Stray or stubborn animals (vv. 4f.).
9. Charge to judges (vv. 6-8).
10. Ill-treatment of a *ger* (v. 9).

There is nothing in the format of these laws which precludes their being attributed to the same author who produced the Ritual Decalogue. I therefore suggest that in 22: 20 (EV 22: 21)—23: 9 we have the original Mosaic Supplementary Code. It must have been appended to Joshua's *mishpaṭim* either by Joshua himself or more probably at some later period.

Morgenstern[1] has argued that the fragmentary nature of the code in 21: 1—23: 9 implies that it is merely a collection of excerpts from a North Israelite code and that other *mishpaṭim* from the same code are to be found scattered throughout Deuteronomy. But it is difficult to imagine why such an incomplete digest should ever have been made. It seems to me that the incompleteness of the code arises from the fact that it represents only the problems actually dealt with by Moses and Joshua.[2] If the "apostolic period" had lasted longer, doubtless the code would be more complete.

Joshua's contribution to the national corpus of law seems in time to have been forgotten and all the laws in Ex. 21: 1—23: 9 were regarded as the work of Moses, constituting his

---

[1] "The Book of the Covenant," *HUCA*, VII (1930), 238ff. E. Robertson, "The Riddle of the Torah: Suggesting a Solution," pp. 374-7, 382, regards the Book of the Covenant as "a running midrash to the [Moral] Decalogue."

[2] Compare the similarly incomplete character of Muhammad's legislation.

The Mosaic Tradition

Supplementary Code. According to the Tradition of the Law-Giving this Supplementary Code was revealed to Moses privately, but the Exodus version of that tradition says nothing about Moses transmitting these laws to the people. In Dt. 4: 46 (cf. 1: 15), however, there is a reference to Moses promulgating a code of laws in Moab. The code alluded to is, of course, the one found in Dt. 12-26. But it has long been recognized that Dt. 12-26 is a revision and expansion of Ex. 21: 1—23: 9, i.e. the Deuteronomic code is a later version of Moses' Supplementary Code. It is highly probable, therefore, that what D says about his code applied in the earlier Tradition of the Law-Giving to the Supplementary Code in Ex. 21: 1—23: 9. In other words, the code which was revealed in Moab was not Dt. 12-26 but Ex. 21: 1—23: 9. Its most likely position in the original tradition is after Nu. 21: 21-35, i.e., after the account of the conquest of Heshbon and Bashan, which is where D places his code (cf. Dt. 4: 44ff.).[1] According to Dt. 27: 1-8 (a passage which seems to be a D rewriting of an earlier tradition) the people were commanded to make a permanent record of this code on stone and to deposit it at Shechem: "Moses and the elders of Israel commanded the people as follows .... On the day that you cross the Jordan ... thou shalt set up some large stones [on Mt. Gerizim; cf. v. 4, Sam. VS[2]] and coat them with plaster; then thou shalt write upon them all the words of this law .... And thou shalt build there an altar to Yahweh, thy god, an altar of stones on which thou shalt not employ any iron [tool]. Out of undressed stones thou shalt build the altar of Yahweh, thy god, and thou shalt offer up upon it burnt-offerings [*'ôlôth*] to Yahweh, thy god, and sacrifice peace-offerings [*shelamîm*] and eat [them] there with joy before Yahweh, thy god. And thou shalt write upon the

[1] This suggestion was first made, I believe, by Kuenen, *The Hexateuch* (Eng. trans.; London, 1886), pp. 260f.).

[2] The Massoretic text of v. 4 reads "Mt. Ebal" but this is manifestly a deliberate Judaean corruption of the original reading, inspired by the refusal of the Southerners to admit that the first written version of Moses' Supplementary Code had been set up in the Samaritan sanctuary on Mt. Gerizim. Is it really likely that an order was given to inscribe the law on Mt. Ebal which is associated in the tradition with a curse? Cf. Dt. 11: 29, 27: 14.

The Tradition of the Law-Giving

stones all the words of this law very distinctly." The carrying-out of this command is related in Josh. 8: 30ff.: "Then Joshua built an altar to Yahweh, the god of Israel, on Mt. [Gerizim[1]], as Moses, the servant of Yahweh, had commanded the Israelites, an altar of undressed stones on which no iron [tool] had been employed, as it is written in the law-book of Moses. And they offered up burnt-offerings ['ôlôth] to Yahweh upon it and sacrificed sacrifices [zebaḥîm]. And he wrote there on the stones a copy of the law of Moses, which [copy] he wrote in the presence of [liphenê] the Israelites."

If the official copy of Moses' Supplementary Code was preserved at Shechem in this form, it is surely reasonable to conclude that the official copy of Moses' decalogue, inscribed on the two stone tablets, was also preserved at Shechem and not at Shiloh as the present form of the tradition asserts. In support of this view is the reference in Ju. 9: 46 to the god of Shechem as *El-berith*, "the god of the covenant."[2] Shechem was the first capital and its sanctuary and priesthood must have enjoyed a leading position among the various sanctuaries taken over by the incoming Hebrews. But Shechem soon lost its importance as a political centre. The flame of religious enthusiasm kindled by Moses and kept alive by Joshua died down at the latter's death and the tribes drifted apart, owning allegiance neither to Shechem nor to any other centre. When, in reaction to Philistine domination, unity was once more restored, it was not Shechem but the newly acquired Jerusalem which appeared in the forefront.

Not content with having attained primacy in the political realm, Jerusalem sought to attain primacy in the religious realm as well. And herein lay the source of the long and bitter rivalry which arose between the South and the North, between the Jews and the Samaritans. Doubtless in

---

[1] The Massoretic text reads "Ebal" in conformity with Dt. 27: 4. But if the reading of the Samaritan Version be adopted there (see the preceding note), it is necessary to read "Gerizim" here.

[2] Of course, in Ju. 8: 33 and 9: 4 the Judaean editors refer to the god of Shechem by the contemptuous term, *Baal-berith*, refusing to identify him with Yahweh at all.

The Mosaic Tradition

an age when politics and religion were closely intertwined, Jerusalem felt it could not afford to recognize the claim of the Shechemite sanctuary on Mt. Gerizim to religious priority, no matter how justifiable that claim might be on historical grounds. And to maintain its own supremacy in the political realm it felt obliged to make bold and ever bolder claims to supremacy in the religious realm. This led to a perversion and falsification of the national tradition with the object of enhancing the prestige of Jerusalem and its sanctuary and priesthood at the expense of Shechem.

It is now possible to give a partial answer to the questions raised above[1] concerning the strange treatment accorded the original Mosaic decalogue as well as the treatment accorded the Mosaic Supplementary Code. The Jerusalem priests could not deny that Shechem possessed a decalogue but they could assert that it was not the original Mosaic decalogue. And so to undermine the primacy of Shechem they put forward a Jerusalem decalogue, the Moral Decalogue, which was manifestly superior to the Shechemite Ritual Decalogue and claimed that it alone was Mosaic. Not content with that, they revised and enlarged Moses' Supplementary Code in Ex. 21: 1—23: 9 to give it the form which it has in Dt. 12-26,[2] thus providing Jerusalem with a version which was superior to that possessed by Shechem. Then they enshrined both codes in a book whose central thesis is that "Jerusalem is the place where men ought to worship" (cf. John 4: 20). But the publication of this book, Deuteronomy, was to lead to complications, for the nation now had on its hands two

---

[1] See p. 40.

[2] The new material now added to the Supplementary Code doubtless represents the practice which had grown up at the Jerusalem sanctuary. This would explain the fact that some of the laws seem to have formed a unit before being incorporated in Deuteronomy; cf. A. Siebens, *L'Origine du code deuteronomique* (Paris, 1929), pp. 207-24, 249. The publication of Deuteronomy furnished an excellent opportunity to canonize this practice. It is doubtful if we are justified in going further back and asserting with E. Robertson, "Temple and Torah: Suggesting an Alternative to the Graf-Wellhausen Hypothesis," *Bulletin of the John Rylands Library*, XXVI (1942), 191ff., that some of the Deuteronomic laws reflect the practice of the Shiloh sanctuary.

The Tradition of the Law-Giving

versions of the Mosaic Tradition, the old one with which it had long been familiar and a new one which was said to have been discovered in the Jerusalem temple and to have been written by Moses himself. What this led to will become apparent later.

THE GIVING OF THE FIRST SET OF TABLETS

Let us turn now to an examination of the sequel to the story of the revelation of the codes. First comes an epilogue, Ex. 23: 20-33, which is generally recognized to be, in part at least, of late origin. Most scholars assign it to Rd but it is probably of even later origin.[1] Then comes chapter 24 with two different accounts of the recording of the laws in permanent form. There has been a good deal of disagreement regarding the documentary analysis of this chapter,[2] although it is generally recognized that vv. 3-8 constitute an intrusive element and that vv. 16f. are the work of P.[3] Verse 18a should probably be assigned to P also.

In vv. 1f., 9-15, 18b we are told that Moses was ordered to ascend the mountain accompanied by Aaron and the latter's two sons, Nadab and Abihu, and seventy of the elders of Israel. A ceremonial feast was celebrated in God's presence, after which Moses was called further up the mountain to receive "the stone tablets and[4] the law [tôrah] and the commandment [miṣwah] which I have written for their instruction." Of course, Moses, being a great man, did not go alone (no oriental chief would be represented as doing that; cf. Elijah and his servant, I Ki. 18: 43f.; 19: 3) but accompanied by his servant Joshua. Aaron and Hur were appointed to act as his deputies during his absence. For forty days and nights he remained on the mountain, during which time, according to the bit of original tradition (ex-

---

[1] For a discussion of the passage, see p. 46.
[2] Cf. Morgenstern, "Psalm 48," *HUCA*, XVI (1941), pp. 72f.
[3] Note the reference to the *kebôd Yahweh* and *Mt. Sinai*, and the dating of the communication of the tablets of the law on the Sabbath.
[4] The LXX and Sam. VSS omit "and." The whole phrase "and the law and the commandment" seems to be an expansion by P.

panded by P¹) in 31:18, he was presented with two tablets inscribed by God's own finger.

Inserted into this tradition, as we have stated above, is another narrative, vv. 3-8, which relates how "Moses came [down from the mountain, apparently] and related to the people all the words and the statutes [*mishpaṭîm*] of Yahweh." He then proceeded to write down these laws in a book, called in v. 7 "the book of the covenant." The following morning he built an altar at the foot of the mountain, set up twelve pillars (*masṣebôth*), and had the young men offer up burnt-offerings (*'ôlôth*) and thank-offerings (*zebahîm shelamîm*). Moses himself disposed of the blood in approved levitical fashion (cf., for example, Lev. 8:22-30) and a covenant was entered into to observe the laws.

Now it is fairly obvious that the "stone-tablet story" in vv. 1f., 9-15, 18*b* refers to the decalogue, the Ritual Decalogue according to the theory here proposed. It would seem inherently probable, then, that the narrative in vv. 3-8, which relates the recording in a book of "all the words of Yahweh" with special emphasis laid on the *mishpaṭîm*, refers to the other Mosaic code, the Supplementary Code.² This is a hypothesis which receives strong support from the fact that the laws of the Supplementary Code are specifically entitled *mishpaṭîm* (21:1). It is customary to assign vv. 3-8 to E, and to regard them as E's account of the inscription of the Moral Decalogue, but there are several considerations which make it evident that they are a late and secondary composition: (i) If they had been present in the Mosaic Tradition at the time when Deuteronomy was composed, could the author of Deuteronomy have ignored them with their assertion that the Supplementary Code was revealed at the mountain, and maintained instead that this code was not revealed until the threshold of the Promised Land had been reached? (ii) They are in disagreement with the rest of the Exodus tradition because according to it Moses' descent from

¹The words "on Mt. Sinai and the two tablets of the testimony" seem to be an addition by P.

²The phrase "all the words of Yahweh" may refer to the hortatory epilogue appended to the code.

The Tradition of the Law-Giving

the mountain was followed, not by the communication of laws to the people and the making of a covenant, but by the incident of the Golden Calf.

Now there are some curious resemblances between these verses and the tradition in Dt. 27 and Josh. 8[1] which suggest that the Exodus narrative was drawn up by P with the other tradition in mind:

(a) The twelve *maṣṣebôth*, which serve no useful purpose in the Exodus narrative, seem to be a reflection of the altar stones of the other tradition.

(b) The *'ôlôth* and *zebahîm shelamîm* sacrificed at the mountain according to Ex. 24 recall the *'ôlôth* and *shelamîm* which were sacrificed at Shechem according to Dt. 27:7 (Josh. 8:31 uses the terms *'ôlôth* and *zebahîm*). In the Mosaic Ritual Decalogue in Ex. 20:24 the terms used for sacrifices are *'ôlôth* and *zebahîm shelamîm*. The change to *'ôlôth* and *zebahim shelamîm* in Ex. 24:3-8 undoubtedly suggests a later period.[2]

(c) The covenant of Ex. 24 recalls the covenant of Dt. 27-8. While there is no specific mention of the making of a covenant in Dt. 27-8, it is obvious from Dt. 29:1 that the ceremony was thought to imply one.

(d) Note also the care taken to dispose of the blood in approved levitical fashion and to have the sacrifices offered by "young men of the Israelites," since the appointment of the Levites as priests is not mentioned until chapter 32.[3]

P's insertion of the 24:3-8 story would be made necessary if it was he who transferred the Supplementary Code from its original position after Nu. 21:21-35 to its present position, for the original story (24:1, 2, 9-15, 18b) refers only to the giving of the decalogue. It was now necessary to amplify the story to make allowance for the giving of the Supplementary Code as well. Hence the specific mention of the *mishpaṭîm*

---
[1] See pp. 40f.

[2] The term *zebahîm shelamîm* is found only in H and P and in I Sam. 10:8, I Ki. 8:63, II Chron. 30:22, 33:16, Prov. 7:14 (Brown, Driver, and Briggs, *Hebrew and English Lexicon*, p. 257b).

[3] Pfeiffer, "The Oldest Decalogue," *HTR*, XXIV (1931), 99, also regards Ex. 24:3-8 as post-exilic, while T. H. Robinson, *History of Israel* (Oxford, 1932), p. 93, admits the late origin of some details of the narrative.

in v. 3. Verses 3-8 are actually one of the clearest proofs that the Supplementary Code is not in its original position.

It was probably P also who composed for the code in its new position the epilogue consisting of 23: 20-33. Its hortatory style and alternation between the singular and plural forms of address, its antipathy to the gods and peoples of the land, its description of the ideal boundaries of the Promised Land, its promise of the *ṣir‘ah* ("hornet") and of a guardian and guiding angel, and its assurance of the blessings which will follow an observance of the code recall passages in Deuteronomy (cf. 7: 1ff.; 11: 13-28; 28: 1ff.). But evidence will be presented below[1] to show that P was quite capable of composing in the Deuteronomic style.

It is interesting to find P maintaining that the laws given at Sinai (he evidently has in mind both the decalogues and the Supplementary Code) were immediately written down by Moses in a book, which is called "the book of the covenant" (v. 7), a term which he manifestly derived from II Ki. 23: 21 where Josiah calls Deuteronomy "this book of the covenant." But the original tradition makes no reference to Moses writing in a book.[2] P's assertion in Ex. 24: 3-8 may reflect the belief current in his day that the law-book at Jerusalem had actually been composed by the great law-giver himself at Sinai. It is worth noting that the post-exilic view, as attested by Dt. 1: 5, was that Moses "expounded" the code in Moab, rather than "revealed" it for the first time.

The results of this enquiry into the Revelation of the Codes may be summarized as follows. Instead of two early versions of the tradition, a J version and an E version, we have only one. In this one original tradition the code which was revealed publicly on Mt. Horeb was the Ritual Decalogue in Ex. 20: 23-6, 23: 10-19 which once stood after 19: 19. The code revealed in private to Moses was the Supplementary

---

[1] See pp. 162-6.

[2] Ex. 34: 27 is by P, as reference to Dt. 10: 4 shows. P, not wishing to attribute to the Deity such an anthropomorphic action as writing, altered the original tradition so that Moses does the writing. For a discussion of v. 28, see pp. 50f., 53f., 60f.

The Tradition of the Law-Giving

Code in Ex. 22: 20—23: 9 which was later incorporated with Joshua's code in Ex. 21: 1—22: 19 and the whole attributed to Moses. This original tradition was corrupted by the authors of Deuteronomy (the priests of Jerusalem, in my opinion[1]) by the assertion that the code revealed in public at Horeb was the Moral Decalogue, although there is no evidence that they tampered with the law-book (the Book of Exodus) to make it conform to this assertion. It was left for the authors represented by the symbol P (the post-exilic priests of Jerusalem) to do that. P no doubt accepted Deuteronomy at its face value as the work of Moses and felt obliged to reconcile the two traditions, the Deuteronomic and the Exodus. In view of the superior character of the Moral Decalogue he preferred, in fact he was compelled, to take it as the original Mosaic decalogue and so he inserted it, with an introduction of his own composing (Ex. 19: 20—20: 1), after Ex. 19: 19. The displaced Ritual Decalogue he distributed at the beginning and end of the Supplementary Code.[2] Its Mosaic character was thus preserved, only it was made a part of the laws revealed to Moses in private.

But this is not the whole story, as we shall see.

The Story of the Golden Calf and the Smashing of the First Set of Tablets

P, as we have seen, inserted into Ex. 24 a composition of his own which purports to relate how the Supplementary Code, as well as the decalogue, was written down by Moses in a book. He then proceeds to give his own version of the

[1] The theory of Welch that the D code is of Northern, Israelite origin is based on a view of the Hebrew priesthood which I believe to be erroneous. Nor can I accept the theory of E. Robertson that the code is the result of a process of collecting, collating, and sifting the legislation and traditions of the various sanctuaries by Samuel and his college of prophets; cf. "The Pentateuchal Problem: Some New Aspects," *Bulletin of the John Rylands Library*, XXIX (1945), 121-42.

[2] May it not be that P broke the decalogue into two parts (20: 23-6 and 23: 10-19) under the influence of the Story of the Smashing of the First Set of Tablets? The broken character imparted to the decalogue may have been deliberately designed to convey the impression that this version had been annulled in favour of the "revised" version which appeared on the second set of tablets (Ex. 34).

construction of an ark to hold the tablets of the law and of a tent-sanctuary to house the ark (Ex. 25-31). With chapter 32 we come to a pre-P tradition relating the Story of the Golden Calf and the Smashing of the First Set of Tablets. This tradition appears in a Deuteronomic version (Dt. 9: 8-29) as well as an Exodus version and a comparison of the two yields interesting results:

(a) The account of the manufacture of the calf in Ex. 32: 1-6 is not repeated in the Deuteronomic version but a knowledge of it is presupposed there.

(b) Dt. 9: 12-14 corresponds to Ex. 32: 7-10.

(c) The Deuteronomic version omits Ex. 32: 11-14 with its account of Moses' appeal to Yahweh to change his mind and not destroy the people because of their sin, as well as its statement that Yahweh did actually repent of the evil which he said he would do unto his people. There can be no doubt that D omitted this deliberately. In his eyes the calf-worshipping Samaritans were worthy of death.

(d) The Exodus account (32: 15-24) of Moses and Joshua descending the mountain and beholding a scene of pagan revelry, of Moses smashing the tablets and grinding up the calf, and of his interrogation of Aaron, appears in summary form in the Deuteronomic version (9: 15-21). But D inserts (in vv. 18f.) a forty-day-and-night intercession by Moses between the smashing of the tablets and the grinding-up of the bull. Obviously his aim is to emphasize the heinousness of calf-worship. He says it took over a month of prayer and fasting on Moses' part to induce Yahweh to change his mind and not destroy the people root and branch.

(e) The story in Ex. 32: 25-9 of how Moses stirred up the Levites to slaughter their fellow-Israelites because of their unruliness has no parallel in the Deuteronomic version. Either the author of Deuteronomy did not know of it or, if he did, he suppressed it.[1] D has, instead, at this point a list of some of the other places where the Israelites provoked Yahweh to anger (9: 22-4).[2]

(f) D winds up his account of the calf incident by reverting to the forty-day-and-night intercession and gives us the gist

[1] A discussion of this passage will be found on pp. 146f. [2] See pp. 130-3.

The Tradition of the Law-Giving

of Moses' petitions (vv. 25-9). But the wording is manifestly derived from Ex. 32: 11-14. Having omitted Ex. 32: 11-14 at its proper place in his version (see point *c* above) he now brings it in at the end. The Exodus version of the calf incident ends with an account (32: 30-5) of Moses re-ascending the mountain and making a second intercession on behalf of the people. But this passage contains a number of features which show it to be of P origin: (i) the reference to the "Book of Life" with names written therein; (ii) the use of the verb *kipper*, "to make atonement," in v. 30; (iii) the fact that the command to depart comes too soon, for Moses has still to go up the mountain to get a second copy of the tablets. In Dt. 10: 11 this command very naturally does not come until the new tablets have been received. P regarded the cult of the Golden Calf as such a heinous sin that the one intercession of the original tradition did not satisfy him and he invented a second, some basis for which he found in the divided form of the Deuteronomic account of the intercession (Dt. 9: 18-20 and 25-9).

A comparison of the Deuteronomic and Exodus versions thus shows that Dt. 9: 8-29 presupposes a knowledge of Ex. 32: 1-24 but knows nothing of the material found in Ex. 32: 25-35. Hence it is altogether likely that the original form of the Story of the Golden Calf and the Smashing of the First Set of Tablets is to be found in Ex. 32: 1-24.

The Story of the Golden Calf is generally and rightly regarded as having been incorporated into the Mosaic Tradition at a relatively late date. Since the story is manifestly a Judaean polemic directed against the bull cult instituted in the Northern Kingdom by Jeroboam I (*c*. 926-907 B.C.), it can only have arisen after the time of Jeroboam. Another indication of its date is the fact that the utterance placed in the mouth of the people in Ex. 32: 4, "These are thy gods, O Israel, who brought thee up from the land of Egypt," is taken from I Ki. 12: 28. The secondary, dependent character of the Exodus statement is revealed by the fact that in Kings the plural "gods," referring to the two bulls which Jeroboam had made, is appropriate but it is not appropriate in Ex. 32 where only one calf is involved.

50 *The Mosaic Tradition*

Pfeiffer[1] dates the first edition of Kings, to which the story of Jeroboam's bulls belongs, to about 600 B.C. This would seem to date the Ex. 32 story after 600 B.C. But the fact that Dt. 9 is based on Ex. 32 shows that the latter was in existence before 621 B.C. S. A. Cook[2] believes that the Golden Calf story is "probably not earlier than the time of Hezekiah" (c. 715-687 B.C.). Evidence of an indirect character will be presented below[3] which suggests that the incorporation of the story into the Mosaic Tradition actually took place in Hezekiah's reign.

Since Ex. 33 has no parallel in the Book of Deuteronomy, let us skip that chapter for the moment and study Ex. 34 with its Story of the Provision of a Second Set of Tablets and the Deuteronomic version of it in Dt. 10.

The Story of the Provision of a Second Set of Tablets

Ex. 34 describes how Moses was ordered to fashion two stone tablets like the ones he had broken and take them up the mountain to be inscribed with the laws which were on the former ones. His ascent was the occasion of a second theophany during which Yahweh revealed himself as a merciful and compassionate god but stern towards evil-doers. A covenant was then announced on the basis of a code of laws detailed in vv. 14-26, referred to in v. 28 as "the ten words." Moses remained on the mountain for forty days and nights, fasting, during which time he wrote the laws on the tablets. Then follows a story (vv. 29-35) of how as a result of this exposure to the Divine Presence a radiance was reflected on Moses' face ever afterwards.

The usual documentary analysis of this chapter sees in the code of laws the J parallel to the E code found in Ex. 20: 23-6, 23: 10-19, while the introductory narrative describing the theophany accompanying the revelation of the code is regarded as the work of J, modified and expanded by Rd. The Story of Moses with the Shining Face in vv. 29-35 is assigned to P.

---

[1] *Introduction to the Old Testament*, p. 377.
[2] *Critical Notes on Old Testament History* (London, 1907), p. 73, n. 1.
[3] See pp. 161f.

The Tradition of the Law-Giving

The interpretation of the chapter has been considerably influenced by the fact that while it pretends to portray the renewal of a broken covenant (see vv. 1-4), vv. 10ff. which describe the actual making of the covenant seem to represent it as something new. There is no allusion to a previous covenant or to any unfaithfulness on the people's part. Therefore scholars have concluded that the references in vv. 1 and 4 to "the former tablets" which Moses broke are later additions by Rd. The chapter, together with 33: 12-23, is said to present us with the J account of the theophany on Mt. Sinai. But fragments of a J theophany are said to be also discernible in Ex. 19 and it is by no means easy to dovetail all the supposed J elements into a smooth-running, consistent account. A problem is also presented by the position of the Ex. 34 code, so far from the theophany in chapter 19.

The answer ordinarily given to this problem is that when J and E were combined, the compiler, Rje, omitted J's code in favour of E's and also omitted part of J's theophany in Ex. 19. Later this discarded J material, which is evidently thought of as having continued to exist in old manuscripts, was reinserted into the tradition by Rd (Rd, because of the numerous Deuteronomic touches now added to the narrative and the laws). Under the influence of the Story of the Golden Calf and the Smashing of the Tablets which was present in the combined JE narrative, Rd utilized the discarded J material to work up a story of a renewal of the broken covenant and the provision of a second set of tablets. It is also maintained that since the laws in 34: 14-26 cannot be arranged in a decalogue (there being at least fourteen), the "ten words" of v. 28 must refer to the Moral Decalogue of chapter 20. In other words, we are asked to believe that Rd made the code of Ex. 34 the renewal, not of the parallel E laws in Ex. 20: 23-6, 23: 10-19, but of the Moral Decalogue, a code of totally different content.[1]

---

[1]Rudolph (*Der "Elohist" von Exodus bis Josua*, pp. 61, 276) regards the Moral Decalogue in Ex. 20 as the code of the original (J) tradition and believes it once stood where the Ex. 34 code now stands. The laws in 20: 23—23: 19 he considers to be an independent code which was attached only later to the Sinai tradition.

The Mosaic Tradition

As a matter of fact, the above interpretation of Ex. 34 has been completely upset by Pfeiffer's demonstration[1] that the code contained in the chapter is a post-exilic version of Ex. 20: 23-6, 23: 10-19 and, therefore, can never have stood in the J Document. Thus it is necessary to search for an entirely new explanation of the problems presented by the chapter.

I believe that the proper approach to the problems is by a comparison of Ex. 34 with Dt. 10: 1-11. According to this Deuteronomic version of the tradition, Moses' intercession for the people as narrated in 9: 25-9 is followed by Yahweh's command to him to cut two stone tablets like the former ones and take them up the mountain to be inscribed. Moses is also to make a wooden ark to put the tablets in. He fashions the tablets and ark and re-ascends the mountain where Yahweh reproduces the Moral Decalogue on them. Moses then descends and places the tablets in the ark.[2]

A comparison of this Deuteronomic account with the Exodus version of the tradition reveals two striking differences:

First, the Deuteronomic version mentions a command to construct an ark after the command to fashion the second set of tablets. The Exodus version, however, says nothing about the ark at this point but places the command to construct it back in chapters 25-30 and hence during Moses' first sojourn on the mountain to receive the tablets of the law. The question arises, Which position is original? Manifestly the command cannot have been given where D places it, for the original tradition knows nothing of a second set of tablets. But neither does it seem possible to accept the Exodus position for it because a perusal of the original narrative of Moses' sojourn on the mountain (cf. Ex. 24: 1, 2, 9-15, 18*b*; 31: 18*) shows that there is no room for it. Hence it is necessary to conclude that the command regarding the ark must have appeared at a later point in the tradition, if at all. A further discussion of the problem must be postponed until we come to a study of the Tent of Meeting.[3]

---

[1] See pp. 31f.
[2] For a discussion of Dt. 10: 6f., 8f., see pp. 74f., 98, 131, 146f.
[3] See pp. 58-61.

The Tradition of the Law-Giving

Second, the Deuteronomic version makes no mention of the theophany related in Ex. 34: 8-18 or of the code given in 34: 14-26. Dt. 10: 1-3 finds its parallel in Ex. 34: 1, 4; the next verse, Dt. 10: 4, finds its parallel in Ex. 34: 28, i.e., at a point after the narration of the theophany and the code. It may be that D deliberately omitted repeating the code, since according to him the Horeb covenant was based on the Moral Decalogue, in which case it was unnecessary for him to mention the theophany. But there are reasons for believing that both the theophany and the code are the work of P and hence cannot have been present in the original Exodus tradition which D used as the basis for his own account.

Let us turn, then, to an examination of the evidences of P authorship. In the case of the theophany, the only clear trace of P's hands is the designation of the sacred mountain as *Sinai* (cf. vv. 2, 4, 29, 32).[1] As for the code, it is necessary first to examine its internal structure.

According to the usual view the code consists of fourteen laws, but actually there are only ten, as follows:

1. A law against worshipping other gods (34: 14-16).
2. A law against making molten images (v. 17).
3. A law regarding the feast of unleavened bread (v. 18).
4. A law regarding firstlings (vv. 19f.).
5. A law regarding Sabbath observance (v. 21).
6. A law regarding the feast of weeks and the feast of ingathering (vv. 22-4).
7. A law against employing leaven with sacrifices (v. 25*a*).
8. A law against leaving any part of the Passover sacrifice unconsumed until morning (v. 25*b*).
9. A law regarding first-fruits (v. 26*a*).
10. A law against boiling a kid in its mother's milk (v. 26*b*).

Comparison with the version of the Ritual Decalogue given in Ex. 20: 23-6, 23: 10-19 shows that the altar-law is missing here, also the law regarding a sabbatical year for the land, and the law against mentioning the names of other gods. Besides these three omissions, there has been one addition, a law prohibiting the worship of other gods (v. 14*a*). There

---

[1] For a discussion of the names of the sacred mountain, see pp. 71-6.

can be little doubt that whoever inserted this law did so under the influence of the Moral Decalogue where such a law appears at the very beginning of the code (cf. Ex. 20: 2f.). The reviser was not content to insert the law alone but appended an extensive statement (vv. 14*b*-16) giving the reasons why it should be observed. Pfeiffer has noted how inextricably the law, and with it the whole code, is connected with the introductory narrative, vv. 1-13, by the particle *kî* at the beginning of v. 14. Thus, if either code or introductory narrative can be shown to be late, it is an additional argument for regarding the other half of the chapter as equally late.

The reviser, having omitted three laws and added one, had to get two more laws in order to bring the total number back to ten. He did this by inserting a law on firstlings and by breaking the festival law into two parts. To keep the two parts separate and prevent them from being taken as one, as they are in Ex. 23: 14-17,[1] he inserted the laws on firstlings and the Sabbath between them. The result is a very unnatural distribution of the festival legislation, enough in itself to brand the Ex. 34 version of the code as secondary.[2] Moreover, D's treatment of the festival law almost certainly rests, not on the Ex. 34 version, but on the Ex. 23 version, another proof of the priority of the latter.

Thus an examination of the internal structure of the code in Ex. 34 strongly supports the theory of Pfeiffer that it is a post-exilic redaction of the code found in Ex. 20: 23-6, 23: 10-19. There is no need to look beyond P for the person responsible for this redaction. However, neither the narrative introducing the code nor its epilogue can be entirely of P origin, for vv. 1, 4, and 28 find a partial parallel in Dt. 10: 1-4. Their true character is apparent from the fact that they form an integral part of the Story of the Golden Calf and the Smashing of the First Set of Tablets. They have, however, been subjected to some amendment by P. In v. 4 an original "the mountain" (cf. Dt. 10: 3) has been altered to "Mt. Sinai," while v. 28 has been reworded so as to have

[1] See the discussion on p. 36.
[2] The fact that v. 24, which has no parallel in Ex. 23: 17, implies centralized worship also points to the late date of the Ex. 34 version of the festival legislation.

The Tradition of the Law-Giving 55

Moses do the writing on the tablets. P may have been anxious to avoid attributing to the Deity such an anthropomorphic action as writing.

The results of our study of the whole Tradition of the Law-Giving may now be summarized. The tradition was corrupted in the first instance by the seventh century B.C. priests of Jerusalem who composed the Book of Deuteronomy. This book was put forth as the *ipissima verba* of Moses and in it the Moral Decalogue replaced the Ritual Decalogue as the basis of the Horeb covenant. This meant that henceforth there were two versions of the Tradition of the Law-Giving, which differed as to the decalogue which was to be attributed to Moses. To have such inconsistency and uncertainty surrounding the very basis of the faith was intolerable, and doubtless steps would soon have been taken to remove them had not the Babylonian exile intervened. But as part of the restoration of the cultus and reconstruction of the national polity following the return from exile, the priesthood of Jerusalem did endeavour to harmonize the two versions of the law-giving. The story of Moses smashing the first set of tablets and going up to get a second set suggested a way out of the difficulty. Why not make the Moral Decalogue the code inscribed on the first set of tablets and the Ritual Decalogue the code inscribed on the second set? In this way a place could be found for both "Mosaic" decalogues. But the Jerusalem priests were not content to take the Ritual Decalogue in the form which had come down to them (as preserved in Ex. 20: 23-6; 23: 10-19), for of that decalogue the Shechemites could claim to possess the original copy engraved on the two tablets. So they resolved to put forward an "improved," revised version of this decalogue, one which Jerusalem alone would possess, just as in the Book of Deuteronomy they put forward an "improved," revised version of the Mosaic Supplementary Code. But the priests, no doubt conservative themselves, had to deal with a conservative public as well and therefore they may have deemed it advisable to preserve the unretouched version of both Mosaic codes. They did so by combining them and placing them at as early a point in the narrative as possible, leaving the impression that the versions which come later are the final, more authoritative forms.

But P's arrangement of the codes presented him with a problem, for by placing the Moral Decalogue after Ex. 19 he thereby deprived the Ritual Decalogue of the theophanic introduction which properly belonged to it. He did not feel it fitting to insert his "improved" version of this Ritual Decalogue into Ex. 34 without an equally impressive theophanic setting and so he was obliged to compose one. Scholars, familiar with the ordinary style of P, will object that this introduction contains little that is characteristic of P. For the present I would merely suggest that P has here made an effort to compose in the "Mosaic" style. A fuller discussion of the whole problem must be reserved till Chapter VII.

IV Tradition of the Tent of Meeting and of Moses' Father-in-Law

LET US TURN BACK NOW AND EXAMINE THE MATERIAL contained in chapter 33. This chapter falls into three divisions: (i) the order to resume the journey to the Promised Land, the promise of a guiding angel, and the order to the people to remove their Mt. Horeb ornaments, vv. 1-6; (ii) the Story of the Tent of Meeting, vv. 7-11; (iii) Moses' request for some evidence of Yahweh's favour and for his presence with them. Yahweh agrees to accompany them and promises to reveal some of his Glory to Moses, vv. 12-23.

This chapter has no parallel in the Deuteronomic version of the tradition except that D does have Moses receive an order to depart. But he places the giving of the order while Moses is on the mountain receiving the second copy of the decalogue and interceding for the people (Dt. 10: 11). It is true that Ex. 33 also places the order to depart after an intercession for the people (32: 30-5) but this intercession is represented as having taken place *before* Moses' ascent to receive the second copy of the laws.

The natural position for the command to be given is immediately after the receipt of the tablets of the law. But the incorporation of the Story of the Golden Calf into the tradition created two occasions when tablets were received. This led D to shift the order to a position after receipt of the second set of tablets, which was certainly the most appropriate place for it as the narrative now stood. However, P, who is responsible for the present arrangement of the tradition in Ex. 33, as we shall see, refused to follow D in this and kept the command in its original position, after receipt of the first set of tablets.[1] His reason for doing so

---

[1] The order to depart in Ex. 33: 1f. is anticipated in Ex. 32: 34. But we have seen that 32: 30-5 is from the hand of P, and the repetition in the present form of the narrative is due to his carelessness.

was probably that he wished to insert a great block of material (Ex. 35-40, Leviticus, Nu. 1—10:28) after the receipt of the second set.

Evidence that the command was originally worded briefly and that it was later amplified by the addition of vv. 2-6 is to be found in the following facts: (i) The pre-Israelite inhabitants of Canaan are not listed in the same order as that which the earlier tradition regularly employs.[1] (ii) Verses 2 and 3a seem to be based on 3:17. (iii) Verse 4, with its reference to the people mourning and putting off their ornaments, has no parallel in Dt. 1:6-8. The reference in v. 2 to the guiding angel suggests that the amplification was the work of P.[2] An examination of the vocabulary of vv. 2-6 also suggests that we have to do with a P composition; note, for example, the employment of *rega‘* in v. 5 and the *Pi'el* of *kalah* in vv. 3, 5 as in Nu. 16:21 (a P passage). It is evident that P expanded the original wording of the command in order to make it appear that the departure from the mountain was a punishment for the sin of the Golden Calf. Yahweh can no longer bear the people's presence. In the parallel versions of the order found in Dt. 1:6-8 and 10:11 there is no suggestion that Yahweh is displeased with the people. On the contrary, he leads them to expect complete success in their new venture.

Turning now to the Story of the Tent of Meeting in vv. 7-11, it is obvious from the abrupt manner in which the tent is introduced that the first part of the story is missing.[3] When we refer to the Deuteronomic version for light on this peculiar problem, our perplexity is increased by the discovery that D makes absolutely no reference to the tent. We are led to ask, What was there about this tent that made it so abhorrent to D that he refused even to mention it? And why was the introduction to the Exodus account of the tent suppressed, presumably by P?

In seeking the answer to these questions, we may begin with the observation that the tent was clearly designed to

---

[1] Cf. p. 162.   [2] Cf. p. 24.
[3] The reading "his tent" in v. 7 by LXX and Syr. is manifestly an attempt to soften the abruptness of the transition.

The Tradition of the Tent of Meeting

serve as an oracular shrine, a place of divination. "Anyone wanting to consult [*mebaqqesh*] Yahweh [that is, to learn Yahweh's will on any matter] would go to the Tent of Meeting which was outside the camp." Since the apparatus regularly employed by the Hebrews for divination was the ephod, containing the sacred lot, the Urim and Tummim, we seem justified in inferring that the Tent of Meeting contained an ephod.

Such an inference is, of course, not in harmony with the P narrative in Ex. 25-30, 35-40, where it is stated that the central object in the Wilderness Sanctuary was an ark, containing the tablets of the law. But it is difficult to see how an ark containing two tablets inscribed with laws that had been publicly revealed could serve as an instrument of divination.

If we examine the original tradition, as far as we have succeeded in identifying it, we are surprised to find that it makes no allusion whatsoever to the ark. We seem driven to the conclusion that the ark was first introduced into the tradition by D. It was his substitute for the tent of the original tradition. This accounts for the difficulty, noted above,[1] of finding a satisfactory place in the original tradition for a command to construct an ark.

D's aversion to the tent may have been due to the fact that it was said to have been in charge of a non-Levite, Joshua (Ex. 33:11). To him a Levitical priesthood was all-important, as is evident from such passages as Dt. 17:9, 18; 18:1; 24:8 and from his care to have the tribe of Levi immediately appointed to look after his ark (10:8).[2]

P was faced with the necessity of combining the tent, presumably containing an ephod, of the original tradition with the ark, containing the tablets of the law, of the Deuteronomic version of the tradition. The content of the introduction to the tent story must have been such that he felt compelled to suppress it in the interests of harmonization. But there is no evidence that he shifted the story to a different

---
[1] p. 52.
[2] It is a mistake to infer from the presence of the itinerary statement in vv. 6f. that D placed the appointment of the Levites at Jotbah. Cf. pp. 75, 146f.

position in the narrative from that which it originally occupied.¹

We have examined the first two sections of Ex. 33. There remain for consideration vv. 12-23. That these verses are from P is clear from their vocabulary. Note the reference to Yahweh's *kebôd* in vv. 18 and 22, the pronoun *'anî* in vv. 16 and 19, the use of *'aḥôr* in the plural in v. 23 (found elsewhere only in P, and in Ez. 8:16 and I Ki. 7:25 = II Chron. 4:4), and the phrase *maṣa' ḥen*, "find favour," in vv. 12f. and 16f. (elswhere only in Gen. 6:8, Ex. 34:9, and Nu. 11:11, 15—all P passages, I believe). Ex. 33:12-23, together with 34:1-13, form P's introduction to the revised version of the Ritual Decalogue which he inserted in 34:14-26.² Being of a conservative temperament, P did not manufacture this introduction, with its account of a second theophany on Mt. Sinai, out of whole cloth but based it on two very natural sources, Ex. 19 and the story in I Ki. 19 of the theophany to Elijah on Mt. Horeb.

According to Dt. 1:6-8 the order to depart from Horeb was followed by a request of Moses to the people to choose assistants for him since their numbers had become so great that the burden of administration was too much for him. So captains (*sarîm*) of thousands, hundreds, fifties, and tens are chosen (vv. 9-18) and immediately thereafter the Israelites set out from Horeb on their way to the Promised Land (v. 19). But the version of the tradition in Ex. 18 attributes this organization of the people to a suggestion of Moses' father-in-law, Jethro, the priest of Midian, who arrives at the Israelite camp accompanied by Moses' wife, Zipporah, and his two sons, Gershom and Eliezer. The story that this Midianite foreigner is to be given credit for the innovation can scarcely be explained as a later invention. It is much more likely that the author of Dt. 1 has reshaped the tradition in

¹Morgenstern believes that the Story of the Tent of Meeting once stood after Ex. 34:28, i.e., it stood where the P story of Moses with the Shining Face now stands ("The Tent of Meeting," *JAOS*, XXXVIII (1918), 125-39; "Moses with the Shining Face," *HUCA*, II (1935), 1-27). He has recently proposed replacing 33:9f. by 34:34f. (*The Ark, the Ephod, and the Tent of Meeting* (Cincinnati, 1945), p. 157).

²Cf. pp. 53-6.

accordance with the national and racial prejudices of a later time. But the chronology of Dt. 1, which places the incident shortly before the departure from Horeb, seems preferable to that of the Exodus version which, in its present form, places it before the arrival at Sinai. As Morgenstern[1] points out, the institution of the judges must have followed, not preceded, the giving of the law.

If we accept the chronology of Dt. 1, Ex. 18 should follow the order to depart from the mountain given in 33:1. But it is necessary to find a place for the Story of the Tent of Meeting, a story which D ignores. The most natural place for it is undoubtedly after 33:1. The sequence in the original tradition would thus be: the order to depart, the Tent of Meeting, the story of Jethro's visit. I believe that it was P who shifted the story of Jethro's visit back to its present position in chapter 18, being animated in so doing by the separatist, puritanical, anti-foreign spirit of his time (cf. Ezra 9-10, Neh. 13:23ff.). He wanted no foreigner to have a part in the foundation of the national faith at the sacred mountain and so shifted the story about Jethro back prior to the arrival at the mountain. But the awkwardness of its present position is obvious from the fact that while in chapter 18 the Israelites are represented as encamped at the mountain of God, they are not definitely stated to have arrived there until 19:1f. When P moved the story from its original position after 33:7-11, he replaced it by a composition of his own, 33:12-23, according to which the Israelites were led on their further journey not by any human guide but by Yahweh himself.

If the above interpretation be correct, the last part of the original tradition in the Book of Exodus must be chapter 18, not Ex. 34:28 as ordinarily maintained. The original narrative is resumed in Nu. 10:29, as has long been recognized, and it forms a very natural sequel to Ex. 18, much more

[1]"The natural implication of the entire Sinai-Horeb narrative is that the first and chief thing to happen after the Israelites came thither was not the visit of Jethro and the appointment of the judges, but the ascent of the mountain by Moses and the revelation of the law..." ("The Oldest Document of the Hexateuch," *HUCA*, IV (1927), 127).

natural than to Ex. 34:28. But two difficulties present themselves: (i) Moses' father-in-law, who in Ex. 18 is called *Jethro*, is in Nu. 10 called *Hobab the son of Reuel*; (ii) the end of Ex. 18 refers to the departure of Jethro to his own land, whereas in Nu. 10:29 Hobab is still present in the Israelite camp.

The problem presented by the two different names for Moses' father-in-law has usually been attacked with the JE hypothesis in mind: Hobab the son of Reuel is regarded as the name used in the J Document, Jethro as the name used in the E Document. But if the basic contention of the present work, that we have to do with only one early document, be correct, then some other explanation of the two names of Moses' father-in-law must be sought. In seeking a new solution of the problem, we may begin with two observations. First, the material separating Ex. 18 (in its original position) and Nu. 10:29 is from P, and we have already seen the tendency of P to make slight alterations in the text of the original tradition immediately preceding and following his own insertions.[1] Thus we are prepared to find traces of his fingerprints in Nu. 10:29. Secondly, Nu. 10:29 sounds incomplete; we naturally expect to find some reference either to Hobab's departure or to his decision to remain. But strange to say, we are left in the dark as to whether he agreed to accompany Moses or not.

The solution of this last problem is probably to be found in regarding Ex. 18:27 as the conclusion of Nu. 10: 29-32. Even so, a reply on the part of Moses' father-in-law is needed between Nu. 10:32 and Ex. 18:27. It must have stated that he refused to accompany the Israelites.

Now if Nu. 10:29-32 was preceded by Ex. 18:1-26, the name of Moses' father-in-law in Nu. 10:29 originally must surely have been Jethro.[2] There would be no need to call him either "the Midianite" or "the father-in-law of Moses" as that has already been done (cf. Ex. 18:1, 2, 5, etc.), although the words "his father-in-law" might have stood there, as in Ex. 18:17, 24.

[1] Cf. p. 28.
[2] Morgenstern, "The Oldest Document of the Hexateuch," pp. 133f., attempts to solve the riddle by altering the name *Jethro* throughout Ex. 18 to *Hobab*.

The Tradition of the Tent of Meeting

We need to remember that in dealing with the problem of Moses' father-in-law, as in dealing with the question of the Mosaic decalogue, P was faced with divergent traditions and had to harmonize them. He had to take into account not only the tradition in Ex. 3 and 18 according to which Moses' father-in-law was called *Jethro the Midianite* but also the tradition in Ju. 4:11 where he is called *Hobab* and made to be the sheikh of the Kenite tribe.[1] It is usually maintained that the name applied to Moses' father-in-law in Nu. 10:29, viz., *Hobab, the son of Reuel, the Midianite*, is an example of P's harmonization. I personally believe that P's assertion that Hobab was a son of Reuel rests on some early tradition. But P was wrong in making Hobab and Reuel Midianites, for Ju. 4:11 states that Hobab was a Kenite. It would seem that P, like most modern scholars, assumed that the Kenites must have been a Midianite tribe.

P was evidently proceeding on the theory that Jethro and Hobab were brothers, the sons of Reuel, who is first mentioned in Ex. 2:18. Now P does not want any foreigner to play a prominent role in the national tradition and so detract from the leadership of Yahweh and Moses. By shifting the story of Jethro back to a position before the arrival of the Israelites at Sinai he disposes of him. But when he changes the name Jethro to Hobab, P is obliged to omit the negative answer of Moses' father-in-law to the request that he accompany the Israelites as a guide, for it was a well-known tradition that Hobab and his Kenites had accompanied the Israelites into Canaan (cf. Ju. 4:11; I Sam. 15:6). P seems to have been anxious to kill this tradition, however, for in his version of it in Ju. 1:16 he deliberately omits the name of the Kenite chief.[2]

It has long been noticed that the name Reuel is introduced in a rather odd manner in Ex. 2. The natural place for it to be mentioned is in v. 16, but it does not appear until v. 18. I believe that this marks it as a later insertion and that

---

[1] The rendering of Ju. 4:11 in the Revised Version which makes Hobab a "brother-in-law" of Moses is not justified. The Hebrew word used is the same as that employed in Ex. 18 for "father-in-law."

[2] LXX^A reads *Hobab* but this reading is probably based on surmise rather than on a Hebrew text.

originally the story did not mention the name of the Midianite priest at all. Notice that in v. 21 he is referred to simply as "the man," whereas if his name had been mentioned previously we should expect it to appear here. P evidently took the name Reuel from the Hobab-Kenite tradition and inserted it here to suggest, without actually affirming it, that Jethro, as well as Hobab, was a son of Reuel. If he had not had some such purpose in mind he could just as easily have inserted the name Jethro in chapter 2 and thus made a smoother transition to chapter 3.

But if we refuse to accept P's solution of the problem of the relationship of Hobab the Kenite to Jethro the Midianite, what alternative solution can we offer? An answer to this question is suggested by Nu. 12 where we have a tradition about Moses' marriage to a Cushite woman. Although many scholars deny that it was a second marriage, this is undoubtedly the most natural interpretation of the tradition for it is very unlikely that Miriam would suddenly go into hysterics over her brother's marriage to the Midianite Zipporah, a marriage which had been a *fait accompli* for a considerable time now.[1] If Moses had two wives, he must have had two fathers-in-law. Is it possible that the Cushite girl whom Moses took to wife on this occasion was the daughter of Hobab ben Reuel the Kenite? Is there any basis for regarding the Kenites as Cushites?

It is a well-known fact that the Hebrews used the term *Cush* to designate Ethiopia and that they reckoned the Yemenite Arabs, as well as the Dedanites of the northern Hejaz, as Cushites or Ethiopians (cf. Gen. 10: 6f.), having doubtless observed what many a modern traveller has noted, namely, the marked resemblance of the Southern Arabs to the Abyssinians or Ethiopians. But the fact that in Gen. 10: 21-31 the Yemenite Arabs are depicted as sons of the Semite Joktan shows that the Hebrews recognized that while from one point of view they should be classified as Ethiopians, from another point of view they should be classed as Semites. Now it is interesting to find the Midianites mentioned in Gen. 25: 1-4 in the same group

[1] Cf. L. E. Binns, *Numbers* (Westminster Commentaries), p. 75.

The Tradition of the Tent of Meeting

as the Sabaeans and Dedanites, and if the latter could sometimes be regarded as Cushites there would seem to be no reason why the other members of the group might not be referred to in the same way. This suggestion receives strong support from Hab. 3: 7 where *Cushan* is used in parallelism with *Midian*.

It was evidently regarded as legitimate, then, for an author to refer to the Midianites as "Cushites." Does the same hold true of the Kenites? Surely the Old Testament with all its wealth of ethnographical information contains some ray of light on the affinities of this tribe whose fortunes became so linked with those of the Israelites. The Hebrew writers are so careful to give the genealogy of everybody who plays a part in their traditions that it is inconceivable that they should have overlooked their friends the Kenites.[1] Now it can surely not be a mere coincidence that the name *Reuel* appears as the name of an Edomite tribe in Gen. 36: 4, 10, 13, 17. This Reuel is a son of Esau's third wife, the Ishmaelitess (i.e., Arab) Basemath, the sister of Nebaioth. In other words, this Edomite tribe was of Arab stock and closely related to the Nabataeans. Is it not highly probable, then, that the term *ben Reuel* applied to Hobab indicates not the name of his father but the name of the tribe to which he belonged, just as *bn hmdn* following many South Arabic names means "a member of the tribe Hamdan."

It may be objected that the tribe to which Hobab belonged could not well possess two names, *Reuel* and *Kain*. In reply it might be maintained that the name *Kain* denoted their occupation (*qain* being the Arabic word for "smith") rather than their tribal designation. Edom was a great copper-mining and refining centre[2] and therefore the logical place to find a group of smiths established. But the story of Cain and his descendants in Gen. 4 suggests that the Kenites regarded themselves as true Beduins. Nor is there anything in their later history to suggest that they were smiths by

---

[1] The reference in Gen. 15: 19 = I Chron. 2: 55 which lists them among the pre-Hebrew inhabitants of Canaan sheds no real light on the problem of who they were.

[2] See Glueck, "Explorations in Eastern Palestine, II," *AASOR*, XV (1935), 48.

profession. Furthermore, the assumed correspondence of Hebrew *ha-qênî* to Arabic *al-qain* is very precarious. The pattern of the Hebrew word is that of a gentilic, not of a noun denoting occupation.

Nu. 24:21 derives *qênî* from *qēn*, "nest," the reference being to some particularly inaccessible crag where the Kenites had their home. While this is merely an instance of popular punning, it may give us the true origin of the term "Kenite" nonetheless. "Kenite" may have been merely a popular designation of a tribe which bore quite a different name. I suggest that the Kenites are identical with the Reuel of Gen. 36. If this be so, the Kenites were of Ishmaelite Arab stock. The Abrahamic-Keturian Midianites might be referred to as Cushites but the Hebrew genealogies lend no support to the theory that the Ishmaelite Arabs could be referred to in the same way. Hence the author of Nu. 12 in using the term "Cushite" of Moses' wife must be basing himself on the occasional application of the term to the Midianites. It would seem, then, that he must have in mind Zipporah, the Midianitess, after all and that Nu. 12 does not refer to a second marriage on Moses' part.

But the hypothesis that Moses had two fathers-in-law, Jethro the Midianite and Hobab the Kenite, offers such a tempting solution of the problem that it is difficult to rest content with the above conclusion. The theory that Nu. 12 refers to a second marriage of Moses receives support not only from the fact that a quarrel over his marriage to the Midianite Zipporah is unintelligible at this stage but also from the fact that it is said to have occurred at Hazeroth, the last camping-place before reaching Kadesh. It seems inherently probable that this second marriage of Moses was motivated by political and security considerations, like some of the marriages of Solomon and Muhammad later on. The Israelites were passing beyond the Midianite area and entering the pasture-lands of a new tribe and Moses may have felt it a wise policy to establish the closest possible ties with his new neighbours by marrying into the family of one of their sheikhs. Just as the fact that he was married to a Midianite wife had secured peaceful entry for himself and his

The Tradition of the Tent of Meeting

followers into Midianite territory, so his marriage to a daughter of the chief of Kadesh would secure admission for himself and his followers into that town and its surrounding territory. So the marriage was arranged and celebrated at Hazeroth, just prior to their arrival at Kadesh. That Kadesh was a town before the Israelites came along is fairly evident from Nu. 20:16 where it is called an '*ir*, which means that it must have had previous inhabitants. But who were these inhabitants? In Chapter v reasons will be advanced for accepting the old tradition that Petra marks the site of Kadesh. Here it may be remarked that in Nu. 24:21f. the abode of the Kenites is said to be "set in the *sela*'" and to possess a perennial stream. The fact that Gen. 36 makes the Reuel tribe, with which in my opinion the Kenites are to be identified, related to the Nabataeans also suggests that their dwelling-place was in or near the region later controlled by the Nabataeans. Now according to Diodorus Siculus XIX. 94-7 (quoting Hieronymus of Cardia, 312 B.C.) the Nabataeans had a law "neither to sow corn nor to plant fruit-bearing plants, nor to use wine, nor to build a house." Exactly the same rule is said by Jeremiah (35:6) to have prevailed among the Rechabites, who, according to I Chron. 2:55, were a branch of the Kenites. This is a very striking coincidence and indicates that the Kenites came from the Nabataean area. We are not told that all the Kenites held to this nomadic rule. I Sam. 30:29 refers to "the cities of the Kenites," while I have suggested above that the Kenites had once dwelt in the '*ir* of Kadesh. But neither did the Nabataean law prevent the Nabataeans from settling in the city of Kadesh and developing it into Petra. There is, however, a striking absence of remains of "built" houses at Petra, most of the homes being hollowed out of the rock. If the inhabitants of Petra were indeed Kenites, then it is almost certain that Moses' marriage at Hazeroth was to a Kenite girl, the daughter of Hobab.

We conclude, then, that behind the present form of Nu. 12 lies an earlier tradition of Moses' marriage to the daughter of Hobab the Kenite. But in Nu. 10:29-33 P has placed Hobab at Sinai rather than at Kadesh and has implied that

Hobab did not accompany the Israelites; he is thus compelled to alter the tradition of a marriage of Moses to Hobab's daughter later on at Hazeroth. He omits all reference to Hobab and turns the Kenite girl into a nameless "Cushite," i.e., Midianite. Why did he use the term Cushite? Probably because he regarded the Kenites as a Midianite tribe and because the term had a contemptuous ring and served to explain why Miriam and Aaron were opposed to the marriage.

Now if we reread Nu. 12, we will be struck by the fact that while the essence of the story is a quarrel between Miriam and Aaron and their brother Moses over his marriage to a Cushite woman, there has been injected into it a defence of the uniqueness of Moses as a prophet—a matter which seems to have little connection with the point at issue. We shall see, however, that P frequently used stories of disputes in the original tradition as pegs on which to hang some of his own ideas and doctrines,[1] and we are led to suspect that he may have done the same here. Our suspicion is increased by the fact that the story of Moses' uniqueness as a prophet forms a natural sequel to the Story of the Seventy Prophetic Elders which P inserted in the preceding chapter (Nu. 11). Clear marks of P authorship are to be found in the expressions "speak against" (*dibber b^e*) in vv. 1 and 8*b*, and "Yahweh heard" (v. 2); in the reference to Yahweh coming down in a pillar of cloud, as in Nu. 11:25 (a P verse); in the implication that Miriam was a prophetess, as in Ex. 15:20 (another P verse)[2] and in the quarantine of Miriam for seven days in accordance with the Levitical law in Lev. 13:4. Gray, McNeile, and Binns regard Nu. 12 as a part of the E Document; Pfeiffer[3] assigns it to E_2. Rudolph,[4] on the other hand, assigns it to J, except for vv. 2-8, 10*a*^{a}, 11, which he regards as secondary additions. Personally I think the story has been so recast by P that little of the original wording remains, although Dt. 24:9 shows that the original tradition referred

---

[1]See the discussion of Nu. 11 on pp. 133-6 and of Nu. 16 on pp. 142-8.
[2]Cf. p. 85.
[3]*Introduction to the Old Testament* (New York, 1941), p. 171.
[4]*Der "Elohist" von Exodus bis Josua*, Beih. *ZAW*, LXVIII (Berlin, 1938), 70-4.

The Tradition of the Tent of Meeting 69

to Miriam being smitten with leprosy. The late date of the present form of the story is indicated by the fact that it assumes that the age of the great prophets is past and that there existed controversies as to the relation in which these stood to Moses.

It may not be amiss to point out the implications of our interpretation of these Sinai-Horeb traditions for the origin of the Yahweh religion. Of recent years a theory of the Kenite origin of Yahweh has been exceedingly popular,[1] but if the above interpretation be correct, the Kenite theory is completely undermined. The Kenites do not appear at the mountain at all but only when Kadesh has been reached. Even if we substitute a Midianite theory for a Kenite, there is little in the Hebrew tradition to support it. We have seen that the proper place for Ex. 18 is at the end of the Horeb story, just prior to the departure for Kadesh.[2] Moses has had his dealings with Yahweh, the laws have been revealed and a covenant entered into before Jethro the Midianite appears on the scene. Moreover, we have seen[3] that P's assertion in Ex. 6:3 that the name Yahweh was first revealed to Moses and that the patriarchs had worshipped God by another name rests on a misinterpretation of Ex. 3. The Genesis tradition asserts that the patriarchs did worship God under the name of Yahweh; Yahweh was "the god of the Hebrews," "the god of Abraham, Isaac, and Jacob."

---

[1] For the literature, see G. A. Barton, *Semitic and Hamitic Origins* (Philadelphia, 1934), pp. 331f.; W. O. E. Oesterley and T. H. Robinson, *Hebrew Religion* (2nd rev. ed.; London, 1937), pp. 147ff.; Morgenstern, *The Ark, the Ephod, and the Tent of Meeting*, p. 152. My colleague, Dr. T. J. Meek, has stood almost alone in opposing this theory (cf. his *Hebrew Origins* (New York, 1936), pp. 86f.).

[2] pp. 61f.   [3] p. 26.

V *The Tradition of the Wilderness Itinerary*

IT HAS LONG BEEN EVIDENT THAT THE PRESENT FORM OF the tradition regarding the route followed by the Israelites during the forty years in the wilderness does not present a simple, straightforward account. The two different names for the sacred mountain (Sinai and Horeb), for the place where Moses brought forth water from the rock (Massah and Meribah), and for the location of Kadesh (the wilderness of Zin and the wilderness of Paran) are only some of the phenomena which indicate the complexity of the narrative. The JE hypothesis promised a solution of the problem, and it was now asserted that the double nomenclature was a result of the fact that the national tradition of the Hebrews either had undergone a bifurcated development, taking on a somewhat different form in the Northern Kingdom from that which it received in the South, or had sprung from two different roots.[1]

But it has become more and more evident that the JE hypothesis does not provide a satisfactory explanation of any of the problems raised by the tradition. Furthermore, the theory has generated an attitude of scepticism and despair. For the assumption that the tradition developed in two different directions, or even that it represents a conflation of the traditions of two originally distinct groups of peoples, has the effect of casting doubt on its trustworthiness. There may be some truth behind it all but it is now impossible to discover precisely what it is. Such a negative conclusion may be the only one possible under the circumstances; the tradition may have undergone so many changes and become so distorted

[1] Cf. T. J. Meek, *Hebrew Origins* (New York, 1936), p. 111; S. A. Cook, *Critical Notes on Old Testament History* (London, 1907), pp. 81f.; *Cambridge Ancient History*, II (1924), 366.

The Tradition of the Wilderness Itinerary

and confused that it is hopeless to try to recover its original form and to ascertain the historical facts lying behind it. But in our study so far we have found no evidence to support the JE theory. Only one early version of the Mosaic Tradition has been found, a version which was later modified by D and then by P. We shall, therefore, approach the study of the Tradition of the Wilderness Itinerary with the assumption that only one early form of it existed, and see if this will lead us to more positive results.

The Sacred Mountain

Any interpretation of the Tradition of the Wilderness Itinerary will be largely determined by the conclusion arrived at as to the location of the sacred mountain. It is, therefore, necessary to make up our minds on this vital matter first of all. I believe we are justified in starting with the assumption that the Jews of a later period were not content to remain in ignorance of the route followed by their forefathers on this memorable trek. The region through which God had led their forefathers was not in some remote corner of the globe but near at hand, and there must have been ardent souls who endeavoured to repeat the sacred pilgrimage. That this last assumption is not without foundation is evident from a comparison of the form of the itinerary as given by P (Nu. 33) with its form in the earlier Exodus narrative. Whereas the early form of the itinerary gives only twenty-four names of camping-places, the P list contains forty-two. These additional names can scarcely be the creation of P's imagination; they must represent the results of later research, probably based on the reports of pilgrims who had endeavoured to repeat the sacred journey.

These pilgrims must have been guided in their movements by some knowledge or theory as to the location of the sacred mountain. Now one of the names given to the mountain in the tradition, viz. *Sinai*, would seem to identify it with some peak in the peninsula which is today called Sinai. Of course, the application of this name to the peninsula is merely an extension of its originally restricted usage as the name of a particular mountain; but the very extension supports the view that the region now called Sinai holds the mountain Sinai somewhere in its embrace. It might be argued, and has been argued, that the name Sinai was originally applied to a mountain in another locality such as Midian, east of the Gulf of 'Aqabah, and was later transferred to a peak on the west side of the gulf. But no other part of the Near East has ever laid claim to the name Sinai, so that there seems to be little basis for assuming a migration or transference of the name. As to the particular peak in the Sinai peninsula which is to be identified with the Mt. Sinai of tradition opinions differ. E. H. Palmer, as a result of the very careful examination of the region made by the Ordnance Survey Expedition to the peninsula of Sinai in 1868-9, of which he was a member, came to the conclusion that "the claims of Serbāl are comparatively modern, . . . the true traditional Sinai is Jebel Mūsa".[1] This view has been accepted by most later investigators,[2] but Mr. C. T. Currelly[3] and others have championed the claims of Jebel Serbal.

However, a decision in favour of the claims of one of these mountains to be Sinai in preference to the other will not give us necessarily the location of the sacred mountain for we still have to take into account the tradition in Ex. 3:1 which calls the mountain *Horeb* and locates it in the land of Midian, which, as we know, lay along the east side of the Gulf of 'Aqabah, and hence to the south of Edom.[4] That the name *Horeb* is an integral part of the early tradition is shown by the fact that it alone appears as the name of the mountain of the law-giving in Deuteronomy (cf. 5:2; 9:8; 18:16; also the later additions 1:2, 6, 19; 4:10, 15; 28:69 [EV

[1] *The Desert of the Exodus* (Cambridge, 1871), I, 5; cf. p. 276 also.
[2] Cf., e.g., S. R. Driver, *Exodus* (Cambridge Bible Series), pp. 177-91, and A. H. McNeile, *Exodus* (Westminster Commentaries), pp. ci-cii.
[3] In Flinders Petrie's *Researches in Sinai* (New York, 1906), pp. 247-54. Cf. also Winckler's article, "Sinai and Horeb," in the *Encyclopaedia Biblica*, IV (London, 1903).
[4] Cf. A. Musil, *The Northern Ḥegâz* (New York, 1926), Appendix 9: "The City of Madian, the Madianites, and the Mountain of God"; W. J. Phythian-Adams, *The Call of Israel* (London, 1934), Appendix 2: "The Boundaries and Topography of Midian"; *Encyclopaedia of Islam:* "Madyan Shu'aib."

The Tradition of the Wilderness Itinerary 73

29:1]; 33:2), in I Ki. 8:9, and in the Elijah story (I Ki. 19:8) where it is stated that a journey of "forty days and forty nights" is required to reach it, a statement scarcely applicable to either Jebel Musa or Jebel Serbal.[1]

While it is clear that the name *Horeb* is an integral part of the early tradition, it is by no means certain that the same is true of *Sinai*. Phythian-Adams, in his stimulating little book *The Call of Israel*, suggested that all the references to Sinai were of post-exilic origin and that the name represents a late attempt to identify the Horeb of tradition. Scholars do not seem to have taken kindly to his suggestion, doubtless because it does not accord with the customary documentary analysis of the Book of Exodus, but the present writer is convinced that it is correct. Phythian-Adams points out that of the thirty-five occurrences of *Sinai* in the Old Testament, seventeen are found in Numbers and Leviticus (in passages of P origin), one in Neh. 9:13 (post-exilic), one in Ju. 5:5 (where it is metrically superfluous and a manifest gloss), two in Ps. 68:8, 17 (post-exilic in its present form), one in Dt. 33:2 (post-exilic).[2] The remaining thirteen instances are found in Exodus; of these, seven are in passages admittedly from P (16:1; 19:1, 2a; 24:16; 31:18; 34:29, 32). Thus the argument as to whether the name *Sinai* existed in the pre-exilic tradition boils down to a discussion of six passages: Ex. 19:11, 18, 20, 23; 34:2, 4. Now it has already been stated that Ex. 19:20-5 is P's introduction to his version of the Moral Decalogue which he inserted in chapter 20,[3] and that Ex. 34:1-13 (except for those few parts which are paralleled in Dt. 10) is his introduction to his version of the Ritual Decalogue which he inserted in chapter 34.[4] This eliminates 19:20, 23 and 34:2, 4. Only two instances remain for consideration, 19:11, 18. In the case of these it is impossible to *prove* that the word *Sinai* is a later insertion, but a comparison of Ex. 34:2, 4 with Dt. 10:1, 3 is very suggestive. Where D has "ascend[ed] the

---

[1] Post-exilic references to Horeb are to be found in Mal. 3:22 (EV 4:4); II Chron. 5:10; Ps. 106:19.

[2] Cf. R. H. Pfeiffer, *Introduction to the Old Testament* (New York, 1941), p. 278.

[3] See p. 33. [4] See pp. 54, 56, 60.

mountain," P in Ex. 34 has altered the wording to "ascend[ed] Mt. Sinai." It would be quite in accordance with his editorial habits, then, that he should alter an original "the mountain" in Ex. 19: 11, 18 to "Mt. Sinai." P's very insistence on the name *Sinai* makes us all the more confident that the name *Horeb* was original to the tradition and that the name *Sinai* represents a post-exilic attempt to identify it.

Having demonstrated that the name *Sinai* was almost certainly not a part of the original tradition, we turn with greater interest to the references to Horeb. We note first that only the passage already mentioned, Ex. 3: 1, definitely states that Horeb lay in Midian.[1] But this statement is supported by all the stories which link Moses with Midian and can be rejected only at the price of rejecting them.

There are, however, two passages (Dt. 33: 2, Ju. 5: 4f.) which place the sacred mountain not in Midian but in Edom. But they both call the mountain "Sinai." The first is definitely of post-exilic date; the second is part of a poem which is usually regarded as one of the earliest surviving specimens of Hebrew literature. Even though we ignore the reference to Sinai in Ju. 5: 5 as a later interpolation (following Burney), still v. 4 states that the sacred mountain was in Edom, an assertion without parallel in all the pre-exilic literature. In fact, this assertion stands in such glaring contrast to the "Horeb in Midian" tradition that, in my opinion, the early date of Ju. 5 in its present form is seriously called in question.[2]

There is another passage to which I should like now to direct attention, viz., Dt. 10: 6f. This passage comes immediately after the account of Moses coming down from the mountain with the second copy of the law and depositing the tablets in the ark. It reads as follows: "The Israelites set out from the wells of the Beneʻ Yaʻaqan for Moserah, where Aaron died and was buried, his son Eleazar succeeding

---

[1] In view of our comparative ignorance of the topography of the land of Midian, the various identifications which have been proposed for Mt. Horeb must be regarded with reserve (cf. Musil, *The Northern Ḥegâz*, p. 263; Pythian-Adams, *The Call of Israel*, p. 212; McNeile, *Exodus*, p. cv).

[2] Nelson Glueck, "The Boundaries of Edom," *HUCA*, XI (1936), 155, regards vv. 3-5 as of post-exilic date.

The Tradition of the Wilderness Itinerary 75

him in the priesthood. From there they set out for ha-Gudgod, and from ha-Gudgod for Yotbah, a land with streams of water." S. R. Driver[1] regards these verses as an interpolation from the E Document but he can suggest no reason for their insertion at this point. Nor, as far as I am aware, has any other commentator divined their real significance. They actually present a theory as to the location of the sacred mountain. Since the preceding verses represent the Israelites as being at Mt. Horeb, the statement that they "set out from the wells of the Bene Ya'aqan" can only mean that the writer located Mt. Horeb in the territory of the Ya'aqan tribe. But who were the Ya'aqanites? If we turn to Gen. 36:27 we get the answer: Ya'aqan (not 'Aqan, as the parallel passage in I Chron. 1:42 shows) was an Edomite, a son of Ezer who was one of the seven sons of Seir. In other words, the Bene Ya'aqan belonged to the Edomite tribe of Ezer. Thus Dt. 10:6f. locates Mt. Horeb in territory which in the author's day was Edomite.

But what is the date of this passage? Is it an insertion by a later hand, as most commentators declare? Certainly it has all the appearance of being an insertion, just as vv. 8f. have; but that does not mean that it cannot be by D. The authors of Deuteronomy wished to insert into the original tradition, which they have been repeating in vv. 1-5, a theory or contention of their own and in doing so were unable to avoid giving to the narrative a broken appearance. What we have in vv. 6f., then, is D's theory as to the location of Mt. Horeb: it was in the land of Edom—or, at least, in territory occupied by an Edomite tribe—not in Midian.

The tradition regarding the location and identity of the sacred mountain thus seems to have developed as follows: (i) In the early form of the tradition it is called *Horeb* and located in the land of Midian. (ii) In the D version, or perversion, of the tradition it is still called *Horeb* but located in Edomite territory.[2] If, as seems probable, the Sinai peninsula was under Edomite control at the time of D, the

---

[1] *Deuteronomy* (International Critical Commentary, New York, 1895), pp. 119f.

[2] The interest shown by the later Israelites in the Edomite traditions was doubtless due to the current belief that the holiest sites of the Hebrew faith lay in Edomite territory.

latter may have located the sacred mountain in that region.
(iii) In the P version of the tradition the mountain is called
Sinai and probably identified with either Jebel Musa or
Jebel Serbal. The references in Dt. 33: 2 and Ju. 5: 4f.
show that the post-exilic Jews located Mt. Sinai in territory
which was regarded as forming a part of Edom. This might
well be the Sinai peninsula.[1] It seems probable, therefore,
that there were only two traditions current as to the location
of the sacred mountain: an early tradition which located
it in Midian, and a later tradition, put into circulation by
D, which located it in the Sinai peninsula.

The existence of these two different traditions or theories
as to the location of the sacred mountain was bound to have a
profound effect on the interpretation of the Tradition of the
Wilderness Itinerary. In the discussion of it which follows
I shall endeavour to demonstrate that the original tradition
represented the Israelites as journeying from Egypt to Mt.
Horeb in the land of Midian but that this tradition was
modified by D and P to accord with their theory that the
sacred mountain lay in southern Sinai.[2] If the tradition was
distorted in this way, it is little wonder that scholars who
have accepted it at its face value have never been able to
work out a consistent theory, on which they are all agreed,
as to the route taken by the Israelites on their way to the
Promised Land.

THE ITINERARY

PART I. FROM EGYPT TO THE MOUNTAIN OF GOD

Stations 1-3: Rameses, Succoth, and Etham

Ex. 12:37a, 39a *The Israelites journeyed from Rameses to
Succoth ... and they baked unleavened cakes out of the
dough which they had brought from Egypt....*

Ex. 13:20 *They journeyed from Succoth and encamped at
Etham on the edge of the desert.*

The long-standing problem of the site of Rameses,
assuming it to be the Hebrew equivalent of the Egyptian

---

[1]For a further discussion, see pp. 100-2, 117.   [2]See the map.

Pi-Ra'messe, seemed to have been settled by the excavations of Montet at Tanis.[1] Rameses was to be located at Tanis (biblical *Zoan*, modern *San el-Ḥagar*). But the fact that Pi-Ra'messe and Tanis are mentioned separately in the Golénischeff Glossary, a list of Deltic towns from the Twenty-First Dynasty and hence from a time when Pi-Ra'messe still existed, made some scholars suspicious that all was not yet well with Rameses. Their suspicions seemed confirmed by the discovery of remains of a palace of Rameses II at Qanṭīr, a village about sixteen miles south of Tanis and six miles north of Faqūs. The presence at this spot of a factory for the production of enamelled tiles on a scale surpassing that of Akhnaten's factory at Tell el-Amarna points to the presence in the immediate vicinity of an imperial residence of first importance. Five ostraca from the site actually bear the name of Pi-Ra'messe.[2]

Even though an identification with Qanṭīr may ultimately prove to be correct, most of the problems connected with the interpretation of the Exodus tradition still remain. It does not, for example, explain the inconsistency of the narrative which at times represents the Israelites as dwelling apart from the Egyptians in the land of Goshen (8: 18, EV 22; 9: 26; 10: 23) and at other times as intermingled with them, so mixed up, in fact, that they are able to borrow clothing and articles of silver and gold from them and despoil them before setting out on their journey (3: 22; 11: 2f.; 12: 35f.).[3]

Nor does this identification solve the problem of reconciling the factors of space and time in the tradition of the departure from Egypt. According to the tradition the

---

[1]Cf. P. Montet, "Tanis, Avaris et Pi-Ramses," *Revue biblique*, XXXIX (1930), 1-28; *Les Nouvelles Fouilles de Tanis, 1929-1932* (1933); also A. H. Gardiner, "Tanis and Pi-Ra'messe: A Retractation," *JEA*, XIX (1933), 122-8.

[2]For an excellent presentation of the case for Qanṭīr, see Père B. Couroyer's article, "La Résidence ramesside du delta et la Ramsès biblique," *Revue biblique*, LIII (1946), 75-98. This identification has been accepted by Père F. M. Abel, *Géographie de la Palestine*, II (Paris, 1938), 430, but Professor W. F. Albright adheres to the identification with Tanis ("Exploring in Sinai with the University of California African Expedition," *BASOR*, No. 109 (1948), p. 15).

[3]Cf. A. H. Gardiner, "The Delta Residence of the Ramessides," *JEA*, V (1918), 265, n. 1.

Israelites reached Succoth after less than a full night's march. Here they seem to have stopped only long enough to partake of a hasty meal of unleavened bread. Then they pushed on to the edge of the desert which was evidently reached at night-fall and there they encamped.[1] It will be perceived at once that whether we take Tanis or Qanṭīr as marking the site of Rameses, a journey of at least thirty miles is required in order to reach the desert. Those familiar with desert life assert that the average day's journey is from ten to fifteen miles.[2] It is very doubtful, then, if a large group, encumbered with women and children and flocks of sheep and goats, could have covered the required distance in part of a night and a day. But even admitting that they could, if they set out from Tanis they would have been unable to enter the desert without passing by one of the strongest Egyptian frontier fortresses, Zilu (Zaru, Thel),[3] which guarded the coastal road to Palestine. Moreover, the nature of the terrain at this point, a narrow strip of land intersected by canals,[4] would have made the Israelites peculiarly vulnerable to attack by the Egyptian garrison. The next nearest point where they could have attempted to enter the desert would be between Lakes Ballah and Timsaḥ. But this would have required an even longer journey and have been even more impossible in the time allotted. If Rameses be located at Qantīr, the difficulty of reconciling the factors of space and time is not as great but is still considerable.

[1] I cannot accept the ordinary interpretation of the tradition which makes Rameses two, or even three, days' journey from the edge of the desert (cf. Gardiner, *JEA*, XIX (1933), 127; Palmer, *The Desert of the Exodus*, p. 270).

[2] A. Lucas, *The Route of the Exodus* (London, 1938), pp. 54f., quotes the opinion of Conder and Jarvis that the Israelites cannot have gone more than ten miles a day. H. C. Trumbull, *Kadesh-Barnea* (New York, 1884), p. 73, states that the average day's journey in the desert is from fifteen to eighteen miles. Musil gives the figure as twenty-two kilometres, i.e., about fourteen miles.

[3] Modern *Tell Abū Ṣēfeh*, 1½ miles east of el-Qantara. Cf. A. H. Gardiner, *JEA*, V (1918), 242f., and VI (1919), 99, 104; and W. F. Albright, *JEA*, X (1924), 6.

[4] See the map from the *Description de l'Égypte* reproduced by Gardiner in *JEA*, VI (1919), 105, which shows this region as it was before the construction of the Suez Canal. Cf. Lucas, *The Route of the Exodus*, p. 40, nn. 1-3, for references to other early maps.

The Tradition of the Wilderness Itinerary 79

These considerations point to the conclusion that the mention of Rameses, the Egyptian capital, as the starting-point is the result of a dramatization of the tradition. It was both more dramatic and more satisfying to Israelite pride to represent the exodus as starting from right under Pharaoh's nose and from the city which had been the scene of their deepest humiliation than to preserve the historical fact, which probably was that Moses and Aaron went home to the land of Goshen where the Israelites were living, reported the failure of the negotiations with Pharaoh, and made plans for a fly-by-night departure from Egypt.

I believe that the inconsistency in the presentation of the dwelling-place of the Israelites, which has been mentioned above, is also to be explained by the striving after dramatic effect rather than by the assumption that two documents, each with a different point of view, have been combined. The historical fact seems to have been that the majority of the Israelites were living apart from the Egyptians in the land of Goshen, usually located in some part of the Wady Tumilat, a thirty mile long avenue leading from about the middle of the modern Suez Canal into the heart of the Delta.[1] But as the tradition developed it was found more satisfying to bring the Israelites occasionally into closer touch with the Egyptians in order that they and their god might "gain glory" at the Egyptians' expense. Actually there are only two such occasions: (i) in chapter 5 (based on chapter 1) where the Israelites are pictured as engaged in building (presumably Pithom and Rameses) for the Egyptians and necessarily intermingled with them for the time being; (ii) in Ex. 12:35f., at the "spoiling" of the Egyptians, where, in order to "spoil" them in a manner satisfactory to the Semitic sense, it was necessary to represent the peoples as intermingled.

---

[1]Cf. A. Lods, *Israel from its Beginning to the Middle of the Eighth Century* (Eng. trans.; London, 1932), p. 173, and Gardiner, *JEA*, V (1918), 128, 218ff. T. E. Peet, *Egypt and the Old Testament* (Liverpool, 1922), pp. 78ff., disputes this identification. If P, like the author of Ps. 78:12, 43, identified Rameses with Zoan = Tanis, he must have thought of the land of Goshen as being in the vicinity of Tanis (cf. Gen. 47:11, a P passage).

Another problem presented by the Exodus narrative which can be explained by the desire for dramatic effect is the inconsistency in the presentation of the manner in which the Israelites left Egypt. In some passages (12: 33, 39; 14: 5) their departure is depicted as extremely hurried, in fact, as a flight; and this must represent the historical truth of the matter. But in other passages (3: 20ff.; 11: 8; 12: 35f.; 13: 18)[1] their departure is represented as a triumphal exodus; the people go out "with a high hand," defiantly, regardless of Pharaoh's wishes. It may be doubted whether the writer was really conscious of any inconsistency in his presentation. It was necessary, on the one hand, to have the Israelites represented as leaving Egypt in a hurry in order to explain the origin of the Feast of Unleavened Bread. But having made this necessary concession, the writer proceeds to forget about it and to emphasize the fact that they left Egypt in triumph. It would scarcely have been consonant with the belief that Yahweh himself led the Israelites to represent them as leaving in ignominious flight, nor would national pride have permitted it. We may be very sure that there would never have been any reference at all to the hastiness of their departure if the story of the origin of the Feast of Unleavened Bread had not required it.

Let us go on now to the problem of the route followed by the Israelites out of Egypt. If we accept Gardiner's identification of Succoth, the first halting-place, with Tell el-Maskhūteh,[2] the line of flight must have been down the Wady Tumilat in which this *tell* is located. The Israelites must have assembled for the flight at a spot five or ten miles to the west of that place. An overnight march would bring them to Succoth; a further march of twelve miles during the day would bring them to Lake Timsah on the frontier, where Etham was evidently located. Here they would have to turn either north or south in order to get around the lake and enter the desert. The modern pilgrim road enters the desert at the north end of the lake. We shall refrain, how-

---

[1] Cf. also Ex. 13: 3, 8f., 14, 16, later accretions to the tradition; and Nu. 33: 3, from the hand of P and, therefore, later still.

[2] Cf. *JEA*, V (1918), 268. See the map.

ever, from drawing any deductions immediately as to the identity of the lake which was crossed until the next part of the Tradition of the Itinerary has been examined.

Station 4: Pi-hahiroth

Ex. 14:1f. *Then Yahweh spoke to Moses, saying, Speak to the Israelites and have them turn back and encamp in front of Pi-hahiroth, between Migdol and the sea, in front of Baal-zephon: you shall encamp opposite it by the sea.*

Instead of being allowed to spend the night at Etham, on the edge of the desert, the Israelites are ordered to turn back and place themselves beside a body of water referred to as "the sea" (Heb. *ha-yam*), a sea they eventually have to cross in order to enter the desert, which shows that they encamped to the west of it. Was the movement to Etham a feint designed to throw a pursuer off the track? Did they on debouching from the Wady Tumilat or some other area strike north as if heading for either the Beersheba road or "the road to the land of the Philistines" in the hope that the news would spread and any Egyptian pursuing force would be sent via Zilu to head them off? Then by retracing their steps for a short distance and using "the sea" as a protection for their flank, did they plan to penetrate into the desert at another point farther south? The ruse, if such it was, failed for we find the Egyptians hot on their trail. Or did they hear that an Egyptian force was approaching from the direction in which they were heading and so turn back? Had Moses hoped to elude the frontier guards and, failing this, was he reduced to the dangerous expedient of trying to ford whatever sea or lake lay in their path? Whether Goshen be located in the Wady Tumilat or in the vicinity of Tanis, the Israelites had been living relatively near the eastern frontier for a long time and some of them must have been acquainted with any feasible crossings of the lakes which lined this frontier.

The location of the spot where the Israelites forded the sea is very carefully defined in Ex. 14:1f. It is customary to assign these verses in their entirety to P, but it is inherently probable that long before the time of P the spot had been pointed out. If the names of the sites where far less notable happenings occurred were preserved by tradition, we may be very sure that the name of the site of this greatest deliverance by their god was similarly preserved. The Crossing is said to have taken place at a spot called Pi-hahiroth, the location of which is defined as "between Migdol and the sea, in front of Baal-zephon." The *'athnah*, marking the main pause within the sentence, appears with the word "sea" but this is almost certainly incorrect because it gives to the sentence the meaning that the Israelites encamped in front of two places, Pi-hahiroth and Baal-zephon, which can scarcely be what the writer intended. It is highly probable that the *'athnah* should be shifted to the word "zephon." The phrase "in front of Baal-zephon" would then define "the sea"; it was the sea which was in front of Baal-zephon.

The reference to "Migdol" without any distinguishing epithet would undoubtedly suggest to the Hebrew mind the same place as the "Migdol" mentioned in Jer. 44:1, 46:14; Ez. 29:10, 30:6, i.e., the Migdol which lay between Pelusium and Zilu (Thel).[1] In the demotic papyrus *Cairo 31169* there is a list of no less than four Migdols. According to Bourdon[2] the third in the list is called "Migdol Baalsephon" and Père Abel accepts this reading. But Gardiner[3] states that "only the first and westernmost of the four Migdols in the Cairo papyrus remains without further epithet or qualification" and refers to the fact that Daressy, whom Bourdon follows, has proposed some new readings which are not to be trusted. He believes that the three lesser Migdols "are probably forts of less importance further along the road to Palestine." If all these Migdols were actually located along this road, it would seem impossible to identify any of them with the Migdol of Ex. 14:2, for we are expressly told in Ex. 13:17 that the Israelites did not take "the road to the land of the Philistines."

The reference to "Baal-zephon," however, points in the

[1] Cf. the discussion of this Migdol by A. H. Gardiner, "The Ancient Military Road between Egypt and Palestine," *JEA*, VI (1919), 107ff.
[2] "La Route de l'Exode," *Revue biblique*, XLI (1932), 543.
[3] *JEA*, VI (1919), 108.

direction of this very road. We know from the Ras Shamrah tablets and from Assyrian inscriptions[1] that there was in Syria a god called *Baal-sapon* whose dwelling-place seems to have been the lofty mountain just above Ugarit, a few miles south of the mouth of the Orontes River.[2] "It is the most conspicuous landmark of North Syria, its summit commanding a view of Cyprus and the Taurus mountains."[3] The mountain is now called *Jebel el-Aqra'*; in Hellenistic and Roman times it was called *Mt. Casius*, and its Baal had become *Zeus Casius*.[4] Strabo (I. ii. 31; iii. 4, 13, 17; XVI. i. 12; ii. 26, 28, 33) and Herodotus (II. 6, III. 6) mention another Mt. Casius, a low mound in the middle of the strip of sand which separates Lake Serbonis (modern Lake Bardawil) from the Mediterranean. It may be that just as the northern Mt. Casius was once called *Sapon* or *Baal-sapon*, so the southern Mt. Casius may once have borne the name *Baal-sapon* (= *Baal-zephon*) also. Sailors may humorously have named this little mound after the great peak which served them as a landmark in the north.[5] While outwardly unimpressive, there is evidence that this mound was a sacred spot for it was crowned with a temple to Jupiter Casius, and Pompey was buried there (Strabo, XVI. ii. 32-3).[6]

[1] Cf. F. A. Schaeffer, "Les Fouilles de Minet-el-Beida et de Ras Shamra," *Syria*, XII (1931), p. 10 and Plate VI; Édouard Dhorme, "Deux Tablettes de Ras-Shamra de la campagne de 1932," *Syria*, XIV (1933), 233f.

[2] The original Safon of North Semitic mythology was probably located much further north (cf. Morgenstern, "Psalm 48," *HUCA*, XVI (1941), 78).

[3] C. H. Oldfather in his translation of Diodorus Siculus (Loeb Classical Library), III, 335, n. 1.

[4] Cf. Diodorus, VI. i. 8-11; Strabo, XVI. ii. 5.

[5] The theory of a transference of the name of the northern Baal to this site was first proposed, I believe, by O. Eissfeldt, Ba'*al Zaphon, Zeus Kasios und der Durchzug der Israeliten durchs Meer*, 1932, a work which, unfortunately, I have not seen. Professor W. F. Albright, *BASOR*, No. 109 (1948), p. 15, follows M. Aimé-Giron in taking a reference in a Phoenician letter to "Baal-zephon and all the gods of Tahpanhes" as proof that the Baal-zephon of Ex. 14: 2, 9 is to be identified with Tahpanhes (= Greek *Daphnae*, modern *Tell Defneh*, about nine miles west of el-Qantara and about eighteen miles east-south-east of Tanis). But does the fact that a *god* Baal-zephon was worshipped at Tahpanhes prove that the *place* Baal-zephon is to be identified with Tahpanhes?

[6] See the maps in *Revue biblique*, XLVIII (1939), facing p. 533, and XLIX (1940), facing p. 239; also *JEA*, VI (1919), facing p. 114, and T. E. Peet, *Egypt and the Old Testament*, map 2.

The Mosaic Tradition

If Baal-zephon be identified with the southern Mt. Casius, then "the sea in front of [i.e., east of] Baal-zephon" must be Lake Serbonis. This is undoubtedly the natural sense of Ex. 14: 2. It is not surprising, however, that scholars have refused to take the passage at its face value for, as we have seen, Ex. 13: 17 definitely states that the Israelites did not go in that direction. The only conclusion that can be drawn is that 14: 2, in its present form, represents a later modification of the original tradition. I would suggest that the original tradition ended with "Pi-hahiroth" and that the rest of the verse represents a later attempt by P to fix the site of this otherwise insignificant spot. If P, like the author of Ps. 78, believed that Zoan (Tanis) marked the site of Rameses, he may very well have assumed that the sea which was crossed was Lake Serbonis.[1] This lake, or bog, and the strip of sand, from one hundred to three hundred yards in width, which separates it from the Mediterranean is a natural feature which has caught the attention of many modern students (Brugsch, Hall, Gardiner, Peet, Jarvis)[2] and led them to regard it as the most fitting setting which the whole Egyptian theatre provides for the events narrated in Ex. 14-15—this in spite of 13: 17. We need not be surprised, then, if it caught the attention of Jewish students in their attempts to fix the sites of the various incidents of the Exodus tradition. P may have felt that the remark in 13: 17 applied only to the route taken after the Israelites had crossed the bog to the strip of sand and followed it to its farther end. Instead of taking the coastal road on up to what is now el-'Arīsh and on to the land of the Philistines, he may have believed that they turned off and headed south into the desert.

When we turn to examine the assumed pre-P form of the tradition, the first thing we observe is that the body of water through which the Israelites passed is called simply "the

[1] On the other hand, he may be responsible for the identification of Rameses with Pelusium which appears in the Targums (cf. Gardiner, *JEA*, V (1918), 262). Such an identification would make P even more certain that the sea of the Crossing was Lake Serbonis, for there is no other body of water beyond Pelusium.

[2] See the striking aerial photograph of this highway through the midst of the sea in C. S. Jarvis, *Yesterday and To-day in Sinai* (Edinburgh, 1931), facing p. 177. Cf. Trumbull, *Kadesh-Barnea*, p. 403.

The Tradition of the Wilderness Itinerary 85

sea" (*ha-yam*) (cf. 14:9, 16, 21-3, 26-30; 15:1, 19, 21).[1] In 15:4 and 22 it is called *yam sûph*, but these verses do not belong to the original tradition. The first verse is part of the poem in 15:2-18, a late expansion of the song of Moses in 15:1. The second verse is clearly by P. McNeile assigns it to J but the deviation from the normal itinerary formula (the *Hiph'il* instead of the *Qal* form of *nasa'*, "to journey," which is used elsewhere; cf. Ex. 12:37; 13:20; 16:1; 17:1; 19:2; Nu. 10:11, 33; 11:35; 12:16; 20:22; 21:4, 10-13; 22:1) betrays its unusual character. It is one of the editorial habits of P when he inserts anything, such as the poem in 15:2-18, to leave his finger-prints in the form of slight alterations and to make additions designed to fasten the new patch on to the old garment.[2] Here his additions consist of 15:19-22a.[3] But why did he employ here, the name *yam sûph* which in Nu. 33:10 he uses for the "Red Sea," if he believed the sea of the Crossing to be Lake Serbonis? We will have to leave this problem in abeyance for the moment.

The original tradition, then, called the sea of the Crossing simply "the sea." It is acquainted with the term *yam sûph* but uses it to designate the Red Sea. Thus in Ex. 13:17f. *yam sûph* clearly denotes that arm of the Red Sea now called the Gulf of 'Aqabah: "Now when Pharaoh let the people go, God did not lead them by the road to the land of the Philistines [i.e. northward], although that was near at hand ... but by the desert road to the Red Sea [*yam sûph*, hence eastward]." The parallel structure of vv. 17 and 18, according to which *yam sûph* in one sentence occupies the place of "the land of the Philistines" in the other, suggests that the *yam sûph* was at a distance from Egypt comparable to that of Palestine. The statement that they had to cross the desert to get to it also indicates that it lay at some distance from Egypt. It is obvious that the Gulf of 'Aqabah

[1]This fact was noticed by Lucas, *The Route of the Exodus*, p. 41, and before him by Chester (cf. Trumbull, *Kadesh-Barnea*, p. 360).

[2]For other examples, see pp. 27f., 62.

[3]It is customary to assign v. 19 to Rp and vv. 20f. to E (J, according to Rudolph) but the reference to Miriam as "the prophetess" and "the sister of *Aaron*" stamps them as the work of P. See p. 68.

best meets the requirements of the situation. The same branch of the Red Sea is denoted by *yam sûph* in passages like Ex. 23: 31, Nu. 14: 25; 21: 4; Dt. 1: 40; 2: 1; Ju. 11: 16; I Ki. 9: 26; Jer. 49: 21. On the other hand, in Ex. 10: 19 (a part of the early Exodus tradition) the term denotes either the main body of the Red Sea or its other northern arm, the Gulf of Suez.[1]

The fact that no part of the Red Sea is characterized by reediness suggests that the popular interpretation of the name *yam sûph* as "sea of reeds" is incorrect. Professor J. A. Montgomery[2] has drawn attention to the fact that in I Ki. 9: 26 the Greek versions render the name by "the farthest sea," which implies a reading *yam sôph* rather than *yam sûph*. The Red Sea was well known from early times as the avenue of commerce with the distant Orient and if regarded as an arm of the Indian Ocean, as it actually is, a name such as *Ultimum Mare* would indeed be appropriate.

To sum up, the complete absence of the term *yam sûph* in the early tradition of the Crossing indicates that "the sea" which was crossed was not any branch of the Red Sea, either the Gulf of Suez or the Gulf of 'Aqabah, while the information given in Ex. 13: 17f. as to the direction taken on leaving Egypt shows that it cannot have been Lake Serbonis. It must, therefore, have been one of the shallow lakes which exist or once existed along the line of the present Suez Canal. Lake Timsah, at the mouth of the Wady Tumilat where the land of Goshen was probably located, fits most naturally into the picture. This is where Lucas[3] and Wright and Filson[4] place the Crossing.

But the vagueness of the primitive tradition, with its reference to the unknown Pi-hahiroth and its designation of the sea of the Crossing as simply "the sea" did not satisfy

---

[1]Lucas, *The Route of the Exodus*, p. 42, thinks it here denotes Lake Manzaleh but the "sea-wind" which lifted up the locusts is most naturally interpreted as a wind from the Mediterranean. It would follow that the *yam sûph* into which the locusts were dumped was the other large body of water in the opposite direction from the Mediterranean.

[2]"Hebraica," *JAOS*, LVIII (1938), 131f.

[3]*The Route of the Exodus*, p. 41.

[4]*The Westminster Historical Atlas to the Bible* (Philadelphia, 1946), p. 38*b*.

The Tradition of the Wilderness Itinerary 87

the later desire for precision. The first attempts to introduce precision are found in the Deuteronomic version of the tradition and in the early portions of the Book of Joshua (cf. Dt. 11:4; Josh. 2:10; 4:23; 24:6). Here *ha-yam* of the original tradition has become *yam sûph*. In post-exilic references to the Exodus we find the same term employed (cf. Neh. 9:9; Ps. 106:9; 136:13, 15). It would seem highly probable that in all these passages, both pre-exilic and post-exilic, the term is used with the same connotation, viz., the Red Sea. Just what particular part of the Red Sea the authors had in mind, we do not know. Perhaps they did not know themselves.

Did P subscribe to this prevalent theory? We have already found some evidence that he did not, that, instead, he identified "the sea" with Lake Serbonis. P was a scholar and given to research and may not have accepted the popular view. But we found that in Ex. 15:22 he definitely calls the sea of the Crossing the *yam sûph*, and that in Nu. 33:10 he uses this term of the Red Sea. As a way out of the seeming impasse at which we have arrived, I would suggest that in 15:22 his use of the term is a concession to the song which he has just quoted (vv. 2-18) where the sea is called *yam sûph* (v. 4). If we adopt Professor Montgomery's suggestion, the original reading in v. 4 will have been *yam sôph* but P, desiring to identify it with Lake Serbonis, interpreted it in v. 22 as *yam sûph*, "sea of reeds," an interpretation doubtless suggested by the definitely reedy character of this lake.[1] It is worth noting, however, that in his summary of the wilderness itinerary in Nu. 33, P is content to call the sea of the Crossing simply "the sea" (v. 8) and does not have the people reach the *yam sûph* (probably originally *yam sôph*) until they have passed Elim (v. 10).

Station 5: Marah

Ex. 15:22f. *Then Moses had the Israelites journey from the* yam sûph *and they went out into the desert of Shur; they travelled in the desert for three days without finding water.*

[1] Cf. C. S. Jarvis, *Yesterday and To-day in Sinai*, pp. 174, 176.

Then they came to Marah, but they could not drink any water from Marah because it was bitter [mar]. *That is why it was called Marah.*

After crossing "the sea" the Israelites entered "the desert of Shur," a term which denoted that part of the Sinai desert next to Egypt (cf. Gen. 25:18; I Sam. 15:7; 27:8). P, in his summary of the itinerary in Nu. 33, avoids the term "desert of Shur" and substitutes instead "desert of Etham" (v. 9; cf. Ex. 13:20). This is evidently an attempt to define more narrowly the region through which the Israelites were moving. A tradition of uncertain origin and date fixes the first halting-place after leaving Egypt at some springs called '*Ayūn Mūsā*, "the Springs of Moses," two hours' ride from Suez. Those scholars who believe that the goal of the Israelites was a mountain in southern Sinai identify Marah with '*Ain Ḥawwārah*, a solitary spring of bitter water three days beyond Suez.[1] But it is significant that Marah is not called '*Ain Marah*. Lucas points out that the throwing of a stick in the water suggests a well. According to the theory of the Exodus route which is being advocated here, the well must have lain along the road to 'Aqabah, though not along the regular route or water would have been met with sooner.

Station 6: Elim

Ex. 15:27 *Then they came to Elim where there were twelve springs of water and seventy palm trees; and they encamped there beside the water.*

This passage is the most crucial for the interpretation of the tradition of the itinerary from Egypt to Horeb. It is to be noted first that P, in Nu. 33:10, turns the Exodus phrase "beside the water" into a further stage in the journey, stating that "setting out from Elim, they camped beside the

[1] Cf. Palmer, *The Desert of the Exodus*, pp. 40, 273; Petrie, *Researches in Sinai*, p. 205; McNeile, *Exodus*, p. ci; G. E. Wright and F. V. Filson, *The Westminster Historical Atlas to the Bible*, p. 39a. Driver, *Exodus*, p. 142, questions this identification, as does Bourdon (*Revue biblique*, XLI (1932), 549) who proposes an identification with Wady Werdān, 60 km. from Suez.

Red Sea." The expansion suggests that he located Elim at some spot that was not on the seashore and so had to insert further journeying in order to bring the Israelites to the sea. This accords with the view of many modern commentators who identify Elim with the Wady Gharandel.[1] Although the wady contains some tamarisks and palms and a perennial stream, it is only two hours' journey from 'Ain Ḥawwārah, which these scholars identify with Marah, and hence does not seem far enough away to constitute a separate camping-place for a group in a hurry. Moreover, this wady does not offer a feasible route to the Red Sea.[2]

Now we have seen that in Ex. 13:18 it is stated that when the Israelites left Egypt they headed across the desert to the *yam sûph*, in this case the Gulf of 'Aqabah. Ju. 11:16 asserts the same thing: "When they came out of Egypt, Israel journeyed through the desert as far as the *yam sûph*." Ex. 15:27 seems to imply that the crossing of the desert ended with their arrival at Elim, a spot characterized by numerous springs and palm trees. Now it is well known that there was a place at the head of the Gulf of 'Aqabah which was called *Elath* (Dt. 2:8; II Ki. 14:22; 16:6) or *Eloth* (I Ki. 9:26; II Ki. 16:6; II Chron. 8:17; 26:2). Whether it be exactly identical with the site of the Roman *Aila* is immaterial; the important fact is that this region is characterized by numerous springs and palm groves.[3] The conclusion seems inescapable that the *Elim* of the itinerary represents a deliberate alteration of an original *Elath* or *Eloth*. It would seem that P, being dominated by the theory that the sacred mountain was in southern Sinai, felt that the camping-place of the tradition could not be the well-known Eloth at the head of the Gulf of 'Aqabah and, to prevent readers from making this natural but, in his eyes, mistaken assumption, altered the form of the

---

[1] See the authors quoted in the preceding foot-note. Cf. Palmer, *The Desert of the Exodus*, pp. 238f., 274.

[2] Phythian-Adams, *The Call of Israel*, p. 126, n. 1, suggests an identification with Tor (Greek, *Phoinikon*, i.e. "Palms") behind which lies a magnificent grove of date-palms.

[3] Cf. Musil, *The Northern Hegâz*, p. 268.

name slightly, substituting the Hebrew masculine plural ending *-îm* for the original feminine plural ending *-ôth*.[1] His own theory seems to have been that the Israelites, on turning off the road to the land of the Philistines, followed the Wady el-'Arīsh to Nekhl, a name whose meaning, "palm," might very naturally suggest an identification with the palmy haven of tradition.[2]

Station 7: The Desert of Sin

Ex. 16:1 *Then they journeyed from Elim, and the whole community* ['ēdah] *of the Israelites came to the desert of Sin, which is between Elim and Sinai, on the fifteenth day of the second month of their exodus from the land of Egypt.*

It is evident from the use of the words *'ēdah*, "congregation, community," and *Sinai*, and the chronological note that the itinerary owes its present form to P. In view of P's geographical theories the use of his chronological data to support the identification of sites here or elsewhere can only be misleading. Those who adhere to the Sinai theory believe that the Israelites moved from the Wady Gharandel (= Elim) along the coast to the plain of el-Markha or inland to the plain of Debbet er-Ramleh, and in each case identify the plain chosen with the desert of Sin. If P located Elim at Nekhl, he must have identified the desert of Sin with the modern *et-Tīh*, the desert plateau between Nekhl and Mt. Sinai. But Lucas points out[3] that manna, which was found in the desert of Sin, does not occur in *et-Tīh* so that this identification is incorrect. Musil, who proposed the identification of Elim with Eloth which we have accepted, places the desert of Sin in the mountain range east of the Gulf of 'Aqabah. In the present state of our knowledge regarding that region it is not possible to be more precise. The original

[1] *Eloth* probably represents the Hebrew, *Elat* the Arabic, pronunciation of the name.
[2] Lucas, *The Route of the Exodus*, p. 48, actually proposes the theory which we have attributed to P, but he objects to an identification of Elim with Eloth.
[3] *Ibid.*, p. 54.

The Tradition of the Wilderness Itinerary

form of the itinerary would probably have been, "Then they journeyed from Eloth and came to the desert of Sin, which is between Eloth and Horeb."

Station 8: Rephidim

Ex. 17:1 *Then the whole community* ['ēdah] *of the Israelites journeyed from the desert of Sin by stages at the command of Yahweh and encamped at Rephidim; but there was no water for the people to drink.*

The occurrence of the word *'ēdah*, "community," and the phrases *lemas'êhem*, "by their journeyings, by stages," and *'al-pî*, "at the command of," show that the original text has been expanded by P. The original form of the itinerary was probably: "Then the Israelites journeyed from the desert of Sin[1] and encamped at Rephidim." In Nu. 33:12-14 P gives the names of the "stages" to which he here alludes, viz., *Dophkah* and *Alush*. The insertion of these names must represent an attempt on his part to point the direction in which he believed Rephidim to lie. We may be very sure that they were stages along the road to Mt. Sinai rather than to Mt. Horeb in the land of Midian. As for Rephidim itself, Palmer places it in the Wady Feiran near Jebel Serbal. Wright and Filson suggest that it is to be identified with the Wady Refayid north-west of Jebel Musa. Musil thinks it has some connection with the mountain range of *ar-Rafîd* about 100 kilometres south of the head of the Gulf of 'Aqabah. It has been maintained that the fact that the Israelites were attacked by the Amalekites at Rephidim shows that the latter place was in the Negeb or in Sinai. But does that necessarily follow? The Amalekites of Sinai were more or less dependent on Egypt and it may have been on the order of Pharaoh that they took up the pursuit of the Israelites. But it would take some time for them to receive the order, assemble, and organize. In the meantime the Israelites had time to reach Eloth, camp there for an unstated period, and move on. It was probably the very

[1] Evidence will be presented below (pp. 131f.) that an encampment at Taberah took place between the desert of Sin and Rephidim (cf. p. 191).

distance of Rephidim from the Amalekite homeland and its nearness to friendly Midian which saved the fugitives from utter disaster.

Station 9: The Mountain of God

Ex. 19:1f. *On exactly the third month of the exodus of the Israelites from the land of Egypt they entered the desert of Sinai. They journeyed from Rephidim and came to the desert of Sinai and encamped in the desert, and Israel encamped there before the mountain.*

The customary analysis assigns vv. 1, 2a to P and 2b to E. There can be no dispute about the assignment of v. 1 to P, but the beginning of v. 2: "They journeyed from Rephidim," follows the same pattern as Ex. 12:37 and 13:20 and is probably original. However, the reference to the "desert of Sinai," like the references elsewhere to "Mt. Sinai," must be an insertion by P, and the double mention of "camping" can hardly be original. One would expect the sentence to read: "They journeyed from Rephidim and came to the sacred mountain, Horeb, and Israel encamped there before the mountain." Now if we cut out v. 1 and the reference to the "desert of Sinai" in v. 2a as the work of P, we are left with the impression that the "sacred mountain" was on the outskirts of the "desert of Sin." For we have seen that although P has the Israelites journey "by stages" from the desert of Sin to Rephidim, the earlier tradition represents Rephidim as quite near the desert of Sin. According to Ex. 17:6 Mt. Horeb was near Rephidim; hence Horeb was also on the outskirts of the desert of Sin. The similarity of the names *Sin* and *Sinai* may have been one of the factors which led to the transference of the site of the sacred mountain from the east side of the Gulf of 'Aqabah to the west side.

PART II. FROM THE MOUNTAIN OF GOD TO KADESH

Stations 10 and 11: Taberah and Kibroth-hattaavah

Nu. 10:11-13 *In the second year in the second month on the twentieth of the month the cloud was lifted from the tabernacle* of the Testimony. So the Israelites journeyed by stages from the desert of Sinai, and the cloud rested in the desert of Paran. They journeyed according to seniority [?] in accordance with the command of Yahweh through Moses.

Nu. 10:33 *They journeyed from the mountain of Yahweh for three days, while the ark of the covenant of Yahweh went a three days' journey ahead of them to spy out [tûr] a resting-place [menûḥah] for them.*

Nu. 10:11-13 is generally recognized as from the hand of P. Verse 33 has a mark of P origin in the word *tûr*; note also the expression "the mountain of Yahweh" instead of "the mountain of God" which the early tradition elsewhere employs. Verses 34-6 are closely dependent on v. 33; it is customary to assign v. 34 to P but vv. 35f. are regarded as the work of J. In favour of assigning them to P is the fact that he was fond of composing liturgies for every suitable occasion.[1] Morgenstern makes much of the reference to "the three days' journey" in v. 33 and interprets it to mean that at the end of the three days the Israelites reached their goal, the land of Canaan. Hence he infers that in his K Document, to which he assigns the verse, the sacred mountain was regarded as being just three days south of the Palestinian border. But there is no other evidence in favour of, and much against, the view that the Israelites ever regarded the sacred mountain as being so close at hand. It is more natural to interpret the verse as meaning that Taberah, the next stopping-place according to the present form of the tradition, was a three days' journey from Mt. Sinai.

Evidence will be given below[2] that the original position of the Taberah incident (Nu. 11:1-3) was before the Massah-Rephidim story of Ex. 17 and that P shifted it to its present position and telescoped it with the Kibroth-hattaavah story in Nu. 11:4-34 so as to give it the appearance of being part of that story. His desire to ignore the Taberah incident

[1]Rudolph assigns v. 34 to Rp and regards vv. 29-33, 35f. as a combination of various traditions. W. R. Arnold, *Ephod and Ark* (Harvard University Press, 1917), p. 139, n. 2, regards vv. 35f. as a later interpolation. Note the ritual in Dt. 27-8 which P devised for the ceremony on Mts. Gerizim and Ebal.

[2]See pp. 131-4.

comes out again in Nu. 33 where he omits all reference to it. The editorial revision to which the Taberah and Kibroth-hattaavah stories were subjected by P resulted in their both losing the itinerary formula with which such stories regularly begin.

Taberah seems to have derived its name, meaning "Conflagration," from a destructive fire which broke out there in the Israelite camp. Kibroth-hattaavah, meaning "the Graves of Craving," also took its name from what happened there—the death of many people from eating too much quail. According to Lucas[1] the references to the quails which appeared in the evening point to a location at the north end of the Gulf of 'Aqabah rather than on the north coast of Sinai where they always arrive about dawn. Palmer's identification[2] of the site with Erweis el-Ebeirig, north-east of Jebel Musa, where there are the remains of a large encampment in the form of small enclosures of stones, has little to commend it.

Station 12: Hazeroth

Nu. 11:35 *From Kibroth-hattaavah the people journeyed to Hazeroth, and they stayed at Hazeroth.*

Palmer identifies Hazeroth with 'Ain Hudherah ('Ain Khuḍrā), a day's journey north-east of Erweis el-Ebeirig. But Hazeroth was the last camping-place before reaching Kadesh and 'Ain Khuḍrā is near no possible site for Kadesh.[3] The reference to Hazeroth in Dt. 1:1 is not particularly helpful in view of our ignorance of the location of the other places which are mentioned in association with it. Remembering the geographical theories of the author of Dt. 1:1—4:43[4] we may be sure that he places it in Sinai.

---

[1] *The Route of the Exodus*, pp. 58-62.
[2] *The Desert of the Exodus*, pp. 257-60, 507.
[3] G. B. Gray, *Numbers* (International Critical Commentary, New York, 1903), p. 120, and Trumbull, *Kadesh-Barnea*, pp. 78, 314f., question Palmer's identification.
[4] For a discussion of his theories, see pp. 164f.

Station 13: Kadesh

Nu. 12:16 *Afterwards, the people journeyed from Hazeroth and encamped in the desert of Paran.*

Nu. 13:26a *They travelled about and then came to Moses and Aaron and the whole Israelite community* ['ēdah] *at Kadesh, in the desert of Paran.*

The bit of itinerary in Nu. 12:16 is followed by chapter 13 with the story of the spies who, after making a reconnaissance, returned to the Israelite camp "at Kadesh, in the desert of Paran." It is a natural assumption that the Israelites had reached Kadesh before the spies were sent out on their mission. At any rate, this tradition, which manifestly owes its present form to P, as the use of the word '*ēdah* shows, locates Kadesh in the desert of Paran. But in Nu. 20:1, which is also from P, it is stated that "the Israelites, the whole community ['*ēdah*], came to the desert of Zin in the first month and the people dwelt in Kadesh. Miriam died there and was buried there."

The present form of the narrative thus gives us two locations for Kadesh, one in the desert of Zin, the other in the desert of Paran. Musil[1] endeavours to harmonize these traditions by locating the desert of Zin in the northern part of the 'Arabah and the desert of Paran in the southern 'Arabah with Kadesh on the border between them so that it could be reckoned as belonging to either. But Nu. 34:3-5 and Josh. 15:1-4 show that P located the desert of Zin not in the 'Arabah but along the southern border of Judah, which is defined as following a somewhat irregular course from the south end of the Dead Sea to the River of Egypt (the Wady el-'Arīsh). Note also Nu. 13:21 (a P verse) where the desert of Zin marks the southern limit of Canaan just as Rehob near Hamath marks its northern border. The most natural inference from this is that the desert of Zin lay west of the 'Arabah in the outer, southernmost reaches of the Negeb.

Now it was precisely in this area, at a spot approximately fifty miles south of Beersheba, that Rowlands discovered a

[1] *The Northern Ḥegâz*, Appendix 5: "The Site of Ḳadeš," pp. 263, 270ff., 278.

spring called 'Ain Ḳadeis or 'Ain Ḳadīs in 1842. Palmer re-discovered it in 1870 and it was visited by H. C. Trumbull in 1881.[1] Trumbull's enthusiastic description of the site convinced most biblical scholars that this spring marked the site of the Kadesh of the wilderness tradition. But the fact is that Trumbull's account was written up a considerable time afterwards from hurried notes made on the spot and in the meantime his pious imagination had been at work with the result that his description bears little resemblance to the actual scene. Instead of being a delightful oasis carpeted with grass and flowers which makes it difficult to realize the proximity of the desert, "the valley of Ain Kadeis is unusually naked, even among the valleys of the south country," being in all its length "a most unmitigated desert."[2] Proof of this assertion is to be found in any photograph of the spot.[3] The flow of water is too small to water the flocks of more than a few families. The pool of water into which Trumbull says his Arabs stripped and plunged is, according to Woolley and Lawrence, "only about a foot or eighteen inches deep, and full of very large and sharp stones." C. S. Jarvis, former governor of Sinai, says: "The wonderful pools of water mentioned by Trumball are two dirty little water-holes."[4] It is evident that the discussion of the wilderness itinerary can never be put on a sane basis until the identification of Kadesh with 'Ain Kadīs is abandoned.

Scholars have tried to defend the identification by extending the application of the term "Kadesh" to include other springs in the vicinity, especially 'Ain el-Qedeirat, five miles to the north, where there are the remains of a fort dating back to at least 1000 B.C.[5] But there is no evidence

[1] Cf. Palmer, *The Desert of the Exodus*, II, p. 350; Trumbull, *Kadesh-Barnea*, pp. 272ff.; for Rowlands' description, see Trumbull, *op. cit.*, p. 213. See also A. Musil, *Arabia Petraea*, II (Vienna, 1907), pp. 177ff., 236.
[2] C. L. Woolley and T. E. Lawrence, "The Wilderness of Zin," *PEF Annual* (1914-15), pp. 73f.
[3] See the photographs in Woolley and Lawrence, *ibid.*, Plates X-XII; G. L. Robinson in *Biblical World*, XVII (1901), pp. 328-35; Olmstead, *A History of Palestine and Syria* (New York, 1931), p. 246.
[4] *Three Deserts* (London, 1936), p. 132.
[5] Cf. Woolley and Lawrence, *PEF Annual* (1914-15), pp. 46, 81-4.

The Tradition of the Wilderness Itinerary 97

that the term ever had this wider connotation. The only general term for the area was "the desert of Zin." Moreover, since 'Ain el-Qedeirat is a more fertile spot than 'Ain Kadīs we should expect it to have given its name to the larger area.

While 'Ain Kadīs cannot be identified with the Kadesh of the wilderness tradition, it can, with great probability, be identified with one of the other Kadeshes mentioned in the Bible. In the story in Gen. 14 of the attack made by four oriental emperors on the five princelings at the south end of the Dead Sea, it is said that the invaders marched from El-paran to "En-mishpat [the Spring of Judgment], that is, Kadesh, and ravaged all the country of the Amalekites . . ." (v. 7). From this it is clear that there was a sacred spring called Kadesh somewhere in Amalekite territory. The story of the first expulsion of Hagar and Ishmael in Gen. 16 also refers to a Kadesh, situated apparently in the same area (v. 14). It is highly probable that these two Kadeshes are identical and that the modern 'Ain Kadīs preserves the name and marks the site.

The fact that these Kadeshes are located in the very area where P places the desert of Zin shows that he identified the Kadesh of the wilderness tradition with 'Ain Kadīs. Confirmation of this opinion is provided by an examination of the P summary of the itinerary from the sacred mountain to Kadesh found in Nu. 33: 16-36. According to Dt. 1: 2 it was an eleven days' journey from Horeb to Kadesh-barnea. For this route P gives a list of twenty-one camping-places, i.e. two a day, the first day being allotted only one since no oriental traveller progresses far on the first day. P's list is composed of four elements: (i) the itinerary of the original tradition, minus Taberah (vv. 16f.); (ii) a list of twelve names peculiar to P (vv. 18-31); (iii) the bit of itinerary containing four names drawn from Dt. 10: 6f. (vv. 32f.); (iv) a P addition of two names (vv. 34-6). To fill up the long interval between Hazeroth and Kadesh (vv. 18-36) P provides eighteen names. It is a natural assumption that section (ii) represents the results of later research and was introduced by P to point the direction in which he believed Kadesh to lie and also as a guide to pilgrims going in the other direction from Kadesh to the sacred mountain. While the locations of the twelve places in this section have not been positively identified, it is significant that three of them, *Rimmon-perez*, *Libnah*, and *Hashmonah*, bear names very similar to those of Judaean towns in the Negeb area, viz., *En-rimmon*, a dependency of Beersheba (Josh. 15:28f.; cf. also the name *Perez*, a son of Judah), *Libnah* (Josh. 10:29; 15:42), and *Heshmon*, which was in the direction of Edom according to Josh. 15:27.

P felt he could not ignore the bit of itinerary given in Dt. 10:6f. which mentions the wells of the Bene Ya'aqan, Moserah, ha-Gudgod, and Yotbah, so he incorporated it as section (iii) of this part of his itinerary. But the position which he allots it bears no relation whatsoever to the position which it has in Deuteronomy. There it comes immediately after the departure from Horeb. Here the Israelites have passed through no less than fourteen camping-sites since leaving the mountain. Moreover, P has altered both the order and the spelling of the names.[1] The introduction of this D itinerary after Hashmonah, which lay in the direction of Edom, indicates that P wishes it to be understood that the four places which it mentions lay in that direction also. Section (iv), containing the names 'Abronah and Ezion-geber, is a further indication that P located the four places of section (iii) along the route from Heshmon to the head of the Gulf. But P's admission of the D itinerary involves him in difficulties. Having brought the Israelites down to Ezion-geber he is compelled to have them make one grand leap to Kadesh ('Ain Kadīs).[2] In spite of this awkward feature the impression left by the P form of the itinerary is that Kadesh lay somewhere on the southern border of Judah, near Edomite territory. A location at 'Ain Kadīs fits most naturally into his picture.

We turn now to an examination of the passage which places Kadesh in the desert of Paran. In Nu. 13:26 the words "in the desert of Paran" are usually assigned to P and the word "Kadesh" to JE. While the passage

[1]The reason for these alterations will appear later. See p. 119.
[2]See Binns' note on Nu. 33:36.

undoubtedly owes its present form to P, there can be little doubt that in locating Kadesh in the desert of Paran, P is in this case basing himself on the original tradition. The desert of Zin is mentioned only in P passages (Nu. 13:21; 20:1; 27:14; 33:36; 34:3; Dt. 32:51; Josh. 15:1, 3). The name was evidently applied to a relatively small area and owed its rise to prominence solely to a late identification of Kadesh with the spring in its midst. The desert of Paran, on the other hand, is mentioned in at least two pre-P passages (Gen. 21:21 and I Ki. 11:18) as well as in several post-exilic passages. In Hab. 3:3 "Mt. Paran" is used in parallelism with "Teman," a place in Transjordan (cf. Am. 1:12; Jer. 49:7, 20; Ez. 25:13), which suggests that it was itself in Transjordan. Jerome and Eusebius (*Onomasticon*, s.v. "Pharan") actually locate it east of Aila (= Eloth). On the other hand, I Sam. 25:1 seems to locate the desert of Paran in the Negeb; but the Massoretic text of this verse is not above suspicion for Codex B reads "the desert of Ma'on" which is more appropriate to the context.

I believe that our best clue to the situation of Paran is to be found in Gen. 21:21, which states that the desert of Paran was where Ishmael settled after his expulsion from the home of his father Abraham. Most commentators, influenced by the fact that the Hagar-Ishmael story has a Negebite setting, interpret this to mean that Paran denotes the region beyond the Negeb, the modern *et-Tīh*.[1] But the Arabs of Sinai were called Amalekites, not Ishmaelites. In the list of the "sons of Ishmael" in Gen. 25:12-18 the inhabitants of Sinai are not mentioned; Ishmael's children are specifically the North Arabian tribes, of whom Nebaioth (the Nabataeans) is the first-born. Are we not justified in inferring from this that Ishmael is thought of as taking up his abode in the region where we later find his first-born son living? In other words, the desert of Paran is to be identified with the homeland of the Nabataeans, the region around Petra. If this be

[1] Cf., e.g., Gray, *Numbers*, p. 91; J. Skinner, *Genesis* (International Critical Commentary, New York, 1910), p. 324; Trumbull, *Kadesh-Barnea*, pp. 67f.; Palmer, *The Desert of the Exodus*, p. 509; Musil, *The Northern Ḥegâz*, Appendix 8: "El Paran and Paran."

true, the site of Kadesh is to be sought in the Nabataean area. Is it possible to ascertain its position more precisely?

According to Nu. 20:16 Kadesh was not in Edom but very close to the Edomite frontier. Trumbull, in his endeavour to fix the location of Kadesh at 'Ain Kadīs in the Negeb, was forced to postulate an extension of Edom westward across the 'Arabah at the time of Moses. But there is no evidence that at that time the Edomites had spread so far afield.[1] In post-exilic times, however, the situation was quite different. Numerous P passages indicate that the region south of 'Ain Kadīs was then in Edomite hands (cf. e.g., Nu. 34:3 and Josh. 11:17; 12:7; 15:1-4, 21-28).[2] The most telling argument against Trumbull's thesis is the fact that in Nu. 20:16 Kadesh is called a town (*'īr*) but there is not the slightest archaeological evidence that a town ever stood at 'Ain Kadīs. Trumbull tried to overcome this difficulty by giving to *'īr* the watered-down meaning of "fortified encampment" or "encircled stronghold," but this can only be termed a desperate expedient.

Petra, in the environs of Edom proper, has attracted attention because of the existence of a tradition associating that spot with Moses. Thus a spring outside Petra is still called *'Ain Musa* ("Moses' Spring"), while the channel along which its waters pass through the site of the city is called *Wady Musa* ("Moses' Valley"). Scholars have tried to account for the rise of this tradition by pointing to the existence at Petra of a striking natural feature called the *sīq*, a tremendous fissure in the rocky ridge on the eastern side of the city which forms the only means of access from that direction. It has been suggested[3] that such a feature would be bound to give rise to a legend explaining its origin and that the story in Nu. 20 of Moses striking the rock is this legend, or at least a Hebraized form of it. But the emphasis in this story is on the production of water, not on

[1] Cf. Glueck, *HUCA*, XI (1936), 144, 152f.; "Explorations in Eastern Palestine, II," *AASOR*, XV (1935) 112f.; Musil, *The Northern Ḥegâz*, p. 252; F. C. Burkitt in the *Schweich Lectures, 1926* (London, 1929), p. 106.

[2] For the probable date of this westward extension of Edom, see pp. 101f.

[3] Cf. Phythian-Adams, *The Call of Israel*, p. 69.

the size of the crack which was produced in the rock by Moses' blow.[1] The association of Petra with the name of Moses must, therefore, have some other basis.[2]

It is frequently asserted or assumed that Petra marks the site of the old Edomite capital, called *ha-Sela'* in II Ki. 14:7. If this were true, it would be at once evident that Petra cannot mark the site of ancient Kadesh, for Kadesh was neither the Edomite capital nor in Edom, although Nu. 20:16 places it very close to the Edomite frontier. But in spite of what is commonly asserted, it seems to me that the results of archaeological examination, as far as it has progressed, are all against an identification of the site with the Edomite capital. The Edomite sherds found on the top of *Umm el-Biyāra*,[3] the great flat-topped peak inside the Petraean rampart, are certainly not sufficient by themselves to prove the existence here of an extensive Edomite settlement.[4]

It is by no means certain that the site of Petra was included within the borders of the early kingdom of Edom. At the time of Moses Edom cannot have extended as far south as the head of the Gulf of 'Aqabah or the Israelites would not have been able to go around Edom. Precisely where the southern border of Edom was at that time we do not know.[5] Later the Edomites did extend their authority to the Gulf. II Chron. 28:16ff. refers to attacks on Judah by Edomites and Philistines in the reign of Ahaz (*c.* 735-715 B.C.) and the loss of many towns in southern Judah. II Ki. 16:6 mentions Rezin, king of Syria, driving out the Judaeans from

[1] The real significance of the Nu. 20 story will be pointed out below; see pp. 149.

[2] Josephus (*Antiquities* IV. iv. 7) identifies Petra with the site of Aaron's death. Cf. Musil, *The Northern Ḥegâz*, Appendix 5: "The Site of Ḳades."

[3] Cf. Glueck, *AASOR*, XIV (1934), 77; XV (1935), 82; Abel, *Géographie de la Palestine*, II, 407f.

[4] The remains of an extensive settlement were found by Nelson Glueck between the modern village of el-Gi and the entrance to Petra. The ground was "covered with thousands upon thousands of fragments of Edomite pottery" (*The Other Side of the Jordan* (New Haven, 1940), pp. 21-6). Glueck suggests an identification of this spot with Teman and of Umm el-Biyāra with Sela', but it is most improbable that two of the leading Edomite cities should have existed so close together. Père Abel (*op. cit.*, II, 479) locates Teman at Shaubak, about twenty miles north-north-east of Petra.

[5] Cf. Glueck, *HUCA*, XI (1936), 144.

Eloth in the same reign and "recovering" Eloth for Syria. However, the passage in Chronicles just referred to suggests that it was the Edomites who recovered control of Eloth, and most commentators emend the text of Kings accordingly. But how long before Ahaz's time they had gained control of Eloth we do not know. It would seem highly probable, at any rate, that this resurgence of Edomite power at the time of Ahaz led not only to hit-and-run raids on southern Judah but to the passing of the Sinai peninsula under Edomite control.

In considering the problem of the site of the Edomite capital we need to remember that in the early period at least there was no permanent capital. Gen. 36: 31-9 attributes the leadership to first one town and then another. Whether one town eventually came to dominate the others we do not know. In the time of Amaziah of Judah (*c.* 800-783 B.C.) the leading town was ha-Selaʻ, a place which is not mentioned in Gen. 36. Amaziah is said to have taken ha-Selaʻ by storm and renamed it Joktheel (Heb. *Yoqthe'el*). I believe that the site of this Selaʻ is to be found not at Petra but near the modern village of Selaʻ, situated a few kilometres west-north-west of Buseirah (biblical *Bozrah*) which is about thirty-five miles north-east of Petra. To the north-west of the modern village is a "completely isolated, jagged, precipitous hill called es-Selaʻ, with the similarly named ancient site on top of it."[1] This ancient site was entered through a narrow *sīq*, just as Petra was. Now the Arabic word *salʻ* means "a crack, cleft, fissure," and there can be little doubt that the common possession of a "cleft" of unusual proportions accounts for the application of the name *ha-Selaʻ* to both this ancient Edomite town, which I believe to have served for a time as the capital, and the later Nabataean city. If this be correct, the centre of gravity of the Edomite kingdom was much further to the north than is ordinarily thought and Petra may well have lain outside the bounds of Edom. Thus there is no insuperable obstacle in the way of identifying Petra with the Kadesh of the Wilderness Tradition.

[1] Cf. Glueck, *AASOR*, XVIII-XIX (1939), 26; *The Other Side of the Jordan* pp. 163, 169.

According to Jerome the real name of the Nabataean Petra was *Recem*. Eusebius derives this name from the Midianite king called Reqem who is said to have been slain by Phinehas. More probably it owes its origin to the many-coloured rocks with which Petra is surrounded and which impart to the site its distinctive charm and character (cf. Ar. *raqama*, "to embroider," *raqm*, "an embroidered or striped robe," Heb. *riqmah*, "variegated stuff"). But *Reqem* and *Kadesh* are quite distinct names, so how can an identification of them be justified? A possible solution of the problem has been suggested indirectly by Nielsen[1] and directly by Phythian-Adams[2] in drawing attention to the high-place at Petra, situated on a peak known today as *Jebel Zibb 'Atūf*. This is the most impressive, as well as the best preserved, high-place in the whole of Transjordan and while it was undoubtedly developed by the Nabataeans, there is every likelihood that it did not originate with them but was sacred from immemorial antiquity.[3] No spot could more appropriately have been named *Kadesh*, "sacred." Israelite tradition may have preferred to remember the name of Reqem's sanctuary rather than the name of Reqem itself. It did not, however, entirely forget the close association of Reqem and Kadesh, for when 'Ain Kadīs in the Negeb came to be identified with Kadesh the name Reqem was also applied to it. Thus in the Targums and the Talmud Kadesh-barnea is frequently called *Reqem*, *Reqam gê'a*, *Reqam degê'a*, etc.[4] The word *gê'a* seems to be the Heb. *gai'*, *gê'*, "valley," although Père Abel[5] regards it as *el-Gī*, the name of the Arabic village near Petra. Trumbull refers to a Rabbinical assertion that there were two Reqems, a Reqem of the mountains and a Reqem of the plain, evidently meaning

[1]"The Site of the Biblical Mount Sinai, a Claim for Petra" (*JPOS*, VII (1927), 187-208); "The Mountain Sanctuaries in Petra and Its Environs" (*JPOS*, XIII (1933), 185-208).

[2]*The Call of Israel*, p. 195. Whereas Nielsen would identify the high-place of Petra with Mt. Sinai, Phythian-Adams would identify it with Kadesh-barnea.

[3]In the second article mentioned in note 1 above, Nielsen gives reasons for believing that the high-places of Petra were of pre-Nabataean origin.

[4]For the exact references, cf. Trumbull, *Kadesh-Barnea*, pp. 167f.

[5]*Géographie de la Palestine*, II, 436.

Petra and 'Ain Kadīs, but this sounds like an attempt to harmonize two divergent traditions.

As if to complicate matters still further, D calls the *Kadesh* of tradition *Kadesh-barnea*, a form which first appears in his own writings in Dt. 9:23. What is the significance of the element *barnea*? I would suggest that just as in the name *Kedesh-Naphtali* the second element denotes a tribe, so in *Kadesh-barnea* the second element is a tribal name. In other words, at the time of D the oasis of 'Ain Kadīs was occupied by the tribe of *Barnea*. It is possible that this tribe was of Kenite stock. Ju. 1:16 states that the Kenites accompanied the Judaeans as far as the Negeb of 'Arad and then went off to live with "the people" (LXX, "the Amalekites"; cf. I Sam. 15:6). The implication of Ju. 1:16 would seem to be that the Kenites went on south of 'Arad. Fifty miles would bring them to 'Ain Kadīs. Did they settle there and was it they who were responsible for originating the idea that the Kadesh of the Israelite tradition was not the Transjordanian Kadesh, the old Kenite home,[1] but 'Ain Kadīs, the hypothetical new Kenite home? Did they find it to their advantage to divert Jewish pilgrims in their direction by associating with the oases in which they were now settled legends relating to the wanderings of the children of Israel? It is a possibility to be reckoned with. Once the site of Kadesh was shifted, it would not be long before Horeb and other sites of the Wilderness Tradition would be similarly shifted.

To sum up our investigation of the location of Kadesh, we have seen that the early tradition places Kadesh in the desert of Paran and that there is some evidence that this desert was situated in the region later occupied by the Nabataeans. This accords well with the modern nomenclature around Petra which attests the existence at one time of a tradition associating that site with Moses. In the D version of the Mosaic Tradition Kadesh has become Kadesh-barnea. This may indicate the rise of a new theory regarding the site of the Kadesh of the wilderness journey. D's theory may have been the same as that which we find in P, viz., that Kadesh was situated in the desert of Zin, a desert which

[1] See pp. 66f.

The Tradition of the Wilderness Itinerary

is placed in the outermost reaches of the Negeb near the Edomite frontier of P's day. In other words, D as well as P may have identified Kadesh with the spring still known as 'Ain Kadīs.

One of the curious features of P's treatment of the itinerary tradition connected with Kadesh is that he has split it into two parts. In Nu. 12:16 he brings the Israelites only to the desert of Paran without explicitly stating that they camped at Kadesh. It is not till Nu. 20:1 that he brings them to the desert of Zin and has them encamp definitely at Kadesh. The reason for this treatment of the tradition will become apparent when the water-miracle story in Nu. 20 is examined.[1] The original form of the itinerary probably was: "Afterwards, the people journeyed from Hazeroth and encamped at Kadesh in the desert of Paran. Miriam died there and was buried there."

PART III. FROM KADESH TO PISGAH

Station 14: Mt. Hor

Nu. 20:22 *They journeyed from Kadesh and the Israelites, the whole community* ['ēdah], *came to Mt. Hor*.

According to the early tradition preserved in Nu. 20:14-21 the Israelites at Kadesh sought permission to cross Edom via "the king's highway," the modern *Darb es-Sulṭān*,[2] to reach which they would have had to go only a few miles east of Petra; but permission was refused, "whereupon Israel turned away from him." Nu. 20:22 gives the first camping-place after leaving Kadesh as Mt. Hor. This verse shows marks of having been expanded by P but there is no reason for doubting that the essence of the verse belongs to the original tradition. At Mt. Hor, Aaron is said to have died. Josephus,[3] writing in the first century A.D., locates the scene of Aaron's death on a mountain near Petra. This must surely be *Jebel Hārūn* ("the Mountain of Aaron"),

[1] See p. 149.
[2] For its position, see Wright and Filson, *The Westminster Historical Atlas to the Bible*, Plates V and VI.
[3] *Antiquities* IV. iv. 7.

about five miles south-west of Petra, where a shrine on top of the mountain is still called "Aaron's tomb."[1] The existence of a tradition as early as the first century A.D. identifying Jebel Harun with the site of Aaron's death is a strong argument in support of the identification of Kadesh with Petra proposed above. I shall, therefore, proceed on the assumption that Kadesh is Petra and Mt. Hor is Jebel Harun.

Leaving Mt. Hor, the Israelites proceeded south for some distance along the road to the Gulf of 'Aqabah before turning off eastward to make a circuit of the land of Edom (Nu. 21: 4).

The account of the departure from Kadesh given in Dt. 2 agrees with the Numbers tradition in having the Israelites set off from Kadesh "in the direction of the Gulf of 'Aqabah [*yam sūph*]" (v. 1). But since the author of Dt. 1: 1—4: 43 clearly located Kadesh at 'Ain Kadīs, in accordance with the prevailing post-exilic theory, he thinks of them as moving away from 'Ain Kadīs in a south-easterly direction, whereas the "turning away" in the original Numbers tradition must have involved a movement in a south-westerly and then southerly direction. Moreover, there is no mention in Dt. 2 of a halt at Mt. Hor. The reason for this omission is that the author is deliberately conforming to the point of view of the rest of the Book of Deuteronomy which places the death of Aaron at Moserah, the first camping-place after leaving Horeb (cf. Dt. 10: 6), whereas the Numbers tradition places it at Mt. Hor, the first camping-place after leaving Kadesh. There is a further difference between the Numbers and Dt. 2 versions which should be noted. From Nu. 21: 4a one gets the impression that the departure from Kadesh was at once followed by the trek around Edom. But the author of Dt. 2 no sooner gets the Israelites uprooted from Kadesh ('Ain Kadīs to him) than he slows down their pace in order to make it conform to his chronological theory according to which nearly thirty-eight years were spent circling about the highlands of Seir after the departure from Kadesh (Dt. 2: 1*b*, 14).

For an understanding of his point of view it is necessary

[1] For descriptions of the tomb, see the references in Trumbull, *Kadesh-Barnea*, p. 128, n. 1.

to remember that he, like other post-exilic authors,[1] uses the term "Seir" or "Mt. Seir" to denote Sinai as well as Edom, doubtless because at that time Sinai was incorporated in the Edomite kingdom.[2] Moreover, at that time Edom extended right to the head of the Gulf of 'Aqabah and as far as the writer was aware had always so extended. Hence he could not take the original tradition in Nu. 21:4 that the Israelites "went around the land of Edom" in its literal sense but was compelled to give it the meaning of "went around in the highland of Seir," by which he means Sinai. After the people have been circling about in Sinai an order comes from Yahweh for them to turn northward. The people are warned that this movement will involve a crossing of the frontier of Seir (evidently Edom proper) and they are to be exceedingly circumspect in their behaviour so as to give no cause for offence. "So we departed from our kinsmen, the sons of Esau who dwell in Seir, off the 'Arabah road [running] from Elath and Ezion-geber; we turned and moved across in the direction of the desert of Moab" (v. 8). They could not turn off the 'Arabah road unless they had been on it; so the writer must have thought of their circling about in Sinai as having finally brought them into the 'Arabah, where the order to turn northward is given. Traversing the 'Arabah to its northern end (a movement which the author regards as a crossing of Edomite territory since the 'Arabah was in Edomite hands in his day), they turn off the 'Arabah road and move eastward through the Wady Zered (cf. v. 13) in the direction of the desert of Moab.[3]

[1]For the connotation of "Seir" in post-exilic times, see Glueck, *HUCA*, XI (1936), 154-7.

[2]Note that he places Hormah "*in* Seir." The Versions, failing to grasp his use of the term, alter *in* to *from*. Once again we are impressed by the accuracy of the Massoretic tradition.

[3]The author has undoubtedly expressed himself a bit vaguely but the difficulties are exaggerated by A. C. Welch, *Deuteronomy: The Framework of the Code* (Oxford, 1932), pp. 168ff. He interprets 2:8 to mean that the Israelites crossed the 'Arabah near the head of the Gulf of 'Aqabah and then struck north via the *Darb es-Sulṭān*. This is also the view of Musil, *The Northern Hegâz*, pp. 254ff. Wright and Filson, *The Westminster Historical Atlas to the Bible*, Plate V, interpret the passage as I have done, and it is an interpretation which is supported by P's version of the itinerary in Nu. 33 (see pp. 112f.)

108   *The Mosaic Tradition*

The story of Aaron's death on Mt. Hor in 20: 23-9 owes its present form to P, as has been generally recognized.[1] It is followed by an account of a movement of the Israelites along the road of the *'atharîm*,[2] a movement which brings them into collision with the Canaanite king of 'Arad (Nu. 21: 1-3). The Israelites suffer an initial defeat at the hands of the king of 'Arad but stage a counter-attack and win an overwhelming victory, the Canaanites and their cities being annihilated. Following this sweeping victory the Israelites are said to journey "from Mt. Hor via the Red Sea road to go around the land of Edom" (21: 4), i.e., they turn southward. But if they had been victorious as 21: 3 asserts, why did they not follow up their advantage and push on into Canaan instead of turning south to make a long arduous trek around Edom and Moab in order to enter Canaan from the east?

Scholars have endeavoured to defend the historical truth of 21: 1-3 by declaring that the passage preserves a tradition of an independent move up into the Negeb on the part of the Calebites,[3] a movement which was successful. They believe that P, wishing to paint a unified picture of the conquest of Canaan, merged a tradition of the settlement of the Calebites

---

[1] For the marks of P authorship, see Gray, *Numbers*, p. 269. Cf. p. 202.

[2] This word is a Hebraized form of the Arabic *'athar*, the plural of which is sometimes used with the meaning "signs, or marks, set up to show the way" (Lane, *Arabic-English Lexicon*, I, 19a). For roads in Sinai marked by little piles of stones, see Palmer, *The Desert of the Exodus*, II, pp. 346, 416, and Trumbull, *Kadesh-Barnea*, p. 316, n. 1.

[3] The chief exponents of the two-movement theory have been S. A. Cook and my colleague, T. J. Meek. "The two leading traditions which underlie the history of Israel are those of an entry into Palestine, one from the south and the other from the east. With the former we can at present associate Caleb and the Kenites, in the latter Joshua is evidently the leading figure. These two views seem to have grown up separately, and there is evidence that each underwent a considerable amount of development." (Cook, *Critical Notes on Old Testament History*, pp. 81f.) See also Cook's chapter, "The Rise of Israel," in the *Cambridge Ancient History*, II (1924), 358-69; T. J. Meek, "A Proposed Reconstruction of Early Hebrew History," *American Journal of Theology*, XXIV (1920), 209ff.; *Hebrew Origins* (New York, 1936), pp. 36-43; H. H. Rowley, "Israel's Sojourn in Egypt," *Bulletin of the John Rylands Library*, XXII (1938), 266f.; T. H. Robinson, *History of Israel* (Oxford, 1932), pp. 118f.; C. A. Simpson, *The Early Traditions of Israel* (Oxford, 1948), pp. 219, 419ff.

with the tradition of the settlement of the Israelites under Joshua, with the result that the Calebite movement is given the appearance of having been a failure since the attackers turn back and set out in the direction of the Red Sea. This interpretation, however, is in manifest contradiction to the whole spirit of the passage which emphasizes the sweeping nature of the Israelite victory. The interpretation rests on the assumption that the Nu. 21: 1-3 story is a variant of the tradition in Ju. 1: 10-17 (cf. Josh. 15: 13-19) which describes a success gained by Caleb in the same general area. But that it is a mistaken assumption is evident from the following considerations: (i) in Nu. 21 the attack is made from the south, in Ju. 1 it is made from the north; (ii) in Nu. 21 the participants in the struggle are "Israel,"[1] i.e., the whole people, and "the Canaanite king of 'Arad," but in Ju. 1 the conquest of the Negeb is made by the tribes of Judah and Simeon, assisted by the sons of Hobab the Kenite, and their adversaries are "the Canaanites" (cf. v. 17). It is, therefore, impossible to regard the two stories as referring to the same incident.

Moreover, the assumption that the name Caleb denotes a group distinct from the Israelites rests on a very precarious foundation. Caleb is introduced in Ju. 1: 12 in a manner which clearly implies that he is an individual. In the P list of spies in Nu. 13, Caleb ben Jephunneh is the representative of the tribe of Judah. He was not, however, the chief of the Judaeans, for Nu. 10: 4 states that Nahshon ben Amminadab was their chief. But Caleb and Joshua are said to have been the only two desert leaders who survived to take part in the Palestinian campaign, and it would be very natural if in that campaign Caleb was the recognized sheikh of the Judaeans. Is that not the most natural interpretation of Ju. 1: 12-20? P, however, states in Josh. 15: 13 that Caleb ben Jephunneh was granted a lot "among the Judaeans, namely ... Hebron," which implies that he thought of him as a non-Jew. In fact, in Josh. 14: 6, 14 he definitely labels him a "Kenizzite," i.e., an Edomite, for we learn from Gen. 36: 11 that Kenaz was

[1] Cook is forced to regard the reference to "Israel" as an attempt to generalize the Calebite tradition.

the name of an Edomite tribe. The reason for P's attitude seems to be that in his day Hebron had fallen into Edomite hands[1] and its inhabitants (regarded as the descendants of Caleb) are looked upon by P, the racial purist, as lost to Judaism; in his eyes they have become Edomites. He finds an Edomite origin for them by relating them to the Kenizzites who inhabited the town of Debir, to the south-west of Hebron.[2] But he wishes to retain a Jewish claim to the territory which they occupied and so points out that their ancestor, Caleb, had been granted an allotment "among the Judaeans" at Yahweh's express command.

If Caleb was really a Judaean leader, and not an Edomite, as P maintains, then there is no basis for interpreting Nu. 21: 1-3 as a tradition of an independent movement up into the Negeb by a group distinct from the Judaeans. Some other explanation must be sought. Since the passage refers to an attack on the Negeb, a natural inference is that it represents a variant of the tradition in Nu. 14: 40ff. about an attack made on the Negeb by the Israelites, even though the latter was unsuccessful, whereas that related in 21: 1-3 was overwhelmingly successful, after an initial failure. There can be no doubt that the tradition in 14: 40ff. comes in the more natural position, immediately following the account of the return of the spies from reconnoitring the Negeb. Hence it would seem to be the earlier tradition.

What, then, can have given rise to the tradition in 21: 1-3? I believe the answer is to be found in the position which the

---

[1] This would seem to be the most likely explanation of the failure of Hebron to play any part in the life of post-exilic Judaism, as far as one can judge from the records. It would also account for P's seeming eagerness to shift the credit for the capture of Hebron and the extermination of its Anakite inhabitants from Caleb to Joshua (cf. Josh. 10: 36-9; 11: 21). Note also the assertion in I Chron. 6: 54-7 that Caleb had not been allotted the town of Hebron proper but only its outlying fields and villages.

[2] When the Judaeans under Caleb moved south and attempted a conquest of the Negeb, they seem to have found allies in the tribe of Kenaz, led by Othniel, a tribe already settled somewhere in the south and having Edomite affiliations. Following the conquest of the Negeb the Kenizzites occupied Debir and seem to have remained henceforth on friendly terms with the Judaean Calebites of Hebron. In course of time the "ancestors" of the two groups were represented in tradition as kinsmen.

The Tradition of the Wilderness Itinerary

tradition occupies in the present narrative. Immediately preceding it is an account of the death of Aaron on Mt. Hor. There would naturally be a desire to know where Mt. Hor, containing the tomb of Aaron, the founder of the Hebrew priesthood, lay. Nu. 21: 1-3 is the answer, P's answer, to that question. Having identified Kadesh with 'Ain Kadīs in the Negeb he is compelled to propose a Negebite site for Mt. Hor, for Mt. Hor and Kadesh were near together. He does so by fabricating an account of a second battle in the Negeb, an account which is obviously modelled on 14: 40ff., as the reference to Hormah shows. He says that "when the Canaanite king of 'Arad[1] who lived in the Negeb heard that Israel was coming along the road of the *'athar̂im*" he attacked them and took some of them prisoner. This is P's version of the attack mentioned in 14: 40ff.; note that he has the Canaanites take the offensive. After this initial reverse, the Israelites make a counter-attack and win a great victory, the Canaanites and their cities being annihilated. One of the places annihilated came to be known as *Hormah*. P does not go so far as to assert the equivalence of *Hor* and *Hormah* but by placing the Hormah tradition immediately after the Mt. Hor story he undoubtedly suggests that there is some connection between them. The antecedent of "that place" in v. 3 can only be " 'Arad"; hence P is really proposing an identification of Mt. Hor with Tell 'Arad.[2] But since according to Ju. 1: 17 it was Zephath which was renamed Hormah, P has here expressed himself with intentional vagueness. Of course, the inconsistency of his identification of Hormah with that given in Judges was not as glaring as it became later when the Book of Judges and the other "Prophetical" Books were appended to the Torah.

We thus see that Nu. 21: 1-3 is not a misplaced fragment of the J Document, as is commonly asserted, but a P

[1] Modern *Tell 'Arād*, about fifty miles north of 'Ain Kadīs and about seventeen miles south of Hebron.
[2] P's eagerness to locate the site of Aaron's tomb in the Negeb comes out in his repetition of part of Nu. 21: 1 in 33: 40. It is curious that in Nu. 34: 7 he seems to identify Mt. Hor with Mt. Hermon. The same identification appears in the Targum of Jonathan. Cf. the *Talmud*: "Gittin," i. 8*a*.

composition designed to serve a dogmatic purpose. Its unhistorical character is apparent from the fact that it makes unintelligible the Israelite decision to turn back and go all the way around Edom in order to get to Canaan instead of pushing straight on north from Hormah. If the elements introduced by P are ignored, we find that the original tradition simply states that the Israelites journeyed from Kadesh to Mt. Hor, where Aaron died. The continuation of the tradition is found in 21: 4.

Stations 15 and 16: Oboth and Ije-abarim

Nu. 21: 4a *They journeyed from Mt. Hor by the Red Sea* [yam sûph] *road to go around the land of Edom.*
Nu. 21: 10 *The Israelites journeyed and encamped at Oboth.*
Nu. 21: 11 *They journeyed from Oboth and encamped at Ije-abarim in the desert which confronts Moab on the side where the sun rises.*

Oboth, the first camping-place after leaving Mt. Hor, can scarcely be 'Ain el-Weiba, as Abel suggests. The next camping-place, Ije-abarim, is stated to have been situated in the desert east of Moab. But it is a statement which causes some perplexity for the Israelites have not yet crossed the Zered, the frontier between Edom and Moab, and it is difficult to believe that a two days' journey took them all the way around Edom to a position in the desert east of Moab. Perhaps the peculiar way in which the location of Ije-abarim is referred to indicates a south-easterly direction from Moab. P, who seems to have identified Mt. Hor with 'Arad in the Negeb, whence it is a considerable distance to the desert east of Moab, felt it necessary to insert two camping-places between Mt. Hor and Oboth (Nu. 33: 42), viz., Zalmonah and Punon (*Pinon* according to the Sam., LXX, and Syr. VSS) The location of Zalmonah is unknown. Punon or Pinon is probably the modern *Feinān*, over thirty miles north of Petra on the map.[1] P's theory seems to be that after leaving Hormah-'Arad, the Israelites circled about in Seir (= Sinai)

[1] Cf. Glueck, *AASOR*, XV (1935), 32-6; Abel, *Géographie de la Palestine*, II, 410f. See Gen. 36: 41; I Chron. 1: 52.

The Tradition of the Wilderness Itinerary 113

for thirty-eight years, then moved across the 'Arabah to Feinān, and proceeded up the east side of the 'Arabah and across northern Edom to the border of Moab.[1] The claim that they actually crossed Edom appears again in Dt. 2, but it is a claim which is contrary to the early traditions in Nu. 20: 20f.; 21: 4 and Ju. 11: 17f.

Stations 17 to 24: The Valley of the Zered, across the Arnon, a well, Mattanah, Nahaliel, Bamoth, the valley in Moab, across from Jericho

Nu. 21: 12 *From there they journeyed and encamped in the valley of the Zered.*
Nu. 21: 13 *From there they journeyed and encamped on the other side of the Arnon, which is in the desert that extends out from the frontier of the Amorites; for the Arnon is the frontier of Moab, between Moab and the Amorites.*
Nu. 21: 16 *And from there to a well; it is the well where Yahweh said to Moses, Assemble the people that I may give them water.*
Nu. 21: 18b *And from the desert [-well] to Mattanah.*
Nu. 21: 19 *And from Mattanah to Nahaliel, and from Nahaliel to Bamoth.*
Nu. 21: 20 *And from Bamoth to the valley which is in the country of Moab, at the peak of Pisgah which overlooks Jeshimon.*
Nu. 22: 1 *The Israelites journeyed and encamped in the steppes of Moab across the Jordan from Jericho.*

From Ije-abarim the Israelites moved to the valley of the Zered (modern *Wady el-Hesā*) which flows into the south-east corner of the Dead Sea. If they were keeping outside of Edomite territory, as we are told they were, their camp must have lain in the upper reaches of this wady. P, however, who has brought them through the valley of the Zered, does not take them so far to the east. His version of the itinerary in Nu. 33: 45ff. does not even mention the camp in the valley of the Zered but follows Ije-abarim with *Dibon-gad* (modern *Dhībān*, about four miles north of the Arnon) and *Almon-*

[1] Cf. Gray, *Numbers*, pp. 282, 448.

diblathaim (probably the modern double ruin of *Kh. Deleilat*).¹ P thus omits any mention of the crossing of the Arnon and of the desert well.² Mattanah, Nahaliel, and Bamoth (all unidentified) likewise fail to find mention in his summary. The "valley which is in the country of Moab, at the peak of Pisgah which overlooks Jeshimon" ("Jeshimon" being the Wilderness of Judaea) is identified by D with "the valley opposite Beth-peor" (Dt. 4:46). In P's version (Nu. 33:47) the valley is not mentioned; instead we read of "the mountains of the 'Abarîm in front of Nebo" (modern *Jebel Nebā*, five miles south-west of Heshbon, modern *Hesbān*).

Nu. 21:23-35 relates how from this valley the Israelites proceeded to the conquest of central and northern Transjordan, which at that time comprised the two Amorite kingdoms of Heshbon and Bashan. No camping-places are mentioned. Evidently these campaigns did not fall within the itinerary scheme. The story of the campaigns is followed in 22:1 by the statement, "Then the Israelites journeyed and encamped in the steppes of Moab across the Jordan from Jericho." But it is quite evident that this statement comes too soon, for the death of Moses on "Mt. Nebo, the top of Pisgah, which faces Jericho" (Dt. 34:1) has not yet been related. The significance of this bit of itinerary becomes clear with a recognition that it is from the hand of P (note the P phrase "the steppes of Moab").³ The original itinerary seems to have ended with the arrival of the Israelites at Pisgah, where Moses died, but P wished to bring them to the Jordan, to the very threshold of the Promised Land, and so bridge the gap between the end of the Mosaic Tradition and the beginning of the next cycle of traditions dealing with

¹Doubtless the *Bt Dbltn* of the Mesha Inscription, line 30, and the *Beth-diblathaim* of Jer. 48:22; cf. Wright and Filson, The *Westminster Historical Atlas to the Bible*, Plate IX.

²Nevertheless it was probably P who added the remarks about this well in 21:16b-18a, also the comment in 21:13b about the Arnon being the frontier between Moab and the Amorites, the quotation from the Book of the Wars of Yahweh in 21:14f., and the poem on the triumph of Heshbon over Ar in 21:27-30. These geographical notes and poetic quotations are comparable to the antiquarian and chronological notes introduced elsewhere by P.

³Cf. Gray, *Numbers*, p. 306.

The Tradition of the Wilderness Itinerary   115

the conquest and settlement in Canaan. In Nu. 33: 49f. he defines their camp as lying along the Jordan "from Beth-jeshimoth as far as Abel-shittim" (called "Shittim" in 25: 1). In the material which P inserted after 22: 1 it is definitely stated or implied that the Israelites have moved on from Pisgah to the Jordan (cf. 23: 13f., 28; 25: 1). In 31: 12, 33: 50, 35: 1, and 36: 13 Moses is represented as present in the camp along the Jordan. But this spoils the dramatic climax of the original tradition which has Moses view the Promised Land from afar, from the top of Pisgah, and then die.

We have already seen[1] that according to Dt. 4: 44-9 the valley opposite Beth-peor was the scene of the promulgation of a Supplementary Code by Moses, which code is to be found in Ex. 22: 20 (EV 22: 21)—23: 9. When P appended the Book of Deuteronomy to the Mosaic Tradition he shifted this code back to Sinai.

Chapters 22-4 contain a number of oracles by the seer Balaam, predicting a glorious future for this new people which has appeared on the scene. They are usually regarded as part of JE—Albright[2] dates them as early as the twelfth century—but whatever be their origin, they have every appearance of being an extraneous element introduced by P. Chapter 25, vv. 1-5, telling of the illicit relations of the Israelites with Moabite women at Shittim, a result of their participation in the immoral rites of the Baal of Peor, is probably not a part of the original Mosaic Tradition. However, the fact that Hosea 9: 10 (cf. 5: 2) refers to the incident shows that the story in Nu. 25 rests on an authentic tradition.[3] JE material has been found in Nu. 32: 1-17, 20-7, 33*a, c*, 34-9, 41f., which relate the allotment of territories in Transjordan to the tribes of Reuben and Gad and the half-tribe of Manasseh, but little can be urged in support of such an assignment and much can be said against it. The rest of the material at the end of Numbers is universally recognized to be from the hand of P.

[1]See p. 40.   [2]"The Oracles of Balaam," *JBL*, LXIII (1944), 207-33.
[3]Not every tradition of the wilderness period necessarily found a place in the official, written version.

The original tradition is not resumed until we come to Dt. 27:1-8, and even this has been recast by D.[1] There follows Dt. 31:14f., 23 which relates the appointment of Joshua to succeed Moses. Then, as a fitting climax, comes the story of Moses' death, in Dt. 34. The original tradition of this event has been worked over and considerably expanded by P, as has been evident to most commentators. S. R. Driver[2] accepts as original v. 1 (omitting "from the steppes of Moab unto Mount Nebo" and "that confronts Jericho"), 2-4, 5 (omitting "at the command of Yahweh"), 6, 10. It seems probable, however, that the detailed description of the extent of Moses' view at the end of v. 1 and in vv. 2f. is an expansion by P, and that v. 6a is linked to the P phrase at the end of v. 5 in that Yahweh is the subject of the verb "bury"; furthermore, the original tradition knows nothing of Beth-peor. Verse 10, which emphasizes the pre-eminence of Moses among the prophets, recalls Nu. 12:7f. and doubtless comes from the same hand, that is, P. The Mosaic Tradition will, therefore, have originally concluded in this dramatic fashion:

"Then Moses went up to the top of Pisgah and Yahweh showed him the whole land. And Yahweh said to him, This is the land concerning which I swore to Abraham, Isaac, and Jacob: To thy descendants I will give it. I have let thee see it with thine eyes, but thou shalt not pass over thither. So Moses, the servant of Yahweh, died there in the land of Moab, but to this day no one knows his burial-place."

A review of the itinerary of the wilderness journey suggests that it has been moulded in the course of time into a schematic form. Each item of the itinerary is couched in a very similar manner, except that to avoid tediousness the verb *nasa‘*, "to journey," has been omitted from the group of names in Nu. 21:16-19. It is quite apparent that P has tampered with the various component parts of the itinerary, adding the word *‘ēdah*, "community," in Ex. 16:1; 17:1; Nu. 20:1, etc., and chronological notes, but this does not mean that the original Wilderness Tradition was minus an itinerary. The very

[1] See pp. 40f., 45.   [2] *Deuteronomy*, pp. 417ff.

The Tradition of the Wilderness Itinerary 117

differences between the itinerary scattered throughout Exodus and Numbers and the P summary in Nu. 33 prove that an itinerary was an essential part of the original tradition. The schematic form of this original itinerary is apparent not only from the common literary pattern of the various elements but also from the number of names preserved. Thus the first leg of the journey (from Rameses to the Mountain of God) contains ten names (Rameses, Succoth, Etham, Pi-hahiroth, Marah, Elim, Desert of Sin, Taberah,[1] Rephidim, Mountain of God). The third leg (from Kadesh to Pisgah) also contains ten (Mt. Hor, Oboth, Ije-abarim, Wady Zered, across the Arnon, a well, Mattanah, Nahaliel, Bamoth, Pisgah).[2] The second leg (from the Mountain of God to Kadesh) contains three names (Kibroth-hattaavah, Hazeroth, Kadesh). It is evident that the names have been selected with an eye to their number in order to facilitate the process of memorization. P added enough names to the original list to bring the number to forty-two (see Nu. 33) but it is probable that in estimating the total he did not take into account either the starting-point, Rameses, because this was not strictly a camping-place, or the steppes of Moab opposite Jericho, because he recognized that the Wilderness Period proper ended with the death of Moses at Nebo. Hence in his reckoning the total number of camping-places was forty, corresponding to the number of years of the wandering. The names which he inserted were added not only to obtain this correspondence but also, of course, to give a Sinai-'Ain Kadīs orientation to the tradition.

Our study of the itinerary has disclosed that at a number of points the D version presents a modification of the original tradition before it was modified still further by P. Thus the nameless sea of the Crossing of the original tradition has become in D the *yam sûph*;[3] the sacred mountain is still called Horeb but it is located in the vicinity of the wells of the Bene Ya'aqan and therefore in Edomite territory; Kadesh has become Kadesh-barnea; and the site of Aaron's tomb has been shifted from Mt. Hor, the first camping-place

---
[1] For the insertion of Taberah at this point, see pp. 131-4.
[2] Station no. 24, "across the Jordan from Jericho," has been shown above to be from P.   [3] See p. 87.

after leaving Kadesh, to Moserah, the first camping-place after leaving Horeb!

It is customary to explain these divergences by the assumption that they reflect two different streams of transmission, a northern and a southern, E and J. I submit that the variations found in D represent a deliberate perversion of the facts. Such a charge requires substantiation. What motive can have possibly inspired these perversions? The answer is to be found once again in the conflicting claims of the Jerusalem and Samaritan priesthoods. It is highly significant that the perversion of the tradition of the site of Aaron's death occurs in connection with an assertion as to who succeeded Aaron. The natural thing would be for Aaron to be succeeded by his eldest son Nadab, who was almost certainly the founder of the Shechemite-Samaritan priesthood, and a good case can be made out for believing that this is what the original tradition actually asserted. But this was unpalatable to the Jerusalemite priests and so in the revised version of the national tradition which they put out under Moses' name, the Book of Deuteronomy, they asserted that Aaron was actually succeeded by his third son Eleazar, from whom the Jerusalemite priests claimed descent. We begin to see that the publication of Deuteronomy involved a great deal more than the promulgation of a new code of laws. It was an attempt to cast doubt on the accuracy of the version of the national tradition which had hitherto been in circulation and of which the Samaritan priesthood were the custodians in a peculiar sense. Whereas the old tradition asserted that the Ritual Decalogue was the one given by Moses at Mt. Horeb, the new "Mosaic" book of which the Jerusalemite priests were the sole custodians asserted that it was the Moral Decalogue. The old tradition claimed that the Supplementary Code of Moses was that which had been written on the altar on Mt. Gerizim whereas the newly discovered book showed that the Samaritans possessed only an abridged copy of it. The old tradition on which the Samaritans relied claimed Horeb was in the land of Midian, whereas it was actually in the territory of the Bene Ya'aqan of Seir; it claimed Aaron died at Mt. Hor, the first stop after

The Tradition of the Wilderness Itinerary

leaving Kadesh, whereas he really died at Moserah, the first stop after leaving Horeb; it claimed (presumably) that Aaron was succeeded by his eldest son Nadab, whereas he was actually succeeded by his third son Eleazar.

P, believing that Deuteronomy was of Mosaic origin, endeavoured to harmonize the two traditions which had come down to him. Wherever they conflict, he very naturally shows a decided preference for the D, "Mosaic," version. Thus he accepts the D theory that the mountain of the lawgiving lay in the Sinai peninsula. The identification with the particular mountain Sinai was probably made before his time; it was part of the oral tradition which he inherited. P also accepted D's identification of Kadesh with Kadesh-barnea in the Negeb. But he dared to differ with D on one point— the site of Aaron's tomb. Here he reverts to the earlier Mt. Hor tradition, although he shifts the site of Mt. Hor to 'Arad in the Negeb (Nu. 21: 1-3). Possibly D's innovation on this matter, one of special concern to priests, was too radical to win acceptance. It is interesting to see how P, in Nu. 33: 32, disposes of the D theory in Dt. 10: 6f. The *wells of the Bene Ya'aqan* become simply the *Bene Ya'aqan*, *Moserah* becomes *Moseroth*, *ha-Gudgod* becomes *Hor-ha-Gidgad*. Instead of D's order: the wells of the Bene Ya'aqan, Moserah, ha-Gudgod, Yotbah, P has Moseroth, Bene Ya'aqan, Hor-ha-Gidgad, Yotbah.[1] Thus P disposes of D's location of Aaron's tomb at Moserah by shifting Moserah before the Bene Ya'aqan and changing the name to Moseroth. This makes ha-Gudgod the first camping-place after Mt. Horeb and therefore the place where Aaron died, and so P prefixes to *ha-Gudgod* (changed to *ha-Gidgad*) the word *Hor*, suggesting Mt. Hor. It is evident from his re-arrangement and corruption of the names that he is anxious to kill the D theory.

The original tradition presents us with an intelligible course of action: Moses leads the Israelites hurriedly across central Sinai to the head of the Gulf of 'Aqabah and thence to Mt. Horeb on the borders of the land of Midian, well out of

---

[1] If we follow Abel in identifying Yotbah with *eṭ-Ṭāba*, 35 km. north of 'Aqabah, in the 'Arabah, this would be additional evidence that D located Horeb and Kadesh west of the 'Arabah.

reach of Egyptian authority. (The D and P versions of the tradition, on the other hand, present us with a course of action which is not intelligible, for a movement into southern Sinai would have brought the Israelites into a region where Egyptian mining expeditions and accompanying troops were frequently to be found.) From Mt. Horeb the Israelites strike north to Kadesh (the later Petra), the home of the Kenites. From here they make an unsuccessful attempt to penetrate into Canaan from the south and an equally unsuccessful attempt to gain permission to cross Edom and Moab, failing which they are obliged to make a long arduous trek around Edom and through the eastern Moabite desert. Then they wheel westward and hurl their weight against the Amorite kingdoms of Heshbon and Bashan which collapse and give them a secure base along the Jordan whence they proceed to make another, and this time successful, assault on the land of their dreams.

VI The Tradition of the Ten Murmurings or Testings[1]

THE REFERENCE IN NU. 14:22 TO THE "TEN TIMES" THAT the Israelites put Yahweh to the test led Carpenter and Harford-Battersby[2] to suggest that the Wilderness Tradition was originally cast in a definitely systematized form. But under the influence of their own elaborate theory of an extensive re-editing and manipulation of the tradition they were discouraged from making any attempt to recover its original form. Nor has any modern scholar, as far as I am aware, taken up the hint which they dropped and endeavoured to do what they failed to do. But the fact that in the present form of the tradition there are precisely ten recorded instances of the people rebelling against Moses and Aaron (although in only four is the verb "murmur" specifically used) encourages us to believe that these are the "ten times" referred to in Nu. 14:22 and that the Wilderness Tradition was originally cast in the form of a series of Ten Murmurings. The Ten Murmurings are as follows:

1. at the sea of the Crossing, Ex. 14:11f.
2. at Marah, Ex. 15:24
3. in the desert of Sin, Ex. 16:2f.
4. at Massah, Ex. 17:2f.
5. at Taberah, Nu. 11:1
6. at Kibroth-hattaavah, Nu. 11:4-6
7. at Kadesh, Nu. 14:1-4
8. at Kadesh, Nu. 16:12-14 (cf. vv. 1-3, 11 and 17:6, 10)
9. at Kadesh, Nu. 20:2-5

---

[1]The substance of this chapter was presented as a paper at the eighth annual meeting of the Canadian section of the Society of Biblical Literature and Exegesis, 1946.

[2]*The Hexateuch*, II (London, 1900), p. 208, n. 17.

10. during the journey around Edom, Nu. 21:5.[1]

The fact that the Story of the Plagues was also cast in the form of a drama of ten scenes strengthens the probability that the reference in Nu. 14:22 to ten testings of Yahweh reflects the actual structure of the original Wilderness Tradition. Significant also is D's assertion that the wilderness journey was a time of repeated rebellion against Yahweh: "Remember, never forget, how thou didst provoke Yahweh thy god to anger in the desert; from the day that thou didst leave the land of Egypt until you reached this place you have been in a state of rebellion with Yahweh" (Dt. 9:7). Of course, these words do not prove that the Wilderness Tradition was cast in the form of a series of murmurings but they would be all the more *à propos* if such were the case.

As soon as one seeks to recover the original form of the tradition, one finds a red herring drawn across the trail in the fact that the reference to the ten testings of Yahweh comes not in the tenth instance listed above but in the seventh. This would seem to indicate that what we have listed as the seventh is really the tenth and last, and that the original order has been altered. It might even lead us to doubt whether Nu. 14:22 really implies that the tradition had a systematized form. But it is worth noting that this verse is from P, not JE (Gray) or Rje (Binns),[2] and it is highly probable that the reference to the "ten times," while coming too soon in the narrative, implies a knowledge of the original pattern of the tradition.[3] I shall, therefore, avoid assuming that the murmuring referred to in Nu. 14 is really the tenth and last and use as the basis of my investigation the ten murmurings listed above.

The First Murmuring: at the sea of the Crossing (Ex. 14)

Ex. 14:11f. *And they said to Moses, Was it because there are no graves in Egypt that thou hast taken us into the desert to*

---

[1] According to the *Talmud*: "'Arakhin 15*ab*" the ten testings were as follows: two at the Red Sea (Ex. 14:11; Ps. 106:7), two in demanding water (Ex. 15:23; 17:2), two food (Ex. 16:20, 27), and two flesh (Ex. 16:3; Nu. 11:4), the worship of the golden calf, and the reaction to the report of the spies.

[2] See pp. 138f.

[3] Note how P anticipates in Ex. 4:21-3 and in 11:10. See pp. 7, 11, 19.

The Tradition of the Ten Murmurings 123

die? Why treat us in this way by bringing us out of Egypt? Is not this the very thing we told thee in Egypt would happen, when we said, Leave us alone and let us serve the Egyptians, for it were better for us to serve the Egyptians than to die in the desert?

Modern commentators see in the Story of the Crossing of the Sea a combination of two versions, J and P, with a few touches of E. McNeile analyses chapter 14 as follows: J—vv. 5-7b, 11-14, 19b, 21b, 24f., 27b, 28b, 30; E—vv. 7a, c, 10b, 15a, 16a, 19a; JE—vv. 10a, 20; P—vv. 1-4, 8, 9a, c, 15b, 16b-18, 21a, c-23, 26, 27a, 28a; Rp—vv. 9b, 29; Rd—v. 31. An examination of this analysis will disclose the fact that it rests in part on a theory of the Plague Story which we have already shown to be fallacious; one error has led to another, or rather to a whole crop of other errors. Thus v. 16a is assigned to E on the ground that a reference to Moses wielding the rod is a mark of E, while vv. 4, 8, and 17 are assigned to P because of the erroneous view that the phrase "Yahweh hardened the heart of Pharaoh" is a mark of P.[1] Again, the assignment to J of v. 21b (which attributes the cleaving of the sea to a strong east wind) and to P of v. 21a, c (which attributes the cleaving to Moses stretching out his hand) rests on the erroneous view that Moses' rod and natural causation are mutually exclusive and presuppose different sources. The statement in 14:21: "Then Moses stretched out his hand over the sea, and Yahweh moved the sea away by a strong east wind all night long and turned the sea into a dry waste" forms an almost exact parallel to 10:13: "So Moses stretched out his staff over the land of Egypt, and Yahweh directed an east wind onto the land all that day and all night. When morning came, the east wind brought the locusts." No evidence was found in dealing with the Story of the Plagues, to which 10:13 belongs, to support the view that two documents have been combined, nor is there any need to assume the presence of two documents here. Yet McNeile assigns the first part of 14:21 to E and the rest to J. It is surely prosaic to ask: If Moses' rod effects the miracles, why the need of

---

[1] For a discussion of these problems, see pp. 4, 6-9f.

an east wind? We must remember that the author is reconstructing a dramatic scene, and it is much more effective to have Moses wielding a magic wand than merely uttering a pious prayer—as we ourselves can testify, if we have ever witnessed a performance by a magician on the stage. The rod is designed to impress the audience; it is the visible link between Moses and the Unseen Powers, to the manipulation of which Yahweh immediately responds. It may well be, of course, that in an earlier form of the tradition the rod was not mentioned. But must its introduction be explained by the theory of the incorporation of another written version of the story where the rod played a leading part? Is it not more natural to suppose that while the story was still in the oral stage the rod was introduced in order to heighten the dramatic effect?

Two different points of view have been detected in the portrayal of the behaviour of the waters. Some verses (21, 25-8) give the impression of a receding and then advancing tide, others (22, 29) picture the waters as forming "a wall for them on their right hand and on their left." It is held that these representations are inconsistent and that the exaggeration of the miracle is a mark of P's hand. But there is nothing of P in the wording of either v. 22 or v. 29. It can be just as well maintained that the heightening of the miracle was the work of an earlier author. We must remember that the author of the Plague Narrative and of the original Mosaic Tradition as a whole was not above using a bit of hyperbole on occasion. It is merely an expression of his sense of the dramatic. To mark off such passages as the work of P is to fail to appreciate the writer's character.[1]

The Story of the Crossing of the Sea, like the Story of the Plagues, undoubtedly contains elements which are of later origin than the main body of the tradition and which are not

---

[1]This is not to deny that the story has been touched up at a few points by P. We have already seen (p. 84) that P added some geographical notes in v. 2, designed to give the location of Pi-hahiroth. In v. 9 he is probably responsible for the expansion "all the horses of the chariots of Pharaoh, his horsemen and his army ... in front of Baal-zephon," while his fingerprints will also be found in v. 10 (see pp. 153f).

The Tradition of the Ten Murmurings 125

always in harmony with it. They seem to represent the last stages in the development of the tradition before it was reduced to written form. There is no need to explain them by the theory that two different documents with divergent points of view have been combined.

The Second Murmuring: at Marah (Ex. 15: 22-6)

Ex. 15: 24 *So the people murmured* [lûn] *against Moses, saying, What shall we drink?*

Brief as the story of the Second Murmuring is, scholars have thought to discern in it elements of diverse origin. Thus McNeile assigns vv. 22-25a to J, 25b to E, and 26 to Rd (Rje, according to Driver). Actually the only secondary bit seems to be v. 22a which owes its present form to P.[1] The problem created by v. 25b ("There he made rules and regulations [*sam ḥoq û-mishpaṭ*, cf. Josh. 24: 25] for them, and there he tested [*nissah*] them") receives clarification from Dt. 8: 2: "Thou shalt remember all the way that Yahweh thy god has made thee go during the past forty years in the desert, afflicting thee in order to test [*nissah*] thee and find out what was in thy heart, whether thou wouldst keep his commandments or not" (cf. 8: 16 also). According to D the trials and hardships to which the people were exposed were part of a divine plan designed to test their temper to discover how much of the Divine Law they were capable of receiving. This interpretation of the wilderness experiences manifestly did not originate with D for we shall see[2] that the Rephidim story had already been shaped with this idea in mind. The mention of the "rules and regulations" in the Marah story was made necessary by the author's desire to use it as the first illustration of this divine testing of the people. The original tradition probably told only of the people murmuring because of the lack of water fit to drink. In order to convert the Murmuring story into a Testing-of-the-People story the author felt obliged to insert a reference to the giving of some laws which tested the willingness of the people to obey. He certainly has no specific body of laws in mind. The Third Murmuring story,

[1] See p. 85.   [2] See pp. 130-3.

as will presently appear,[1] was likewise converted into a Testing-of-the-People story. Yahweh there lays down a rule that only one day's supply of manna is to be gathered at a time "in order that I may test [*nissah*] them [to see]whether they will walk in my law or not" (Ex. 16: 4). The moulding of the Wilderness Tradition into a pattern of ten murmurings or testings led to the frequent employment of both the verb *lûn*, "to murmur," and the verb *nissah*, "to test."

S. A. Cook,[2] failing to grasp the pattern of the tradition as a whole, suspected that any passage which contained the word *nissah* was a fragment of the Massah story. He was fortified in his opinion by the observation that the length of the pilgrimage which the Israelites had requested permission of Pharaoh to make (Ex. 5: 3; 8: 27; cf. 3: 18) agrees with the actual distance to Marah, viz., three days (Ex. 15: 22f.). This suggested that there was more to Marah than a pool of bitter water. It was evidently situated near Massah-Meribah, for the Massah-Meribah story comes shortly after the Marah story. In Nu. 20 Meribah is identified with Kadesh; therefore, Marah was near Kadesh. In Gen. 14: 7 Kadesh is called *En-mishpaṭ* ("the Spring of Judgment") which suggests that it was an ancient centre of law-giving. But Marah is also said to have been the scene of a law-giving. These observations led Cook to the belief that in the early form of the Wilderness Tradition the Israelites journeyed straight from Egypt to Kadesh (= Marah) and there the law-giving took place. He believes that many of the legends now associated with Sinai and Horeb had their original setting at Kadesh but were later transferred to the sacred mountain in order to magnify its importance.

This theory was first suggested by Wellhausen[3] and it has been very widely adopted.[4] But no theory has done more to

[1] See pp. 129f.

[2] *Critical Notes on Old Testament History* (London, 1907), pp. 78f.; *Cambridge Ancient History*, II (1924), 361.

[3] *Prolegomena to the History of Israel* (Eng. trans.; Edinburgh, 1885), pp. 343ff.

[4] e.g., by A. Lods, *Israel from its Beginning to the Middle of the Eighth Century* (Eng. trans.; London, 1932), pp. 176ff.; von Rad, *Das formgeschichtliche Problem des Hexateuchs* (Beiträge zur Wissenschaft vom Alten und Neuen Testament, Folge IV, Heft 26; Stuttgart, 1938); and C. A. Simpson, *The Early Traditions of Israel* (Oxford, 1948), pp. 219, 419ff.

The Tradition of the Ten Murmurings

bedevil and confuse the subject of early Israelite history. It is based on what I believe to be a mere coincidence, viz., the agreement of the distance from Egypt to Marah with the length of the journey for which the Israelites had originally requested permission. The Israelites had asked for *three* days because anything less would not have given them a sufficient head-start in their dash for freedom and anything more would have aroused suspicion and would almost certainly have met with refusal. There is not the slightest evidence that Marah was a centre sacred to Yahweh, a place to which Hebrews in Egypt would want to make a pilgrimage. The tradition seems to represent it as a spot previously nameless, or at least as a spot whose name the Israelites did not know, but which was given a name suggestive both of the quality of its waters (*mar*, "bitter") and of the rebelliousness of the people (*marah*, "to rebel"). That Marah was nowhere near Kadesh is evident from the examination of the wilderness itinerary made above.[1]

The Third Murmuring: in the Desert of Sin (Ex. 16)

Ex. 16: 2f. *And the whole community* [ēdah] *of the Israelites murmured* [lûn] *against Moses and Aaron in the desert. And the Israelites said unto them, Would that we had died by the hand of Yahweh in the land of Egypt when we sat by pots of flesh, and ate our fill of food, for you have brought us out to this desert to kill this whole assembly with famine.*

Although the present form of the story of the Third Murmuring bears numerous marks of having been expanded by P, the references in Dt. 8:2f., 16 to the provision of the manna show that D found a manna story in the original Exodus tradition. Just how much of the present story is original and how much due to P is a little difficult to determine. McNeile assigns only vv. 4 and 15 to the original tradition (E); Driver allows to it vv. 4, 5, 13b-15a, 27-30 (J?); Rudolph allows vv. 1a (omitting "the whole community of the Israelites"), 2 (omitting the same phrase and the words "and against Aaron"), 3 (reading "unto him" and "thou hast brought us out"), 4a, b^a, 13b-17, 21, 31 (J). Rudolph

[1]See p. 88.

is certainly right in regarding the bit of itinerary in v. 1*a* as original, for although the wilderness itinerary has been worked over by P in some cases, there is every evidence, as we have seen, that the original did contain an itinerary, one, moreover, that was arranged in a somewhat schematic form.[1] Rudolph is also right in including vv. 2f. among the original portions (although his alterations and omissions are quite uncalled for), for they contain the statement of grumbling which immediately follows the itinerary in the introduction to each Murmuring story. There is nothing in these verses distinctive of P. Verse 4 has similarities with the style and vocabulary of earlier parts of the original Exodus narrative (cf. 9: 18 and 5: 9, 13), while the latter part of the verse finds an echo in Dt. 8: 2, thus proving its originality. Verses 5-12 have numerous marks of P's interests and style, while the reference to the quails in v. 13*a* is of a piece with the promise of meat in the P verses immediately preceding.[2] The original quail story comes in the story of the Sixth Murmuring at Kibroth-hattaavah, Nu. 11. That vv. 13*b*-14 are part of the original tradition is proved by the fact that the later P verse, Nu. 11: 9, is based on them, while Dt. 8: 3, 16 presuppose the etymology of the word "manna" given in v. 15. Verses 16-20, 22-30, 32-6 contain marks of P authorship, but v. 21 conforms so closely to the description of the manna given in v. 14 and is so little in harmony with the P accounts of it in vv. 23f. and Nu. 11: 8 that it must be regarded as original also. The dependence of Nu. 11: 7, 8*c* upon v. 31 shows that it also is part of the original tradition. The definition of an *omer* in v. 36 would seem to imply that some of the verses which mention the *omer* must be original. But the passages in which the word occurs, viz., vv. 16, 18, 32f., all seem to be by P. It seems necessary to conclude that P's use of the word is a conscious archaism without any basis in the original narrative.

The original form of the Third Murmuring story, there-

---

[1]See pp. 116f.

[2]P probably introduced a reference to the quails here because of his knowledge of the annual arrival of large numbers of them in Sinai (see C. S. Jarvis, *Yesterday and To-day in Sinai* (Edinburgh, 1931), p. 170).

The Tradition of the Ten Murmurings 129

fore, is to be found in vv. 1a,[1] 2 (omitting "the whole community"), 3f., 13b-15, 21, 31. Putting these verses in sequence, the story reads as follows: "2 And the Israelites murmured [lûn] against Moses and Aaron in the desert. 3 And the Israelites said to them, Would that we had died by the hand of Yahweh in the land of Egypt when we sat by pots of flesh and ate our fill of food, for you have brought us out to this desert to kill this whole assembly [qāhāl] with famine. 4 Then Yahweh said to Moses, Behold I am going to rain food for you from the sky. The people shall go out and collect one day's supply at a time in order that I may test [nissah] them [to see] whether they will walk in my law or not. 13b In the morning there was a layer of dew around the camp, 14 and when the layer of dew evaporated, there, on the face of the desert was a fine scaly substance, as fine as hoar-frost on the ground. 15 When the Israelites saw it, they said to one another, What [Heb. *man*] is it?—for they did not know what it was. Moses said to them, It is the food which Yahweh has given you to eat. 21 So they collected it morning after morning, each according to his eating capacity; and when the sun grew hot it melted. 31 The house of Israel called it manna [Heb. *man*]; it was as white as coriander seed, and its taste was like that of wafers made with honey."

The statement in v. 4 that the people were commanded to gather no more than one day's supply of manna at a time in order to test their faith in the providence of their god and to see whether they would follow his instructions or not, led S. A. Cook[2] to assert that this implies a previous law-giving and that, therefore, the manna story finds its most logical place after the departure from Sinai, in the great desert where the duplicate story in Nu. 11 actually places it. But the content of v. 4 is of a piece with the statement in 15: 25b regarding the bitter waters of Marah. Yahweh is testing the people, trying them out with a few laws, before he issues his full set of rules and regulations for them to observe. The incidents before the arrival at the mountain are regarded

[1]For the probable original form of v. 1a, see pp. 90f.
[2]*Critical Notes on Old Testament History*, p. 65.

by the author as a progressive education of the people, designed to prepare them for the revelation of the divine Torah. The present position of the manna story gives a certain balance to the arrangement of the tradition—the question as to how the people were provisioned during the desert journey is answered by the story of the manna in the desert which was traversed before reaching Horeb and by the story of the quails in the desert which was traversed after leaving Horeb.

The Fourth Murmuring: at Rephidim-Massah-Meribah (Ex. 17: 1-7)

Ex. 17: 1b-3 *They encamped at Rephidim; but there was no water for the people to drink. So the people disputed* [rîbh] *with Moses and said, Give us water to drink. Moses said, Why do you dispute* [rîbh] *with me? Why do you put Yahweh to the test* [nissah]? *The people thirsted there for water, and the people murmured* [lûn] *against Moses and said, Why didst thou ever bring us up from Egypt to have me and my sons and my livestock die of thirst?*

McNeile's analysis of the Massah-Meribah story is as follows: J—vv. 2b, 3, 7a, c; E—vv. 1b, 2a, 4-6, 7b; P—v. 1a. There can be little doubt that v. 1a owes its present form to P.[1] Verse 3 with its awkward "me" and "my" also seems to have been expanded by P. The division of the rest of the narrative, vv. 4-7, between two sources is highly questionable, as Rudolph has perceived, although he regards v. 5b as a later gloss. The presence of the two names, Massah and Meribah, has been used as a support for the JE hypothesis, but the names are clearly synonymous, being religious substitutes for Rephidim. It was a "Place of Testing" (*massah*) and a "Place of Contention" (*merîbah*). At the time that the tradition was reduced to writing both titles of Rephidim were in circulation. D, however, uses the name Massah only (cf. Dt. 6: 16; 9: 22).[2] It has sometimes

[1] See p. 91.
[2] The reference in Dt. 33: 8 is of post-exilic date.

The Tradition of the Ten Murmurings

been inferred from this that the name Meribah originally designated a different locality but one associated with a similar story,[1] and that this led to the eventual insertion of the name Meribah in Ex. 17 where it does not properly belong. Its proper place is said to be in Nu. 20 where v. 13 identifies it with Kadesh. But Nu. 20:13 is by P and we shall reserve judgment on the value of that identification.[2] In the meantime it may be reasonably argued that both names, Massah and Meribah, were present in the Ex. 17 story which D used but that, for the sake of convenience, he elected to use only one name, the first one mentioned, i.e. Massah.

It has been maintained that Dt. 9:22-4, which mentions Massah between Taberah and Kibroth-hattaavah, shows that the Massah incident should be placed after the Taberah incident, hence in the great desert which the Israelites encountered after leaving Horeb. But Yahweh's remark in Ex. 17:6, "I am going to stand *before thee* there upon the rock in Horeb," implies that the Israelites encamped at Rephidim-Massah have not yet reached Horeb, let alone the great desert which lay beyond it. On the other hand, there seems no reason for doubting that the order of mention in Dt. 9:22-4 is chronological. The solution of this problem requires a careful examination of the Deuteronomic passage. The first thing which strikes the reader is that the passage constitutes an interrupting element in its context, the Story of the Golden Calf, being in this respect exactly similar to Dt. 10:6-9. We have seen[3] that Dt. 10:6-9 is a composition by D himself, inserted into the tradition which he is quoting in order to give it the interpretation he desired. It is therefore probable that in Dt. 9:22-4 we are faced with a similar situation. But what was the object of the insertion? I believe the answer is to be found in D's desire to include the Golden Calf incident, which took place at Horeb, among the Ten Murmurings or Testings. It is a striking fact that this incident is not mentioned in the original list of the Ten.[4]

---

[1] Cf. S. A. Cook, *Critical Notes on Old Testament History*, p. 65.
[2] For a discussion of P's use of the name Meribah, see pp. 149f.
[3] pp. 74f.   [4] See pp. 121f.

Moreover, it has not been cast in the Murmuring mould, which shows that it was incorporated into the Mosaic Tradition some time after the latter had been cast in schematic form. The story was present, however, in the form of the tradition which reached D, and, of all the incidents related in the tradition, that of Aaron's making an image of Yahweh in the form of a bull seems to have made the greatest impression on his mind. If anything could be called a "provoking" or "testing" of Yahweh, it was that. Surely it should be reckoned among the Ten Testings. The insertion of vv. 22-4 in chapter 9, by associating the Golden Calf incident with four other notable instances of "testing," accomplished this object. But it was not necessary for D to distort the chronological sequence of the testings in order to achieve this aim. Hence it would seem altogether likely that D has preserved the original sequence of the events. This conclusion will receive support from the examination of the Taberah incident when evidence will appear that it, rather than the Massah story, was tampered with by P and shifted by him to a different position from that which it had originally occupied.

At Rephidim, *alias* Massah, *alias* Meribah, a battle is said to have taken place with the Amalekites (Ex. 17: 8-16). McNeile assigns this passage to E because of the mention of Moses' magic wand and the role played by Joshua, Aaron, and Hur. But we have already seen that these elements belong to the original homogeneous tradition and are not an indication of the presence of a separate literary source.[1]

The Fifth Murmuring: at Taberah (Nu. 11: 1-3)

Nu. 11: 1 *Now the people were complaining of misfortune in the hearing of Yahweh. When Yahweh heard* [them] *he became angry and the fire of Yahweh burned among them and consumed the outskirts of the camp.*

That the Taberah incident was regarded as a Murmuring or Testing story is evident from the reference to it in Dt. 9: 22. P, however, omits all reference to it in his summary of the

[1] See pp. 4, 6, 43, etc.

The Tradition of the Ten Murmurings 133

wilderness itinerary in Nu. 33 (cf. v. 16). I believe that his reason for doing so was that, following D, he regarded the Golden Calf affair at Horeb as one of the Ten Murmurings or Provokings of Yahweh. The inclusion of the Story of the Golden Calf meant that one of the original ten had to go. P decided to omit the Taberah incident, probably because he regarded it as the least important. But while he omitted it from his summary of the itinerary, he did not dare to obliterate all mention of it. He did, however, reduce the story to insignificant proportions and telescope what was left of it with the Kibroth-hattaavah story. To prevent anyone from persisting in regarding it as one of the Ten Murmurings, he altered the verb *lûn* ("to murmur"), which was regularly employed in the introductions to these stories, to *'anan* ("to complain"), a late word found elsewhere only in Lam. 3:39. S. A. Cook[1] perceived that the Taberah story had been abbreviated but believed that the lack of detail in it was due to the fact that the story is merely an attempt to explain the meaning of the place-name, viz., "Conflagration."

As pointed out above,[2] Dt. 9: 22-4 places the Taberah incident before the Massah incident and there seems no reason for doubting that this order is chronological. It is interesting to discover that the adoption of D's order puts five testings or murmurings before Horeb and five after it— another indication of a schematic arrangement of the original tradition.

The Sixth Murmuring: at Kibroth-hattaavah
(Nu. 11: 4-34)

Nu. 11: 4-6. *Now the rabble who were among them had a craving; the Israelites also again wept and said, O that we had meat to eat! We remember the fish that we used to eat for nothing in Egypt, the cucumbers, the melons, the leeks, the onions, and the garlic. But now we are famished, and there is not a thing, except that the manna is still with us.*

---
[1] *Critical Notes on Old Testament History*, p. 68.
[2] p. 131.

When P telescoped the Taberah and Kibroth-hattaavah stories together,[1] the introduction to the second of these stories naturally underwent some modification. Thus the customary itinerary statement is missing, and the verb *lûn*, "to murmur," does not appear. But the frequent references to the people "weeping" (vv. 3, 10, 18, 20) and the presence of a complaint (vv. 4b-6) justify the assumption that the story once conformed to the regular Murmuring pattern.[2]

The Kibroth-hattaavah story, in its present form, is a conflation of two originally independent stories, one relating the provision of quails as a meat supply (vv. 4-13, 18-24a, 31-4), the other the appointment of seventy prophetic elders (vv. 14-17, 24b-30). I shall examine the latter story first.

The functions of the seventy elders are nowhere clearly defined. It is said that they prophesied once (proof that the spirit of Moses had really descended upon them) "but never again" (v. 25). Prophesying was, therefore, not their primary function. They were appointed in response to Moses' complaint that the burden of the people was too much for one pair of shoulders to carry. This indicates that their functions were of a judicial and administrative character. But Ex. 18 and Dt. 1 have already related the appointment of an unstated number of *sarîm* (Dt. 1:15 adds *shoṭerîm*) to assist Moses in administering the law, and there has been no suggestion in the succeeding narrative that their powers have been terminated. It would seem that we are faced with two conflicting traditions respecting the institution of these judges. But closer examination will show that the Nu. 11 story cannot be explained by the simple theory that it is just a variant of the Ex. 18 and Dt. 1 story. For one thing, it places the appointment of the seventy elders at Kibroth-hattaavah, whereas the appointment in Ex. 18 and Dt. 1 is at Horeb. For another, it limits the number to seventy, whereas the other story has an official (*sar*) appointed for every ten members of the population. If the two stories concern the same incident, then seventy officials would imply a population of only seven hundred, which is

[1]Cf. pp. 93f., 132f.   [2]See pp. 152f.

absurd. Furthermore, the Nu. 11 story has the elders appointed from those who are already elders and *shoṭerîm* of the people, whereas in Ex. 18 and Dt. 1 the only qualification is that they be men of integrity. We are led to the conclusion that the author of the Nu. 11 story is describing the institution of an inner court of judges, a supreme tribunal. Now it is a well-known fact that post-exilic Judaism possessed just such a court, called the Sanhedrin, composed of exactly seventy members.[1] It is surely legitimate to infer that the writer is giving us what he believes, or would have us believe, to have been the origin of the Sanhedrin.[2] He does not go so far as to push its origin right back to Sinai-Horeb but he does locate it in the Wilderness Period. He confers on it divine sanction and authority; its members are endowed with the Spirit of Moses. But by the story of Eldad and Medad the author wishes to make clear that this judicial body is not to be regarded as having any monopoly of the gift of prophecy and divine inspiration.

Gray and Binns assign the Story of the Seventy Prophetic Elders to the E Document; Rudolph regards it as a later addition to J. I believe it comes from the hand of P. In composing the story P leaned heavily on Ex. 18 and Dt. 1, particularly the latter; for example, Nu. 11:14 is based on Dt. 1:9, not on Ex. 18:18; the "burden" of Nu. 11:17 reflects Dt. 1:12, not Ex. 18:22. In fixing the number at seventy P was no doubt reflecting the actual composition of the Sanhedrin in his day, which in turn was doubtless determined by the divine preference for that number manifested on the occasion of the giving of the tablets (Ex. 24:1, 9). A linguistic mark of post-exilic origin is the use of the expression "the recorded" or "registered" (*kethûbhim*)[3]

---

[1] Cf. Josephus, *Wars* II. xx. 5; IV. v. 4.

[2] The Story of the Seventy Elders is a good illustration of Cook's remark regarding Jewish history that "the past is often presented in such a way as to furnish authority and precedent for that which is contemporary" (*Notes on Old Testament History*, p. 62).

[3] To maintain an E authorship for the story this word has had to be regarded as a late gloss (see *Enc. Bib.*, 1256) or the possibility raised that the practice of registration may have extended back to the eighth or ninth century B.C. (see Gray, *Numbers*, p. 114).

in reference to Eldad and Medad in v. 26 (cf. Neh. 12: 22, I Chron. 4: 41, etc.). It is significant that the same emphasis on the spirit of prophecy is found in two post-exilic writers, Ezekiel (cf. 11: 19f.) and Joel (cf. 3: 1f., EV 2: 28f.). The assonance between Eldad and Medad also recalls the Gog and Magog of Ezekiel, while the rare verb *'aṣal*, used in vv. 17 and 25, appears in Ez. 42: 6.

Having disposed of the Story of the Seventy Prophetic Elders and shown that it is in all probability a P insertion, let us turn to the Story of the Quails in vv. 4-13, 18-24*a*, 31-5. Binns regards the story as a literary unity and assigns it to JE but thinks vv. 11f., 14f. were transferred here from their original position after Ex. 33: 1-3.[1] Certainly the connection of vv. 11f., 14f. with the Story of the Quails is very loose. I believe they, and v. 10 as well,[2] represent matter composed and inserted by P in order to graft his story of the Seventy Prophetic Elders on to the original tradition.[3] In vv. 7-9 we have further material from the hand of P, for the description of the manna which they give (i.e., that it was something that could be ground and made into cakes and had an oily taste—a reflection of later attempts to identify it) corresponds to that given in the P verses in Ex. 16 (cf. v. 23), whereas according to the original tradition it was like hoar-frost and evaporated as soon as the sun rose.

The Seventh Murmuring: at Kadesh (Nu. 13-14)

Nu. 14: 1-4 *Then the whole community* ['ēdah] *proceeded to give vent to its feelings and the people wept that night. All the Israelites murmured* [lûn] *against Moses and Aaron, and the whole community said to them, Would that we had died in the land of Egypt! Or would that we had died in this desert! And why is Yahweh bringing us into this land, only to fall by the sword? Our wives and our little ones will become a prey. Would it not be better for us to return to*

[1] Through an oversight Gray's text reads "23: 1-3."
[2] Note the phrase "by their families," a mark of P (cf. Gray, *Numbers*, p. 107).
[3] The reference in v. 15 to Moses "finding favour in Yahweh's sight" recalls Ex. 33: 12f. (a P passage). See p. 60.

The Tradition of the Ten Murmurings

Egypt? Let us appoint a leader, they said to one another, and return to Egypt.

The Seventh Murmuring of the people ensued upon the return of the spies from reconnoitring the Negeb with a report that its inhabitants were giants. They all wanted to turn around and go back to Egypt. The tradition of their murmuring has been preserved not only in Nu. 13-14 but also in Dt. 1: 20-46 and a comparison of the two versions will aid us in recovering the original form of the Numbers version.

1. The statement in Dt. 1: 20f. that as soon as the Israelites reached Kadesh Moses proposed an attack on the Promised Land and that spies were appointed to reconnoitre the ground is missing at the beginning of Nu. 13. But it must surely have once stood there as it provides the necessary introduction to what follows. Of course, the author of Dt. 1 has not preserved the exact wording of the original, for his account is cast in the first person, and he may have made other changes.

2. Nu. 13: 1-16 amplifies the tradition preserved in Dt. 1: 22f. by giving the names of the twelve spies. The passage is generally recognized to be from the hand of P.

3. The account of the mission of the spies in Nu. 13: 17-33 finds a brief parallel in Dt. 1: 24f. The first part of Nu. 13: 17 is clearly by P because of the use of the verb *tûr*, while the last three words, embodying a command to "go up to the highland," not only sound redundant after the preceding command to "go up into the Negeb" but are in line with P's conception of the mission of the spies as embracing the whole land of Canaan (cf. v. 21). Verses 19f. are redundant after 18 and probably constitute an expansion of the original narrative by P. All of v. 22 after "Negeb" seems to be by P. Probably P, anxious to bring Caleb on this occasion into contact with the place which was afterwards to be his, introduced into the narrative information about Hebron and its Anakite inhabitants drawn from Josh. 15: 13f. The term *yelîdhê* is definitely a P word, while the chronological note also suggests P's hand. Furthermore, a reference at

this point to the Anakites mars the dramatic effect of the story. The proper place for such a reference is in v. 33, where they are actually mentioned—mentioned, moreover, with the word *benê* and not with the P word *yelîdhê*. The Anakites are the trump card played by the other spies to offset the effect of Caleb's optimistic report. The references to the Nephilim are, of course, awkward and may with some confidence be regarded as insertions by P. The fact that v. 24 does not conform to the pattern of Ex. 15:24, 17:7, 15f., Nu. 11:3, 34 suggests that it is from P. Verse 25 is marked as P's handiwork by the employment of the verb *tûr* and by the chronological interest. Verse 26 seems to belong to the original tradition except for the phrases, "and unto all the *'ēdah* of the Israelites" and "and all the *'ēdah*." Verse 27 is original and also v. 28, except for the clause "moreover, we saw the *yelîdhê* of the 'Anaq there." The precise information in v. 29 about the location of the various inhabitants of Canaan makes no contribution to the progress of the popular tradition and seems to be a scholarly note introduced by P. We shall see later[1] that it conforms to P's conception of the distribution of these peoples. Verses 30f. must be original; otherwise the promise that Caleb would enter the Promised Land is unintelligible. The whole of v. 32 must be regarded as the work of P.

4. Nu. 14:1-9 is paralleled by Dt. 1:26-33. Verse 1 is generally recognized as being from P. Verses 2-4 contain the usual introduction to a Murmuring and have suffered only one P expansion, the words "all the *'ēdah*" in v. 2. Verses 6-9 relate the expostulation of Joshua and Caleb with the people. In the Dt. 1 version, it is Moses who does the expostulating. The sequel to the story, vv. 34-9, suggests that only Caleb did the expostulating. Hence both versions would seem to have been tampered with. The use of the root *tûr* in v. 6 and the fact that the speech of Caleb has already been given in 13:30 point to the conclusion that vv. 6-9 are by P. P loved composing speeches as they gave him an opportunity to preach.

5. Nu. 14:10-22 has no parallel in Dt. 1. That v. 10 is

[1] See p. 141.

The Tradition of the Ten Murmurings 139

from P is generally recognized. As for vv. 11-22, Gray remarks: "It has been very generally felt that in its present form this section is not derived from the early prophetic sources." Kuenen assigned it to the seventh century B.C.; Binns to Rje. I believe it comes from the hand of P for the following reasons: (i) The phrase *'adh 'anah* at the beginning of v. 11 is found elsewhere in the Hexateuch only in Ex. 16:28 (a P verse) and Josh. 18:3, and outside the Hexateuch only in passages from the seventh century on. (ii) Verse 12 is based on either Ex. 32:10 or Dt. 9:13f.; vv. 13 and 16 are based on Ex. 32:12 and Dt. 9:28. Therefore these verses must be dated later than the seventh century. (iii) The whole section, vv. 13-17, has close affinities with the thought of Ez. 20. (iv) Verse 18 is a quotation from Ex. 34:6f., a P composition.[1] (v) The statement in v. 21 that "the whole earth shall be full of the glory of Yahweh" recalls post-exilic passages like Ps. 72:19 and Hab. 2:14. (vi) The reference to the *kebôd Yahweh* in v. 22 is a clear mark of P authorship.

6. Nu. 14:23-35 is paralleled by Dt. 1:34-40. A curious feature of the Numbers account is that the oath of Yahweh that none but Caleb should enter the Promised Land is repeated. The first version in vv. 23f. is the simpler of the two and therefore no doubt the earlier.

It is interesting that the Deuteronomic version explicitly includes Moses in the group condemned not to enter Canaan (cf. Dt. 1:37). There can be little doubt that the author was here basing himself on the original tradition, for the passage provides the necessary explanation why Moses was condemned to suffer the same fate as the people: he was manifestly engulfed in the same pessimism and lack of trust in Yahweh which swept over the people following the report of the spies. Indeed Nu. 14:41-3 definitely states that he advised against an attack. Only Caleb was confident of success. The author of Dt. 1, however, has endeavoured to shield Moses from the charge of lack of faith and actually makes him, rather than Caleb, take the lead in expostulating with the pessimists, although he thereby leaves unexplained

[1] See pp. 54, 60.

the grounds for the divine promise concerning Caleb. Note also how he phrases the condemnation of Moses in v. 37: "Yahweh was angry with me *for your sakes*," as though Moses' guilt arose solely out of the fact that he was the leader of the people and not out of anything that he personally had done or failed to do. When P revised the original Nu. 14 account, he altered the tradition still further by omitting from that chapter all reference to a sin of Moses. We shall see that he transferred it to Nu. 20:12.[1]

The condemnation of Moses is followed in the Dt. 1 version by a statement excluding Joshua from the sentence passed on the rest of that generation. This would seem to be the most natural place for him to be mentioned—after the mention of Moses. But P, having omitted the condemnation of Moses, felt it best to omit also the reference to his successor and found a convenient place for him beside Caleb (14:30, 38). It may very well be that P's association of Joshua with Caleb was animated by a desire to deprive Caleb, whom he regarded as an Edomite,[2] of part of the unique glory that was his in the original tradition. His treatment of Caleb would thus be on a par with his treatment of Jethro,[3] another non-Hebrew who plays a prominent role in the early annals of the nation.

The mention of Joshua, which must once have appeared after Nu. 14:24, was followed by a reference to the "little ones" (*taph*), as Dt. 1:39 shows. This order is actually preserved in the second version of the oath which P places in Yahweh's mouth (vv. 30f.). Then came a command to turn about and journey into the desert in the direction of the Red Sea (cf. Dt. 1:40). When P inserted an expanded form of Yahweh's oath, he should have transferred this command to a position after v. 35. His failure to do so has imparted a certain awkwardness to the join at v. 26.

7. Nu. 14:36-45 is paralleled by Dt. 1:41-6. Verses 36-8 of the Numbers version have unmistakable signs of P authorship. The reference in v. 44 to the "ark of Yahweh's covenant" also seems to be due to P, for the original tradition knows nothing of an ark,[4] and the designation of it used here

[1] See p. 150. [2] See pp. 109f. [3] See pp. 60f., 63. [4] See p. 59.

The Tradition of the Ten Murmurings 141

is derived from Deuteronomy.[1] The rest of the narrative is probably a part of the original tradition. It describes an unsuccessful attack which the Israelites made on southern Canaan. There is one difference between the Deuteronomic and Numbers versions of the attack which calls for comment. Dt. 1: 44 calls the enemy "Amorites" (cf. also 1: 7, 19f., 27) whereas Nu. 14: 43, 45 calls them "Amalekites and Canaanites." It is usually asserted that the J Document used the term "Canaanites" for the pre-Israelite inhabitants of Canaan, whereas E and D used "Amorites." As a matter of fact, it is not D but the author of the secondary introduction to Deuteronomy (1: 1—4: 43)[2] who uses the term "Amorites." D himself, in the only two passages (7: 1 and 20: 17) where he refers to the pre-Israelite inhabitants by name, does not employ a collective name but lists the peoples individually. In Nu. 13: 29 P puts into the mouth of the spies the learned remark that "Amalek is living in the land of the Negeb, and the Hittites, Jebusites, and Amorites are living in the highlands, while the Canaanites are living along the sea and the banks of the Jordan." It is interesting to discover that the author of Dt. 1: 1—4: 43 conforms to this theory, for in giving his version of the attack on southern Canaan he alters the "Amalekites and Canaanites" of the original tradition (Nu. 14: 43, 45) to "Amorites," that is, he regards the highland of southern Canaan as inhabited by "Amorites." He doubtless omitted any reference to the Hittites and Jebusites, the other inhabitants of the highland according to Nu. 13: 29, for the sake of convenience.

We now perceive the significance of the remark in Nu. 14: 25 (which seems so out of place in its present context) that "the Amalekites and the Canaanites inhabit the plain ['*emeq*]." It was as much as to say, If anyone wonders why the adversaries of the Israelites are called "Amorites" in Dt. 1, let him remember that the Amalekites and Canaanites dwelt on the plain, so that the highlanders who were attacked should properly be called "Amorites." P uses the term

---
[1]Cf. S. R. Driver, *Deuteronomy* (International Critical Commentary, New York, 1895), pp. 122f.

[2]For his identity, see pp. 164-6.

'*emeq* in this context with the negative meaning of "non-highland country"; it has not the specific positive connotation of "coastal plain" which it has in Ju. 1:19, 34.¹

The above comparison of the Deuteronomic and Numbers versions of the story of the Seventh Murmuring shows that the original tradition in Numbers may be reconstructed approximately as follows: On reaching Kadesh Moses proposes an attack on southern Canaan and appoints spies to reconnoitre the ground (cf. Dt. 1:20f.). The spies are instructed to go up into the Negeb and discover how numerous and how strong the inhabitants are (Nu. 13:17*, 18). They set out and reach the valley of Eshcol where they cut down a huge cluster of grapes requiring two men to carry it (13:22*, 23). Returning to the Israelite encampment at Kadesh in the desert of Paran, they display the fruit which they have brought back as evidence of the fertility of the land but report that the inhabitants are powerful and their towns strongly fortified (13:26*, 27, 28*). Caleb urges an immediate attack but the other spies dissent and report having seen giants (13:31, 33*). At this news the Israelites murmur against Moses and Aaron (14:2*, 3f.). Yahweh becomes angry and swears an oath that none but Caleb shall enter the Promised Land (Nu. 14:23f.; for the introduction to the oath, see Dt. 1:34). Moses is also included in the condemnation (Dt. 1:37), but Joshua is excluded (Dt. 1:38), as are also the little ones (Nu. 14:31). Then comes an order to turn about and head southward in the direction of the Red Sea (14:25*b*), but the rebellious people decide to attack instead and as a result suffer a reverse (14:39-45).²

The Eighth Murmuring: at Kadesh (Nu. 16)

Nu. 16:12-14 *Moses sent for Dathan and Abiram, the sons of Eliab, but they said, We will not come. Is it such a*

¹In Ju. 1:34 the Amorites are represented as inhabiting the *shephelah*, the foothills between the *har* and the '*emeq*, and as preventing the Danites from penetrating down into the '*emeq*.

²The narrative will be found in full in the translation of the original tradition at the end of the present volume.

The Tradition of the Ten Murmurings   143

trifling matter that thou has brought us up from a land flowing with milk and honey to kill us in the desert that thou dost play the prince over us as well? Certainly, it is to no land flowing with milk and honey that thou hast brought us, and it is no heritage of fields and vineyards that thou hast given us! Art thou trying to blind the eyes of those men? We will not come!

It is generally recognized that Nu. 16 is a conflation of two traditions, one (vv. 12-15, 25-34) dealing with a revolt on the part of the Reubenites, Dathan and Abiram, against the temporal authority of Moses, the other (vv. 1-11, 16-24, 35-50) dealing with a revolt led by Korah against the priestly status and spiritual authority conferred on Aaron and his sons.

The Story of Dathan and Abiram is assigned by Binns and Gray to JE. The weakness of the JE hypothesis again appears in their inability to divide the story into two strands. It is manifestly a unity. We have seen that the Israelites have been in a state of incipient or open revolt against the leadership of Moses ever since leaving Egypt. In the Seventh Murmuring story they are represented as seriously considering the election of a new leader and returning to Egypt. In the story of the Eighth Murmuring the underlying spirit of revolt is represented as coming to the surface once more in the refusal of Dathan and Abiram to comply with a request of Moses that they appear before him. It is significant that they were Reubenites, for it was this tribe which had once held, but had lost, the senior position among the Hebrew tribes (cf. Gen. 49:3f.). Dathan and Abiram, probably the head men of this tribe, may have felt that the leadership should properly be theirs. It was a revolt of traditional privilege against upstart ability.

The story of how the ground opened up beneath the feet of Dathan and Abiram and engulfed them and their families has a fictitious sound unusual in the Mosaic Tradition. But the reference to the story in Dt. 11:6 shows that it was present in the Mosaic Tradition which D knew. If the story was cast in the form of a Murmuring, it is probable that more than Dathan and Abiram were involved in the revolt against Moses' authority, for in all the other Murmurings either the people as a whole or a sizable group is implicated. As a matter of fact, v. 1 does associate with them "On, the son of Peleth" but who he was is unknown, and it is not certain that the reference to him is a part of the original tradition. The present form of the story shows signs of having been amplified by P but the original is believed by Gray and Binns, with considerable probability, to be preserved in vv. 12-15, 25, 27b-31, 32 (omitting "and all the men who belonged to Korah"), 33f.

As pointed out above, there has been merged with the story of the revolt led by Dathan and Abiram a story dealing with another revolt led by Korah (vv. 1-11, 16-24, 35-50). Korah and two hundred and fifty other Israelites are said to have registered an emphatic protest against allowing Aaron and his sons a monopoly of the priesthood. The disgruntled element seems to be the other members of the tribe of Levi, who refuse to be content with the sub-priestly, "levitical," status which has been accorded them and demand elevation to full priestly status.[1] They find a spokesman in Korah, the senior uncle of Moses (cf. Ex. 6: 16ff.), and, therefore, a man of some influence in the tribe.[2]

The Story of Korah is usually regarded as coming in its entirety from the hand of P. The question arises, Is it a P recasting of a story which stood in the original tradition, or is it a projection back into the Kadesh period of a dispute which only arose at a much later period? As long as it is assumed that the distinction between priest and levite did not arise until a comparatively late period, the answer can only be that the story had no basis in the original tradition but reflects later disputes within the priesthood. But I believe it can be demonstrated[3] that the distinction between

---

[1] The story implies that an account of the institution of the priesthood has preceded. See pp. 146ff.

[2] It will be recalled that the descendants of Muhammad's senior uncle, al-'Abbās, became the recognized leaders of the opposition to the Umayyads.

[3] Such a demonstration would involve a study of the whole history of the Hebrew priesthood, which cannot be undertaken here.

The Tradition of the Ten Murmurings 145

priest and levite dates back to the very institution of the Israelite priesthood. If that be admitted, it is highly probable that a form of the Korah story once stood in that part of the narrative dealing with the events at Kadesh. I would suggest that it is to be found in Nu. 16: 1*, 2*, 3*, 4, 16*, 17*, 18, 35. The story would read as follows:

"1 Now Korah, the son of Izhar, the son of Kohath, the son of Levi ... 2 along with two hundred and fifty of the Israelites stood before Moses .... 3 And they assembled [*Niph'al* of *qahal*][1] against Moses and Aaron and said to them, We have had enough of you! ... Why do you exalt yourselves above the assembly of Yahweh? 4 When Moses heard this, he fell on his face. 16 And Moses said to Korah, ... Thou and they and Aaron are to appear before Yahweh tomorrow. 17 Each of you is to take his fire-pan and place incense on it and present his fire-pan before Yahweh .... 18 So each of them took his fire-pan and put fire on it and placed incense on it and then stood at the entrance of the Tent of Meeting, along with Moses and Aaron. 35 And fire came forth from Yahweh and consumed the two hundred and fifty men offering the incense."

It seems to be implied, without being directly asserted, that Korah suffered the same fate as the two hundred and fifty. But when P merged the story with the Dathan and Abiram story, he seems to have wished to convey the impression that Korah perished in the same manner as Dathan and Abiram (cf. vv. 32f. and Nu. 26: 10), by the ground opening and swallowing him. We should probably be on more historical ground if we were to assume that the rebel leader was appeased by Moses granting to him and his sons a special position in the newly organized cultus, that of singers, for according to the genealogies Korah was the founder of the guild of singers (cf. the titles of Ps. 42-9). Korah may have been satisfied with the arrangement but his descendants were not and seem to have renewed their claim to full priestly status. We learn from Josephus[2] that in the first century A.D. they were still pressing their claim, for they are said to have asked King Agrippa II to use his

[1] This verb seems to be a substitute for an earlier "murmured" (cf. pp. 148, 153).
[2] *Antiquities* XX. ix. 6.

influence with the Sanhedrin to have it grant them permission to wear the white priestly dress.

In Nu. 17, which immediately follows the combined Dathan-Abiram-Korah stories, there is an account, recognized to be from P's hand, of how any latent dissatisfaction of the other tribes with the appointment of Levi to the priesthood was nipped in the bud by placing twelve rods inscribed with the names of the twelve tribes in front of the tablets of the law in the Tent of Meeting and how the one bearing the name of Aaron, the representative of the tribe of Levi, sprouted, a visible manifestation of his divine election. But we have not yet met in the original tradition an account of the appointment of Levi to the priesthood. Of course, there is the tradition in Ex. 32: 25-9 of how the Levites *won* their right to the priesthood by their fanatical loyalty to Yahweh at the time of the Golden Calf episode. But the Deuteronomic version of the Golden Calf episode betrays no knowledge of the events narrated in Ex. 32: 25-9, a suspicious circumstance. D's story about the appointment of Levi comes in Dt. 10: 8f. The two stories about Levi are inconsistent with each other, for Ex. 32 places the appointment of Levi after Moses' first descent from the mountain, whereas Dt. 10 places it immediately after the second descent. However, the inaccuracy of both stories is proved by the fact that according to the original tradition the Tent of Meeting, which was the only sanctuary that the Israelites possessed in the wilderness, was in charge not of a Levite, but of the non-Levitical Joshua.[1]

If the priesthood was not instituted at the mountain, it is inherently probable that it was not instituted until settled life was once more resumed, that is, at Kadesh. And that is what the Story of Korah in Nu. 16 and the Story of the Sprouting of Aaron's Rod in Nu. 17 imply. The very fact that all this dissatisfaction broke out at Kadesh suggests that the institution of the priesthood took place there, for it would seem more natural for the unrest to appear at the time of the appointment than long afterwards.

But it was intolerable to the Levitical priests of Jerusalem that their appointment did not date back to the sacred

[1] See p. 59.

The Tradition of the Ten Murmurings 147

mountain, and wishful thinking led in time to the rise of a tradition of their mountain origin. The assertion in Dt. 10: 8f. that "at that time [the time of the provision of a second set of tablets] Yahweh set apart the tribe of Levi to carry the ark of the covenant of Yahweh," etc., probably represents the first appearance in written form of this claim to a Horeb-Sinai origin. It is interesting to observe that no attempt is made to state the grounds on which the selection was made. It is simply affirmed as an historical fact. The post-exilic priests of Jerusalem were not satisfied with this and invented the story, which now appears in Ex. 32: 25-9, of how the Levites *won* their right to the priesthood. The late date of the story is proved by its dependence on the Golden Calf story, which we have already seen[1] to have been of comparatively late origin and not a part of the original Mosaic Tradition.

The original tradition dealing with the appointment of Aaron and his sons to the priesthood and of the other members of the tribe of Levi to the position of priestly assistants must have stood in Nu. 17 where the P story of the sprouting of Aaron's rod now stands. P has converted the story of their appointment into a re-appointment, or miraculous confirmation of what he maintains took place at Sinai. It is not without significance that the following chapter, Nu. 18, gives the laws which are to govern the relations of the levites with the priests and of both with the people. Such a series of laws would follow naturally after an account of the institution of the priesthood. Although they come from the hand of P, their appearance at this point suggests what may have preceded in the original narrative.

It seems very unlikely that the tradition of the institution of the priesthood was cast in the form of a Murmuring. But the Story of Korah might very easily have been. This story, as we have seen,[2] implies that an account of the institution of the priesthood has preceded. The Levites were angry at the restriction of the priesthood proper to one family among them, that of Aaron, and this would form a very natural subject for a Murmuring story. While the verb

[1] pp. 49f., 131f.   [2] p. 146.

lûn, "to murmur," is not actually used in the Korah story, its place being taken by the *Niph'al* of *qahal*, "to assemble," the narrative undoubtedly has a murmuring atmosphere about it. The references in chapter 17 to the "murmurings" of the Israelites seem to reflect the spirit, if not the wording, of the original tradition at this point. P has shifted the story of the institution of the priesthood back to the mountain but left the stories of the unrest which followed in their original Kadesh setting.

If the Story of Korah be a Murmuring, where does it fit into the scheme? An answer will be provided in the next section.

The Ninth Murmuring: at Kadesh (Nu. 20: 1-13)

Nu. 20: 2-5 *There was no water for the community* ['ēdah] *so they assembled* [Niph'al of qahal] *against Moses and Aaron. The people disputed* [rîbh] *with Moses and said, If only we had perished when our brothers perished before Yahweh! Why did you bring the assembly of Yahweh to this desert to die, both us and our cattle? Why did you bring us up from Egypt to bring us to this miserable place, since it is no place for grain or figs or vines or pomegranates, nor is there any water to drink?*

This story is assigned by Binns to P, except for the reference in v. 1b to the death and burial of Miriam, which is assigned to E, and v. 5 which is assigned to J. But we have already seen[1] that the notice of Miriam's death finds its logical place at the end of the itinerary in Nu. 12: 16 (in its original form). As for v. 5, there are no real grounds for assigning it to a different source from its context.

The contending of the people with Moses is said to have been due to the absence of water at Kadesh, and from this contending or disputing (*rîbh*) the place came to be called *Meribah*, "Place of Disputing." The incident is dated at the very end of the sojourn at Kadesh, but if there was no water there we should have expected to hear about it immediately following their arrival. The people could hardly

[1] See p. 105.

The Tradition of the Ten Murmurings 149

have resided at Kadesh for any length of time without an ample supply. Moreover, the fact that Kadesh is referred to as a town ('*îr*) in Nu. 20:16 implies that a water supply had previously existed there. It was probably a recognition of this difficulty which led P to alter the original itinerary in Nu. 12:16 so as to bring the people at first only to the desert of Paran and not specifically to Kadesh.

P's location of a water miracle at Kadesh creates further difficulties, for the story of Moses bringing forth water from the rock has already been related in Ex. 17, where it is localized at Rephidim. Moreover, the account of the Kadesh miracle shows signs of literary dependence on the Rephidim miracle. Thus Nu. 20:3a = Ex. 17:2a, while Nu. 20:5 has points of contact with Ex. 17:3b and 1b. But why did P repeat the water-miracle story at Kadesh? I would suggest that the reason is to be found in P's desire to cast a halo of sanctity about the waters of 'Ain Kadîs, whither some of the Jews of the post-exilic period doubtless made pilgrimages. We have already seen [1] in dealing with the theophany prefixed to Ex. 34 that P was anxious to avoid manufacturing stories without any basis in the original tradition. Here, this tendency leads him to base his water-miracle story on the Rephidim story in Ex. 17. The fact that D uses only the name *Massah* in referring to the Rephidim incident may have suggested to P the adoption of the name *Meribah* for Kadesh. In view of the squabbles which took place there, the name was certainly appropriate. P was too conservative, however, to take the logical step of wiping out the name Meribah in Ex. 17 where it denotes Rephidim and restricting its application to Kadesh. But there is no doubt that from P's time on, the name Meribah would suggest Kadesh, not Rephidim.

P also seems to have given a new content to the name *Massah*. Thus in Dt. 33 (a P composition, or one at least reflecting P's point of view) we read: "Whom thou didst test at Massah, With whom thou didst contend at the waters of Meribah" (v. 8b). Cook remarks that the tradition records no special testing of the Levites at either place. However, P is probably using Massah as a title of *Horeb* (and the

[1] See p. 60.

incident of the Golden Calf made it a paramount "Place of Testing" in his eyes), in which case he must be thinking of the story which he inserted in Ex. 32:25-9 of how the devotion of the Levites was tested at Horeb, while the reference to the contending with the Levites at Meribah must refer to the revolt of the non-Aaronid Levites under Korah at *Kadesh*. Thus Massah and Meribah, originally religious titles of Rephidim, have by P's time come to denote Horeb and Kadesh, the two paramount places of testing and contention in the revamped tradition.

P transferred the divine sentence debarring Moses and Aaron from entering Canaan from its proper place in Nu. 14 to Meribath-Kadesh. In the discussion of that chapter,[1] P's attempt to shield Moses from being implicated in the same sin as the people was pointed out. Here P invents a special sin for him: Moses strikes the rock when Yahweh had told him only to speak to it,[2] thus displaying a lack of faith in Yahweh's omnipotence. P does not use the word "omnipotence" but the root *qadash* conveying the idea of "holiness" because he wants to suggest how Kadesh (Qadesh) got its name.

Although P seems to have based his Kadesh story on Ex. 17, it is worth noting that he uses the term *ha-sela‘* to denote the rock which Moses smote rather than the term *sur* employed in Ex. 17. P evidently knew of a tradition which identified Kadesh with *ha-sela‘* but refused to admit that this *sela‘* was Petra. Hence he tried to give a new interpretation to the tradition by applying the term *ha-sela‘* to the rock from which the waters issued at ‘Ain Kadīs. The correctness of this reading of P's mind becomes clear when we turn to examine his use of *ha-sela‘* in Ju. 1:36, "The frontier of the Amorites ran from the ascent of ‘Aqrabbim, from *ha-sela‘* upwards."[3] Aware that *ha-sela‘* properly denotes Petra, scholars have wished to alter "Amorites" to "Edomites," but this is because they have failed to grasp P's use of *ha-sela‘*

---

[1] See p. 140.
[2] Cf. H. C. Trumbull, *Kadesh-Barnea* (New York, 1884), p. 23.
[3] I regard the secondary introduction to the Book of Judges, 1:1—2:5, as the work of P, although based in part on older materials.

to denote 'Ain Kadīs. The passage in Judges finds a very close parallel in Nu. 34:4 and Josh. 15:2-4 (both from P) where the southern frontier of Judah is represented as running south of the ascent of 'Aqrabbim and south of Kadesh-barnea. A comparison of the three passages strongly suggests that Ju. 1:36 is merely a summary of the other two and in this summary *ha-sela'* manifestly takes the place of Kadesh-barnea in the other two passages. Scholars have also failed to grasp P's use of the term "Amorite."[1] According to him the early inhabitants of the highland country above (i.e. north of) what was the southern boundary of Judah in his day were Amorites.

We conclude, then, that although the story in Nu. 20:1-13 of Moses bringing forth water from the rock at Kadesh is cast in the form of a Murmuring, it is entirely a P composition without any basis in the original tradition. It was devised for the sole purpose of casting an aura of sanctity about the waters of 'Ain Kadīs.[2] What, then, can have been the content of the Ninth Murmuring? I would suggest that it consisted of the Story of Korah which, as pointed out above,[3] has some of the characteristics of a Murmuring story.

The Tenth Murmuring: during the journey around Edom (Nu. 21:4-9)

Nu. 21:4b-5 *And the people grew impatient over the journey, and the people spoke against God and against Moses, Why have you brought us up from Egypt to die in the desert? For there is neither food nor water, and our souls loathe this miserable food.*

Gray assigns this story to JE (Binns to E, Rudolph to J), except for the words "they journeyed from Mt. Hor," which he assigns to P (Binns and Rudolph to Rp). But this

---

[1] See p. 141.
[2] The same tendency appears in Gen. 14:7, where P would have us believe that the ancient name of the spring was *En-mishpaṭ*, "the Spring of Judgment." See p. 126.
[3] See pp. 147f.

analysis is certainly not correct. The itinerary in v. 4 is a necessary part of the original tradition, as we have seen.¹ On the other hand, a suggestion of P is to be found in the employment in vv. 5 and 7 of the expression *dibber bᵉ*, "to speak against, reproach," found elsewhere with this meaning only in Nu. 12:1, 8 (P, not E₂), Job 18:18, Ps. 50:20; 78:19—all late passages. The coupling together of God and Moses in v. 5 is also without parallel in the original tradition. In spite of these indications that the story has been worked over by P, it is most unlikely that the story as a whole owes its origin to him. It is obviously not the sort of story which he was apt to fabricate. It may, therefore, be regarded as a genuine part of the original Wilderness Tradition.

At the beginning of this chapter there was put forward the hypothesis that the reference in Nu. 14:22 to the "ten times" that the Israelites had put Yahweh to the test actually reflected the original form of the Wilderness Tradition. The results of our study strongly confirm this hypothesis, for we have succeeded in recovering exactly ten Testing stories. We have seen² that these stories were cast in the first place in the form of "murmurings against Moses and Aaron." But in time the tradition was subjected to a religious interpretation and the "murmurings against Moses and Aaron" became "testings of Yahweh" (Dt. 9:7) or "testings of the people" (Dt. 8:2). This process of religious interpretation had already begun before the stories assumed written form, for the verbs *lûn*, "to murmur," and *nissah*, "to test," both appear in some stories.

Each Murmuring or Testing story seems to have possessed originally a more or less stereotyped introduction. The first element in this introduction is a bit of itinerary relating the journey to a new camping-site. Then comes a statement that the people found something wrong with the place and "murmured" against Moses and Aaron.³ But we have found that only four of the stories have the original "murmuring"

___
¹See pp. 106-8.   ²See pp. 125f.
³See the quotations at the head of each of the stories above.

The Tradition of the Ten Murmurings 153

introduction preserved intact. Thus the verb *lûn* appears in No. 2 (Ex. 15:24), No. 3 (Ex. 16:2), No. 4 (Ex. 17:5), No. 7 (Nu. 14:2) but it does not appear in Nos. 1, 5, 6, 8-10. This might seem to indicate that the tradition has only an approach to a stereotyped form and that the theory upon which we have been working is devoid of adequate support. But it is significant that the verb *lûn* never appears in the introductions to any of the incidents after No. 7,[1] at which point P refers to the "ten times" that the people have put Yahweh to the test. It begins to appear that P wants us to think of the Seventh Murmuring as the Tenth and last. But why should he wish us to think that? Simply because he has falsified the tradition more than usual after that point in order to obliterate the account of the origin of the Levitical priesthood at Kadesh which once stood there. He admits that there were ten testings but he does not want anyone to inquire too diligently as to what the ten were. He wants the original structure of the tradition to be forgotten. So he deliberately omits the verb *lûn* in the introductions after No. 7 and substitutes something else instead. In Nos. 8 and 9 he employs the verb *qahal* (Ni.), "they were assembled against Moses and Aaron" (Nu. 16:3; 20:2; cf. 17:7), in No. 10 the expression "spoke against." His desire to make the Story of the Golden Calf into a Testing also leads him to attempt to break up the original pattern of the tradition by transferring the Taberah story from before Rephidim-Massah and burying it in the Kibroth-hattaavah Testing, thus spoiling the original arrangement of five murmurings before Horeb, five after. He also alters the Murmuring introduction of this story by employing the late word *'anan* instead of *lûn*. The introduction to No. 6 is changed by making the people "weep" instead of "murmur" (cf. Nu. 11:4, also vv. 10, 13, 18, 20).[2] P also reworded the introduction to the First Murmuring story so as to leave out the verb *lûn* (cf. Ex. 14:10b, 11). But the retouched text

---

[1] Although it appears in the main body of No. 8 (Nu. 16:11), also in 17:20, 25.

[2] P was very fond of representing the people as weeping. See his introduction to the story of the Seventh Murmuring in Nu. 14:1, whereas the original introduction in 14:2 has them murmuring. Cf. also Ju. 2:4.

sounds a bit awkward for it has the words "and the Israelites cried unto Yahweh" followed by "and they said unto Moses," an awkwardness which has led commentators to assign the clauses to different sources. There can be little doubt that the former clause is P's substitute for an original "and the Israelites murmured against Moses" (cf. Ex. 15:24; 17:3).

Thus in every case where the Murmuring introduction is missing from the story, there is reason to believe that the text has been tampered with by P. All the evidence supports our thesis that the Wilderness Tradition was originally cast in the form of a series of Ten Murmurings.

VII The Corruption of the Mosaic Tradition by the Jerusalem Priests

THE THEORY OF A DEUTERONOMIC REDACTOR (Rd)

The presence in the Mosaic Tradition of passages which are undeniably Deuteronomic in tone has suggested the theory that the tradition was subjected to a revision after 621 B.C. (the date of the publication of Deuteronomy) by persons under the influence of the ideas and language of that book, these persons being denoted by the symbol Rd. This is a theory, however, which requires very careful examination. The passages in Exodus which are assigned by McNeile[1] to Rd are as follows: 3: 8*b*, 17*b*; 10: 1*b*, 2; 12: 25-27*a*; 13: 3 (except the words "And Moses said to the people"), 5, 8f., 14-16; 14: 31; 15: 26; 19: 3*b*-6; 22: 21*b*, 22, 24; 23: 9*b*, 13, 20*b*-33; 32: 7-14; 33: 2; 34: 1*b*, 4 (the words "like unto the first"), 10*b*-16, 24, 28 (the phrase "the ten words"). I shall not attempt an exhaustive discussion of all these passages, since an examination of the more important should suffice to test the accuracy of the accepted theory regarding them.

Let us begin with a discussion of the three laws in Ex. 12-13 which are thought to have received amplifications at the hand of Rd.

I. *The Passover Law*

That 12: 1-14 represents the P version of the Passover Law has long been recognized. An earlier tradition which describes the institution of the festival is preserved in 12: 21-7. But these verses do not give a law for the observance of the Passover; they only relate the origin of the custom of smearing blood on the door-posts at the Passover

[1] *Exodus* (Westminster Commentaries), pp. xii-xxxviii.

season. Nothing is said about the disposal of the carcasses of the victims slaughtered in order to procure blood for the door-post ceremony. However the D form of the law in Dt. 16: 1ff. refers to the eating of the Passover victims as a matter of course. Therefore one feels justified in inferring that the narrative in Ex. 12: 21-7 either implies the eating of the victims or, more probably, at one time actually mentioned it. We now begin to see significance in the fact that P has seen fit to make an insertion (v. 28) in the earlier tradition just where we would expect a statement regarding the disposal of the Passover victims. He has obviously suppressed the regulations which once stood there in favour of his own regulations. These he introduced in a very awkward manner at the beginning of the chapter, before the institution of the rite has been narrated. What the nature of this original Passover legislation was we can only guess.

It is a very curious and important fact that neither the Mosaic Ritual Decalogue nor the Mosaic Supplementary Code refers to the Passover. The rite may have been a Canaanite one which was gradually adopted and merged with the specifically Israelite Festival of Unleavened Bread. II Chron. 30 refers to the observance of a Passover by Hezekiah and it is probable that this was the first time that the festival had been celebrated as a national festival, although there is no doubt that it had been observed at many of the local sanctuaries long before this. By the time of Josiah (639-609 B.C.) the festival was firmly entrenched in official Yahwism, as we see from Dt. 16: 1ff. The priests of the post-exilic period seem to have felt that the Mosaic laws in Exodus, as well as the Mosaic laws in Deuteronomy, should somewhere refer to the Passover. They found a possible reference to it in the Mosaic Ritual Decalogue, in Ex. 23: 18*b*: "The fat of my festival-sacrifice shall not remain overnight until morning." Actually, the regulation applied to the three festivals mentioned in 23: 14-17, but P interpreted it as referring only to the Passover. Hence in his version of the law in Ex. 34: 25*b* he changed the wording to read: "The sacrifice of the Passover-festival shall not remain overnight until morning."

The Corruption of the Mosaic Tradition 157

The Passover is referred to again in 12: 43-9, and again P's hand is evident. It is usually asserted that the position of this supplementary legislation indicates that vv. 43-9 represent a secondary stratum of P (P_2), but P_2 could just as easily have inserted it after v. 13 as after v. 42. The real reason for these laws appearing where they do is surely that they are quite foreign to anything in the earlier Deuteronomic version of the law in Dt. 16. So P inserted them, along with some other notes he was adding, at the end of the chapter.

II. *The Law of the Festival of Unleavened Bread* (*maṣṣôth*)

Unlike the Passover, this festival is definitely legislated for in the Mosaic Ritual Decalogue, in Ex. 23: 15. It is said to have been instituted as a commemoration of the Exodus. The narrative in 12: 33f. relates the origin of the custom of eating unleavened bread. The second stage in the development of the *maṣṣôth* law is clearly to be found in Ex. 13: 3-10, since there is no mention there of the necessity of observing the festival at Jerusalem. This requirement appears for the first time in Dt. 16: 1-8 which, therefore, marks a further stage in the evolution of the law. The final stage is the P law in Ex. 12: 15-20.

III. *The Law of Firstlings*

The earliest form of the law on the dedication of firstlings is found in Ex. 22: 28*b*-29 (EV 29*b*-30) as part of the Mosaic Supplementary Code: "The first-born [*bekôr*] of thy sons thou shalt give me. Thou shalt do the same with thine ox and thy sheep; for seven days it shall remain with its mother; on the eighth day thou shalt give it to me." This law clearly presupposes the actual sacrifice of first-born sons, since no distinction is made between the treatment of the first-born of men and of animals. It also presupposes a plurality of sanctuaries, for it would be manifestly impractical to offer a child or animal to Yahweh on the eighth day after its birth unless it could be done at the local sanctuary. The next stage in the development of the law is found in 13: 11-16.

This version is characterized by provision for the redemption of first-born sons,[1] by a special regulation covering the treatment of the firstling of an ass, and by new terminology: the first-born are referred to as *peṭer-reḥem*, although *bekôr* is used of human first-born in v. 13, and the verb denoting their dedication or sacrifice to Yahweh is the seemingly technical *we-haʻabarta*, not the simple *tittēn*, "thou shalt give," of the earlier legislation.[2] But there is still no mention of the necessity of bringing the firstlings to a central sanctuary. The D form of the law in Dt. 15: 19-23, which insists on this very point, is manifestly of later origin. Apart from the rule that the firstlings must be offered at "the sanctuary which Yahweh shall choose," the principal changes are: the substitution of "year by year" for the "eighth day" as the time of offering (evidently the sacrifice is now to be made at one of the three annual pilgrimages to Jerusalem), the omission of the term *peṭer-reḥem* and the application of the term *bekôr* to the first-born of animals, the employment of the verb *taqdîsh* instead of the earlier *we-haʻabarta*, and the omission of any reference to the treatment of first-born sons.

As mentioned above, a law on firstlings appears first in the Mosaic Supplementary Code; it does not appear in the Mosaic Ritual Decalogue. P, however, was not satisfied with this. Firstlings constituted an important source of revenue for the post-exilic priests of Jerusalem and so P inserted a law on firstlings into his version of the Mosaic decalogue in Ex. 34: 19f. For his wording of the law he turned to Ex. 13: 11-16, of which he offers a summary. He also inserted a law on firstlings in 13: 2 where his phrasing is dependent on both the Ex. 34 and the Dt. 15 forms of the law. It may seem odd that P should take the trouble to mention the law of firstlings at all at this point, all the more so since his statement of it is incomplete and interrupts the narrative. The logical place for it would seem to be before v. 11. The reason for its insertion here seems to be that P

---

[1] The law must have specified the price of redemption but this section has been omitted by P in favour of his own legislation on the subject in Nu. 18: 15-18.

[2] The *Hiphʻil* of *baʻar* was sometimes used of the sacrifice of children (cf. II Chron. 28: 3). Was the *Hiphʻil* of *ʻabar* a deliberate substitution?

The Corruption of the Mosaic Tradition 159

desired to conform, as far as possible, to the Deuteronomic (in his eyes Mosaic) arrangement where the law of firstlings comes before the law of *maṣṣôth* and so to suggest that the proper time to offer firstlings was at this springtime festival.[1]

The three laws in Ex. 12-13 which we have just examined are usually assigned to the J Document, but they cannot have belonged to the original Mosaic Tradition because that tradition contains only laws of Mosaic date whereas these have been shown to be of later origin, standing between their Mosaic prototypes and the corresponding laws in Deuteronomy. Is there anything in the content of the laws which will enable us to assign to them a definite date? A clue may be found in the fact that Ahaz, king of Judah, "made his son pass through (*heʻebîr*)[2] the fire" (II Ki. 16: 3; cf. II Chron. 28: 3). This suggests that Ahaz (*c.* 735-715 B.C.) knew of no law such as that in Ex. 13: 11-16 providing for the redemption of the first-born. A second clue may be found in the reference in II Chron. 30 to a unique observance of the Passover by Hezekiah (*c.* 715-687 B.C.). This suggests that the Passover Law, which we have found reason for believing once stood after Ex. 12: 21-7, was promulgated by this latter sovereign. These facts, taken in conjunction with the account in II Chron. 29-32 of the extensive reforms undertaken by Hezekiah, make it appear highly probable that the three laws were issued in the reign of this particular sovereign.

Some confirmation may be found in an examination of these laws from a slightly different angle. In the Mosaic Ritual Decalogue the three annual festivals are: the Feast of Unleavened Bread, the Harvest Festival (or Feast of Weeks, which was really a dedication of first-fruits, cf. Ex. 23: 16), and the Feast of Ingathering (or Feast of Tabernacles, which was the real "Harvest Festival" in the ordinary sense of that term). While three festivals are prescribed, there is no doubt that the greatest and most popular was the Feast of Ingathering. "Throughout the O.T. *the* feast *par excellence* is the autumn festival, the 'feast of ingathering at the end of the year.' "[3] "It was probably for a long time

[1] Cf. the remarks on Ex. 12: 43-9, p. 157.
[2] See the comment on this verb on p. 158, n. 2.
[3] J. Skinner, *Kings* (Century Bible), p. 140.

the only feast celebrated by the whole people, or at least by the population of a whole district, at one of the greater sanctuaries (I *Kings* viii. 65; xii. 32; *Hos.* xii. 10 [9]; *Zech.* xiv. 16-19; *Ezek.* xlv. 25; cf. *Judges* xxi. 19; I *Sam.* i. 3, 21; ii. 19). But although this remained the chief festival up to the captivity, we also hear of 'feasts' in the plural as early as the eighth century (*Am.* v. 21; viii. 10; *Hos.* ii. 13 [11]); and in Isaiah they seem to be spoken of as held at Jerusalem (xxix. 1; xxxii. 9 sqq.; cf. xxxiii. 20)."[1]

In Ex. 12-13 the three things selected for special emphasis are the Passover, the Feast of Unleavened Bread (the two forming a combined festival) and the Dedication of Firstlings which took place at this combined festival. Surely this reflects a new departure in Jewish religion, a concentration of emphasis on the springtime festival. Now we know from II Ki. 18:22 that Hezekiah tried to centralize the Yahweh religion at Jerusalem some time before Sennacherib's invasion in the fourteenth year of his reign. And it seems highly probable that one aspect of this centralization policy was the celebration of the Passover at Jerusalem, of which so much is made in II Chron. 30. There we are expressly told that invitations were sent out to the Israelites of the Northern Kingdom who were under the cloud of a recent disaster, a reference to the fall of Samaria to the Assyrians (in the sixth year of Hezekiah's reign according to II Ki. 18:9f.). It begins to appear that it was shortly after the fall of Samaria in 722 that the priests of Jerusalem endeavoured to capture for their own temple the position of leadership previously held by the Mt. Gerizim sanctuary at Shechem. As part of this attempt they seem to have put out a revised version of the national law-book (hitherto common to North and South), into which they inserted the three laws stressing the springtime festival in opposition to the old autumn festival which had been characteristic of the past and probably had close Shechemite associations.

We now can turn to the supposedly Rd verses (12:25-27*a*; 13:8f., 14-16) which have been appended to the three laws. They consist of exhortations to the Israelites to explain the

[1]Kuenen, *The Hexateuch* (Eng. trans.; London, 1886), p. 207. See his note 19, p. 208.

The Corruption of the Mosaic Tradition

significance of the rites to their children. The fact that the Book of Deuteronomy contains exhortations of a similar character (cf. 6:7f., 20f.; 11:1f., 18f.) has led scholars to assume that the Exodus exhortations were composed by Rd. This splitting-up of the narrative into two parts, assigning the legal portions to J and the appended exhortations to Rd, was a result of the theory that the "Deuteronomic age" began with the publication of the Book of Deuteronomy in 621 B.C. All passages with a "Deuteronomic" flavour must be dated after 621; hence the necessity of divorcing the exhortations from the laws to which they are appended. But if we assign the laws to the reign of Hezekiah (c. 715-687 B.C.), about eighty-five or ninety years before the composition of Deuteronomy, there would seem to be no reason why we should not regard the exhortations as coming from the same period. Just how long a period of time is covered by the term "Deuteronomic age" cannot now be determined, but it would seem preferable to assume that it can be extended backwards to include the reign of Hezekiah rather than that it began in Josiah's reign and that every writing which shows marks of the "Deuteronomic" style must be dated later than 621 B.C. S. R. Driver gave it as his opinion that many so-called Deuteronomic passages are of pre-Deuteronomic origin.[1] He then had to find an author for them who was not too far removed from the Deuteronomic period, as he conceived it, and so he assigned them to Rje. But if there be no JE, as we hope to have demonstrated, then there is no Rje either. Hence we cannot drag in a non-existent Rje to account for the presence of "Deuteronomic" colouring. We seem driven to the conclusion that the "Deuteronomic age" began at least as early as the reign of Hezekiah, when the priests of Jerusalem put out a revised edition of the national law-book containing the three laws in Exodus 12-13, designed to enhance the position of Jerusalem.

The hand of Rd has also been detected in Ex. 32:7-14 because of its similarity to Dt. 9:12-14, 25-9. But we have seen[2] that the Story of the Golden Calf in Ex. 32:1-24 is not

[1] *Exodus* (Cambridge Bible Series), pp. xviif., 87, 98. [2] See pp. 49.f, 131f.

an original part of the Mosaic Tradition but a later accretion. If Hezekiah did put out a revised edition of the national law-book, as suggested above, the occasion would have presented an excellent opportunity for inserting an attack on the Northern cultus and priesthood, such as Ex. 32 undoubtedly is. In that case the "Deuteronomic" colouring observable in Ex. 32: 7-14 is to be explained in the same way as the "Deuteronomic" colouring of the exhortations appended to the laws in Ex. 12-13.

Let us look now at the lists of the pre-Israelite inhabitants of Canaan in Ex. 3: 8*b*, 17*b*; 13: 5; 23: 23, 28; 33: 2; 34: 11 which are also regarded as insertions by Rd. What is the basis of this contention? Simply that in Deuteronomy there are *two* such lists of peoples, 7: 1 and 20: 17. But neither of them has the same order as the Exodus lists, and if the Exodus lists are later than those in Deuteronomy it is strange that none of them mentions the Girgashites of Dt. 7: 1. Moreover, D's specific enumeration of the pre-Israelite peoples as "seven" makes it difficult to believe that any later writer would reduce the number to six. P, who comes after D, does not fail to mention the Girgashites (Gen. 15: 19-21 and cf. Josh. 3: 10; 24: 11). The order in the Exodus lists is always *Canaanites, Hittites, Amorites, Perizzites, Hivvites, and Jebusites* (cf. 3: 8*b*, 17*b*; in 13: 5 the Perizzites seem to have been accidentally omitted). There seems to be no reason why these lists may not have been a part of the original tradition. There would be no point in inserting them into the revised edition of the tradition put out by Hezekiah. We may be sure that any additions or alterations would have been of a significant character. The insertion of lists of the pre-Israelite inhabitants of Canaan cannot be termed such.

"Deuteronomic" Compositions by P

While some of the so-called Rd passages in Exodus may be accounted for by assuming that the "Deuteronomic age" began as early as the reign of Hezekiah, there are others which are manifestly of later origin and which must, in my opinion, be regarded as the work of P. We must remember that the

The Corruption of the Mosaic Tradition 163

Book of Deuteronomy claims to be the *ipissima verba* of Moses, and devout minds must have been steeped in its thought and phraseology and have been quite able, if the occasion demanded it, to compose in the "Mosaic" style. There are at least two places in the Book of Exodus where I believe P did this, viz., 19: 3b-8 and 34: 10b-16, both instances being found, let it be noted, in descriptions of theophanies on Mt. Sinai.

The first one, 19: 3b-8[1] is assigned to Rd on the following grounds: (i) The reference in v. 4 to Yahweh bearing the Israelites "on eagles' wings" to his mountain-home recalls the metaphor in Dt. 32: 10f. (ii) in vv. 5f. Yahweh promises, if the people heed his commandments and keep his covenant, to make them his *segullah* ("peculiar treasure"), a "kingdom of priests," and "a holy nation"—phrases which recall Dt. 7: 6, 14: 2, 26: 18f., 28: 9. But Dt. 32 is a P composition, or at least dates from the fifth century.[2] Moreover, the use of "the house of Jacob" in parallelism with "the Israelites" in v. 3 recalls the similar parallelism between "Jacob" and "Israel" in Nu. 23: 7, 10, 21, 23; 24: 5, 17, 18f.; Dt. 33: 10, 28. The monotheistic point of view expressed in the declaration that "all the earth is mine" (v. 5) also finds its most natural setting in the post-exilic period, that is, in the period of P rather than of D. P probably inserted the passage here because he desired to have the divine promise that Israel would be God's "peculiar treasure" explicitly stated at a most solemn moment.[3]

As for the second passage, 34: 10b-16, it can reasonably be argued that the passage is dependent on Dt. 7: 1-5, for a command to have nothing to do with the inhabitants of Canaan and to smash their sanctuaries to bits has a more appropriate setting in Deuteronomy than in the Exodus account of a theophany on Mt. Sinai. The fact that Ex.

---

[1]Verses 7f. are regarded by McNeile as from E_2 but they are almost certainly from the same hand as those preceding; note their similarity to 24: 3, a P passage. See pp. 44f.

[2]Cf. R. H. Pfeiffer, *Introduction to the Old Testament* (New York, 1941), p. 280.

[3]Carpenter and Harford-Battersby regard vv. 3b-8 as a fragment which has found its way into the wrong place.

19: 5f., a passage just shown to be from P, is dependent on Dt. 7: 6 is an additional argument for assigning 34: 10*b*-16 to P. Moreover, we have already seen in Chapter III that the code of laws in Ex. 34 represents a P version of the Mosaic Ritual Decalogue and there is, therefore, a strong *a priori* probability that the narrative framing the code is likewise of P origin. It becomes increasingly evident that P was quite capable of composing in the Deuteronomic, "Mosaic," style.

I believe that a recognition of this fact provides us with a solution of the problem presented by the secondary introduction and conclusion to the Book of Deuteronomy. If Ex. 19: 3*b*-8 and 34: 10*b*-16 be by P, is there any reason why this secondary material in Deuteronomy cannot be by P also? The secondary introduction consists of four parts: (i) a title (1: 1-5), (ii) a historical review (1: 6—3: 29), (iii) a hortatory discourse (4: 1-40), (iv) a note regarding the setting apart of three cities of refuge in Transjordan (4: 41-3). While the title outwardly conforms to the Horeb tradition, the statement that it is an eleven days' journey from "Horeb" to Kadesh-barnea shows that the writer really has Mt. Sinai in mind, for according to modern investigators 'Ain Kadīs is about ten or eleven days of ordinary camel-riding from Mt. Sinai.[1] This interpretation is confirmed by the reference in 1: 19 to the "great and terrible desert" which the Israelites traversed on the way from "Horeb" to Kadesh-barnea—manifestly the desert *et-Tīh*. There is no such desert between northern Midian and Petra. Moreover, the original tradition embedded in Nu. 10: 29, 12: 16 of the journey between Horeb and Kadesh says nothing about crossing a desert. The late point of view of the author appears also in his use of "Seir" in 1: 2, 44 to denote a region west of the 'Arabah.[2]

With regard to the historical review (1: 6—3: 29), Addis has presented what at first appear to be strong arguments for believing that it cannot be by P. "In the numerous points on which the two accounts [of the spies, by JE and D] differ, the Deuteronomist agrees with the older narrative,

[1] Cf. H. C. Trumbull, *Kadesh-Barnea* (New York, 1884), p. 215.
[2] See pp. 106f.

The Corruption of the Mosaic Tradition 165

and shows no sign of acquaintance with the 'Priestly Writer.' "[1] But we must remember that P has already presented his own interpretation of the story of the spies in Nu. 13-14 and would be quite willing to let the original tradition stand here comparatively unaltered. He was anxious to preserve the original book of tradition as far as possible but at the same time desired to present his own interpretation of it. A good illustration of his method is provided by his treatment of the story of the appointment of assistants to Moses. He lets the original tradition stand in Ex. 18 but presents his own interpretation of it in Dt. 1: 16-18. The elimination of the figure of Jethro the Midianite in this interpretation strongly suggests that it comes from the post-exilic period when we know that an exclusive, anti-foreign sentiment prevailed. Similarly, he lets the original tradition of the journey around Edom stand in Nu. 20: 14-22 (except that he inserts the phrase "the whole community of them" in v. 22), 21: 4ff., but presents his own interpretation of it in Dt. 2: 1-8, according to which the Israelites do not go around Edom but across its northern edge, a point of view which is in agreement with his version of the itinerary in Nu. 33: 41f.[2] He was unable, however, to insert in Deuteronomy his theory of a movement north from Kadesh against Hormah (cf. Nu. 21: 1-3), a movement which was closely associated with the death of Aaron, because this would not agree with the rest of the Book of Deuteronomy which places the death of Aaron much earlier, at the first camping-place after leaving Horeb (cf. Dt. 10: 6). Thus Dt. 2: 1-8 presents us with only a partial picture of P's theory of what happened after the departure from Kadesh.

As for the hortatory discourse in 4: 1-40, Addis regards it (at least vv. 9-40) as of later date than the preceding material. "It seems to have been written by one who had accustomed himself to the Deuteronomic style, but was at the same time familiar with the style and language which appears in Ezekiel and the 'Priestly School.' "[3] Actually

---
[1] *The Documents of the Hexateuch* (London, 1898), II, 36, n. 1.
[2] See pp. 112f.
[3] *The Documents of the Hexateuch*, II, 21f.

there is no basis for marking off 4: 9-40 from what precedes. The reason for the peculiar stamp of this passage is that here the author is expressing himself, whereas in what precedes he is largely quoting the original Exodus-Numbers tradition. The fact that when the writer is "on his own" he reflects the style of P and Ezekiel[1] is, then, highly significant and must be taken as the determining factor in dating the whole secondary introduction to Deuteronomy.

If the secondary introduction be by P, it is highly probable that the secondary conclusion, comprising most of Dt. 27-34, is also by P; and that is what an examination of the language suggests. As Addis remarks: "Although the language is Deuteronomic, it approximates here and there to that of Ezekiel and the 'Priestly Writer.' " We have seen, however, that the concluding portions of the original narrative of the Mosaic Tradition are to be found embedded in these last chapters of Deuteronomy. Thus Dt. 27: 1-8 preserves the original sequel to the story of the promulgation of the Supplementary Code, although the Deuteronomic phraseology shows that the narrative has suffered some recasting.[2] Dt. 31: 14f., 23 preserves the original tradition of the appointment of Joshua to succeed Moses,[3] and 34: 1*, 4, 5*, 6* the original tradition of Moses' death.[4] Apart from these bits, chapters 27-34 seem to be P compositions modelled on the Deuteronomic style.

THE LITERARY HISTORY OF THE MOSAIC TRADITION

We are now in a position where it is possible to discern the various stages through which the Mosaic Tradition passed before attaining its final written form.

During the first stage, of course, the tradition circulated orally. How early it was cast in the schematic form revealed in the course of our study is uncertain. The national feeling which permeates the tradition suggests that it took shape after the development of a national consciousness among the Israelites. Such a consciousness had been created by Moses,

---

[1] For details, see Addis, *op. cit.*, p. 51.
[2] See pp. 40f., 45, 116.   [3] See p. 116.   [4] See p. 116.

The Corruption of the Mosaic Tradition 167

but after Joshua's death the flame died down and the tribes drifted apart. There was a resurrection of national feeling under Saul but the times were troubled and men's minds must have been preoccupied with the struggle against the Philistines. Israelite national consciousness did not come to maturity until the reigns of David and Solomon. These reigns witnessed considerable literary activity,[1] as we know, and this seems the most likely time for the national tradition to have taken shape. The sober, non-fanciful character of most of the tradition should warn us, however, against postulating too great a lapse of time between the Mosaic period and the fixing of the main outlines of the tradition.[2]

Even after the tradition had been cast in a schematic form to facilitate the process of memorization, it did not remain completely static but underwent modification. In studying the Story of the Plagues traces of three different stages in the growth of the story were found.[3] Likewise in the Story of the Ten Murmurings in the wilderness, we noted a tendency to convert what were originally stories of Murmurings against Moses and Aaron into Testings of Yahweh.[4] All these changes seem to have taken place while the tradition was still in the oral stage.

Precisely when the national tradition was committed to writing cannot now be determined, but the date suggested for the composition of the J Document, the middle of the ninth century B.C., seems as likely a date as any.

In 722 B.C. the Northern Kingdom of Israel was overthrown by the Assyrians, leaving Jerusalem, capital of the Southern Kingdom of Judah, as the principal centre of Jewish life. Hezekiah, king of Judah, at once seized the opportunity to popularize the Jerusalem sanctuary by instituting a springtime festival of national proportions, in which the Passover was combined with the Feast of Unleavened Bread. At the same time he seems to have issued

---

[1] A written literature is not necessarily implied.
[2] H. M. and N. K. Chadwick believe the main outlines were fixed as early as the eleventh century B.C. (*The Growth of Literature* (Cambridge, 1926), II, 704-7).
[3] See p. 14.   [4] See pp. 125f.

a revised version of the national law-book, inserting into it a violent attack on the Northern cultus and priesthood in the form of Ex. 32: 1-24.

Not satisfied with this, the Jerusalem priests developed a completely distorted version of the national tradition which eventually took the form of the Book of Deuteronomy (4: 44—26: 19). In this a decalogue of moral character was substituted for the original Mosaic decalogue of a ritual character, and an enlarged, "improved," version of the Mosaic Supplementary Code took the place of Ex. 21: 1—23: 9. The main theme of the book is that Jerusalem is the true centre of Yahweh worship. The book was hidden in the temple and "found," probably not long afterwards, in 621 B.C. King Josiah seems to have been completely deceived by the fraud, if he was not a party to it, and the Code of Deuteronomy became the law of the land.

The acceptance of Deuteronomy as a genuine work of Moses meant that the Jewish people now had on their hands two versions of the national tradition, an Exodus (in a Hezekian recension) and a Deuteronomic, which differed radically at a number of points. After the exile the priests of Jerusalem (denoted by the symbol P) undertook a harmonization of these two versions. The problem of the two Mosaic decalogues was solved by making the Moral Decalogue of Deuteronomy the one inscribed on the first set of tablets, and the Ritual Decalogue of Exodus the one inscribed on the second set. P was not content, however, to leave the Ritual Decalogue as it was but had an "improved" version of it inscribed on the second set of tablets. He did not discard the original version of this decalogue but distributed it around the Supplementary Code. The problem of the two Supplementary Codes was solved by shifting the Exodus version (Ex. 21: 1—23: 9) from its original setting in Moab back to the mountain, and leaving the Deuteronomic form (Dt. 12-26) in its original position. P not only endeavoured to harmonize the two conflicting versions of the Mosaic Tradition which had reached him but added a great deal of material, chiefly of a legal and genealogical character, drawn rom a variety of sources. There is no evidence that this diversified material ever existed as a separate, continuous document. It seems rather to consist largely of the oral tradition which had grown up in Jerusalem around the written tradition.

The literary history of the Mosaic Tradition may, therefore, be summarized as follows:

I. The Original Tradition[1]

The Call of Moses: Ex. 3: 1—4: 18, 27-31.
The Story of the Plagues
  Introduction: Ex. 5: 1—6: 1.
  The Ten Plagues: (i) 7: 14-25; (ii) 7: 26—8:11; (iii) 8: 12-15; (iv) 8: 16-28; (v) 9: 1-7; (vi) 9: 8-12; (vii) 9: 13-35; (viii) 10: 1-20; (ix) 10: 21-7; (x) 11: 1-8a; 10: 28f.; 11: 8b.
The Exodus: Ex. 12: 29-39.
The Five Murmurings before Horeb
  (i) at the Crossing of the Sea: Ex. 13: 17-22; 14: 1, 2†, 3-8, 9†, 10†, 11-18, 19b—15: 1.
  (ii) at Marah: Ex. 15: 22†, 23-6, 27†.
  (iii) in the Desert of Sin: Ex. 16: 1†, 2†, 3f., 13†, 14f., 21, 31.
  (iv) at Taberah: Ex. 17: 1a+ . . . ; Nu. 11: 1†, 2†, 3.
  (v) at Rephidim: . . . +Ex. 17: 1b-7.
The Battle with the Amalekites: Ex. 17: 8-16.
The Revelation of the Law: Ex. 19: 2†, 3a, 9a, 10†, 11†, 12-17, 18†, 19; 20: 1, 23-6; 23: 10-19; 20: 18-21; 24: 1f., 9-15, 18b; 31: 18†.
The Order to Depart from Horeb: Ex. 33: 1.
The Institution of the Tent of Meeting: . . . +Ex. 33: 7-11.
The Visit of Jethro to the Israelite Camp: Ex. 18: 1, 2†, 3-26; Nu. 10: 29†, 30-2,+ . . ., Ex. 18: 27.
The Sixth Murmuring—at Kibroth-hattaavah: . . . +Nu. 11: 4†, 5f., 11†, 13†, 16†, 18†, 19, 20†, 21-24a, 31-4.

---

[1]By "original tradition" is meant the form which the tradition possessed before it was revised in the reign of Hezekiah. Verses marked by a dagger have been retouched by P. The nature and extent of the retouching in each case can be determined by using the Index of Scriptural Passages. An ellipsis . . . indicates that the original tradition is missing at that point.

Moses' Marriage to the Daughter of Hobab, the Kenite: Nu. 11:35+ ....

The Story of the Spies: Nu. 12:16†; 20:1b;+ ..., 13:17†, 18, 22†, 23, 26†, 27, 28†, 30f., 33†.

The Seventh Murmuring—at Kadesh: Nu. 14:2†, 3f.,+ ..., 23†, 24,+ ..., 31, 25b.

The Abortive Attack on Southern Canaan: Nu. 14:39-43, 44†, 45.

The Eighth Murmuring—at Kadesh (led by Dathan and Abiram): Nu. 16:12-15, 25, 27b-31, 32†, 33f.

The Institution of a Priesthood: the original tradition is missing.

The Ninth Murmuring—at Kadesh (led by Korah): Nu. 16:1†, 2†, 3†, 4, 5†, 6†, 7, 16-18, 35.

The Attempt to Cross Edom: Nu. 20:14-21.

The Death of Aaron at Mt. Hor and the Appointment of his Successor: Nu. 20:22†, 23†, 24†,+ ....

The Tenth Murmuring—during the journey around Edom: Nu. 21:4, 5†, 6-9.

The Journey to Pisgah: Nu. 21:10-12, 13†, 16†, 18b, 19f.

The Conquest of the Amorite Kingdoms of Heshbon and Bashan: Nu. 21:21-35.

The Promulgation of a Supplementary Code: ... +Ex. 22:20 (EV 22:21)—23:9.

The Command to Inscribe this Code on the Altar on Mt. Gerizim: Dt. 27:1-8 (a D recasting of the original tradition).

The Appointment of Joshua as Moses' Successor: Dt. 31:14f., 23.

The Death of Moses: Dt. 34:1†, 4, 5†, 6†.

II. *The First Judaean Recension*

(from the early part of the reign of Hezekiah, *c.* 715-687 B.C.)

The original Israelite tradition was expanded by adding: (i) the account of the Institution of the Passover in Ex. 12:21-7 (verse 27 was probably followed by a regulation regarding the disposal of the Passover victims but this regulation was later displaced by P in favour of his own

The Corruption of the Mosaic Tradition

regulations in 12: 1-20, and v. 28 added as a sort of compensation); (ii) the Law of the Feast of Unleavened Bread in 13: 3-10, designed to supersede the old law in Ex. 23: 15; (iii) the Law of Firstlings in 13: 11-16, designed to supersede the old law in Ex. 22: 28*b*-29, EV 29*b*-30 (a law specifying the price of redemption for first-born sons must have stood after 13: 13 but it has been omitted by P in favour of his own legislation on the subject in Nu. 18: 15-18); (iv) the Story of the Golden Calf, the Smashing of the Tablets, and the Provision of a Second Set, in Ex. 32: 1-24; 34: 1, 4†, 28.

III. *The Book of Deuteronomy* (4: 44—26: 19)
(a Judaean distortion of the Mosaic Tradition, promulgated by King Josiah of Judah in 621 B.C.)

IV. *The Second Judaean Recension*
(promulgated by Ezra, *c.* 397 B.C.)

This recension took the form of a harmonization of the First Judaean Recension and the Deuteronomic distortion of it. To the harmonized account was added a great variety of material drawn from different sources and of widely different date.

Appendix: The Original Form of the Mosaic Tradition[1]

THE CALL OF MOSES[2]

Ex. 3:1 Once when Moses was shepherding the flock of his father-in-law, Jethro, the priest of Midian, he led the flock to the back of the desert and came to the sacred mountain, Horeb. **2** There the angel of Yahweh appeared unto him as a flame of fire in the midst of a thorn-bush. He noted with surprise that although the bush was burning, the bush itself was not being consumed. **3** So Moses said, I will go over and see this great sight [and find out] why the bush does not burn up. **4** Yahweh saw him going over to look, and God[3] called to him from the midst of the bush and said, Moses! Moses! Here I am, he replied. **5** Do not come any nearer, he said; remove thy sandals from thy feet, for the place on which thou art standing is holy ground. **6** I am the god of thy father, he said, the god of Abraham, the god of Isaac, and the god of Jacob. Then Moses hid his face, for he was afraid to look at the Deity. **7** I have indeed seen the humiliation of my people who are in Egypt, said Yahweh, and their cry because of their taskmasters I have heard, so that I know their sufferings. **8** And I have come down to deliver them out of the hand of the Egyptians and to bring them up out of

---

[1]By "original form" is meant the pre-Hezekian form of the tradition. Omissions which consist of less than half a verse are given in the foot-notes in order that the student may the more readily perceive how much of the received tradition is regarded as later accretion. All passages which have been omitted are to be regarded as the work of P unless otherwise indicated. Reasons for any omissions are given in the main body of the book. These may be found by using the Index of Scriptural Passages. The translation is my own, but it is deeply indebted to the translation of my colleague, Dr. T. J. Meek, found in *The Old Testament: An American Translation* (University of Chicago Press, 1935).

[2]Reasons for believing that chapters 1 and 2 belong to another Life of Moses have been presented on pp. 27f.

[3]Heb. *'elohim* and *ha-'elohim* have been differentiated in the present translation by rendering the former by "God" and the latter by "the Deity."

that land unto a splendid, spacious land, a land flowing with milk and honey, the home of the Canaanites, Hittites, Amorites, Perizzites, Hivvites, and Jebusites. **9** The cry of the Israelites has now reached me, and I have also seen the way the Egyptians are oppressing them. **10** Come now that I may send thee unto Pharaoh and bring forth my people, the Israelites, from Egypt. **11** But Moses said to the Deity, Who am I to go unto Pharaoh and to bring forth the Israelites from Egypt? **12** He said, I shall be with thee, and this will be the sign for thee that it is I who have sent thee: When thou bringest the people out of Egypt, you shall worship the Deity upon this mountain. **13** Moses said to the Deity, When I come to the Israelites and say to them, The god of your fathers has sent me unto you, they will say to me, What is his name? What shall I say to them? **14** God said to Moses, I am who I am [*'ehyeh 'asher 'ehyeh*]. He said, Thus shalt thou say to the Israelites, I AM [*'ehyeh*] has sent me unto you. **15** God said further to Moses, Thus shalt thou say to the Israelites, Yahweh, the god of your fathers, the god of Abraham, the god of Isaac, and the god of Jacob, has sent me unto you. This is my name eternally, and this is my designation to all generations. **16** Go and assemble the elders of Israel and say to them, Yahweh, the god of your fathers, the god of Abraham, Isaac, and Jacob, has appeared to me, saying, I have indeed visited you and [seen] what is being done to you in Egypt. **17** And I have said, I will bring you up from the humiliation of Egypt unto the land of the Canaanites, Hittites, Amorites, Perizzites, Hivvites, and Jebusites, unto a land flowing with milk and honey. **18** They will hearken to thy voice, and then thou and the elders of Israel shall go in unto the king of Egypt and you shall say to him, Yahweh, the god of the Hebrews, has met with us; now, therefore, let us go a three days' journey into the desert that we may sacrifice to Yahweh our god. **19** I know, of course, that the king of Egypt will not give you permission to go, except under compulsion. **20** So I shall stretch forth my hand and smite the Egyptians with all my wonders which I shall perform in their midst; after that he will let you go. **21** And I shall grant this people such favour in the eyes of the Egyptians that when you go, you shall not go empty-handed. **22** Each woman is to borrow from her neighbour and from any foreigner residing in her house articles of silver and gold and clothes; these you shall place upon your sons and daughters, and you shall despoil the Egyptians.

Original Form of the Mosaic Tradition

4:1 Moses replied, Probably they will not believe me nor heed my talk, but will say, Yahweh did not appear to thee. **2** Yahweh said to him, What is that in your hand? He said, A staff. **3** Throw it on the ground, he said. So he threw it on the ground and it became a snake, and Moses fled from it. **4** Then Yahweh said to Moses, Put out thy hand and catch it by the tail. So he put out his hand and caught it, and it became a staff [again] in his hand— **5** in order that they may believe that Yahweh, the god of their fathers, the god of Abraham, the god of Isaac, and the god of Jacob, has appeared to thee. **6** And Yahweh said to him further, Put thy hand in thy bosom. So he put his hand in his bosom, and when he drew it out, lo, his hand was leprous like snow. **7** Then he said, Put thy hand back in thy bosom. So he put his hand back in his bosom, and when he drew it forth from his bosom, behold, it was restored like his [other] flesh. **8** If they will not believe thee nor heed the import of the former sign, they may believe the import of the latter sign. **9** But if they will not believe even these two signs nor heed thy voice, then thou shalt take some of the water of the Nile and pour it on the ground, and the water which thou shalt take from the Nile shall become blood on the ground. **10** Moses said to Yahweh, Please, Lord, I have never been a fluent speaker, either in the past or now when thou art speaking to thy servant, but I am awkward-mouthed and awkward-tongued. **11** Yahweh said to him, Who ordained a mouth for man? Or who ordains dumbness or deafness or sight or blindness? Is it not I, Yahweh? **12** Now then, go, and I will be with thy mouth and instruct thee what to say. **13** Please, Lord, he said, send whom thou wilt. **14** Then Yahweh became angry with Moses and said, Is there not thy brother, Aaron, the Levite? I know that he can speak well. Furthermore, he is coming out to meet thee, and when he sees thee he will be glad. **15** Thou shalt speak to him and put the words in his mouth, while I will be with thy mouth and with his mouth and I will instruct you both what to do. **16** He shall speak to the people for thee, acting as a mouthpiece for thee, while thou shalt act as a god for him. **17** And thou shalt take in thy hand this staff with which to perform the signs. **18** Moses then went back to Jethro,[1] his father-in-law, and said to him, Let me go back to my folk who are in Egypt that

---

[1] The Hebrew text reads *Yether* instead of the usual *Yithro*. The change is probably deliberate, designed to suggest a meaning for the name by connecting it with the Hebrew word *yether*, "remainder, excellence."

I may see whether they are still living. Jethro said to Moses, Go in peace.[1]

27 Yahweh said to Aaron, Go to meet Moses in the desert. So he went and met him at the sacred mountain and kissed him. **28** Then Moses related to Aaron all the words with which Yahweh had sent him and all the signs with which he had commissioned him. **29** Moses and Aaron then went and assembled all the elders of the Israelites. **30** Aaron spoke all the words which Yahweh had spoken to Moses and performed the signs in the sight of the people. **31** The people believed, and when they heard that Yahweh had visited the Israelites and had seen their humiliation, they bowed down and prostrated themselves.

THE STORY OF THE PLAGUES

INTRODUCTION

5: 1 Afterwards Moses and Aaron went in and said to Pharaoh, Thus saith Yahweh, the god of Israel, Let my people go that they may make a pilgrimage to me in the desert. **2** Who is Yahweh, said Pharaoh, that I should heed his request to let Israel go? I am not acquainted with Yahweh. Furthermore, I will not let Israel go. **3** They said, The god of the Hebrews has met with us. Pray let us go a three days' journey into the desert that we may sacrifice to Yahweh our god, lest he fall upon us with pestilence or the sword. **4** The king of Egypt said to them, Why, O Moses and Aaron, do you make the people neglect their tasks? Be off to your burdens! **5** Behold, said Pharaoh, the people of the land are too numerous now and you would have them rest from their burdens! **6** On that day Pharaoh commanded his taskmasters and officials over the people, saying, **7** You shall no longer give straw to the people for making bricks as hitherto. They shall go and collect straw for themselves. **8** But you shall make them responsible for the same quota of bricks as they have been making hitherto. You shall not reduce it, for they are lazy. That is why they are crying, Let us go and sacrifice to our god. **9** Let the labour be heavy upon the men and let them keep busy with it instead of busying themselves with seditious talk. **10** So the taskmasters and officials of the

---

[1]For evidence that 4: 19f., 24-6 belong to another Life of Moses and that 4: 21-3 are a later addition by P, see pp. 19, 27.

Original Form of the Mosaic Tradition 177

people went out and said to the people, Thus saith Pharaoh, I am not going to give you any straw. **11** Go and get straw for yourselves wherever you can find it, but there is to be no reduction whatsoever in your labour. **12** So the people scattered all over the land of Egypt to collect stubble for straw. **13** The taskmasters kept pressing them, saying, Finish each day's task on time just as when there was straw. **14** And the officials whom the taskmasters of Pharaoh had placed over the Israelites beat them, saying, Why have you neither yesterday nor today carried out the regulation that you must make bricks as hitherto? **15** Then the Israelite officials went in and complained to Pharaoh, saying, Why dost thou treat thy servants in this way? No straw is being given to thy servants, yet they are saying to us, Make bricks! Thy servants are being beaten and thy people have sinned. **17** He said, You are utterly lazy. That is why you are saying, Let us go and sacrifice to Yahweh. **18** Now get to work; no straw will be given to you and the quota of bricks you must produce. **19** The Israelite officials saw themselves placed in an unpleasant position in having to say, Do not reduce the daily number of your bricks. **20** As they came out from Pharaoh's presence they encountered Moses and Aaron who were waiting to meet them. **21** They said to [the two of] them, May Yahweh look upon you and judge you who have made the smell of us so offensive in the eyes of Pharaoh and of his servants as to put a sword in their hand to slay us. **22** Then Moses returned to Yahweh and said, Lord, why hast thou treated this people badly? Why didst thou ever send me? **23** From the time of my coming unto Pharaoh to speak in thy name he has done nothing but evil to this people and thou hast not delivered thy people at all. **6: 1** Yahweh said to Moses, Thou wilt now see what I shall do to Pharaoh, for under compulsion he will let them go and under compulsion he will drive them out from his land.

THE TEN PLAGUES

1. *The Water of the Nile changed into Blood*

7: 14 Yahweh said to Moses, Pharaoh's heart is hard; he refuses to let the people go. Go unto Pharaoh in the morning, when he goes forth to the water, and station thyself so as to meet him on the bank of the Nile, and take in thy hand the staff which was changed into a snake. **16** And say to him, Yahweh, the god of the Hebrews, has sent me unto thee to say, Let my people go that they may worship me in the desert. Since thou hast not hearkened hitherto, **17** thus saith Yahweh, By this thou shalt learn that I am Yahweh: I am going to strike the waters which are in the Nile with the staff which is in my hand and they will be changed into blood. **18** The fish which are in the Nile shall die and the Nile shall stink and the Egyptians shall tire themselves out trying to get drinking-water from the Nile. **19** Yahweh said to Moses, Say to Aaron, Take thy staff and stretch out thy hand over the waters of the Egyptians, over their rivers, their canals, their pools, and every collection of water, that they may become blood, so that there will be blood throughout the whole land of Egypt, and in [vessels of] wood and stone. **20** Moses and Aaron did exactly as Yahweh commanded: he raised the staff and struck the waters which are in the Nile in the sight of Pharaoh and his servants, and all the waters which were in the Nile were changed into blood; **21** the fish which were in the Nile died and the Nile stank so that the Egyptians were unable to drink any water from the Nile, and there was blood throughout the whole land of Egypt. **22** But the magicians of Egypt did the same by means of their spells, so the heart of Pharaoh became stubborn and he did not listen to them, just as Yahweh had said. **23** Pharaoh turned and went into his house, paying no attention even to this. **24** And all the Egyptians dug round about the Nile for water to drink because they were unable to drink any of the water from the Nile. **25** Seven days elapsed after Yahweh's smiting the Nile.

2. *The Frogs*

7:26 Then Yahweh said to Moses, Go in to Pharaoh and say to him, Thus saith Yahweh, Let my people go that they may worship me. **27** If thou refusest to let them go, I am going to smite thy whole territory with frogs. **28** The Nile shall swarm with frogs, and they shall come up and enter into thy house and thy bedroom and upon thy bed and into the house of thy servants and thy people and into thy ovens and thy mixing-bowls. **29** Both on thee and thy people and on all thy servants shall the frogs come up. **8:1** Then Yahweh said to Moses, Say to Aaron, Stretch out thy hand with thy staff over the rivers, the canals, and the pools, and

Original Form of the Mosaic Tradition 179

bring up the frogs upon the land of Egypt. **2** So Aaron stretched out his hand over the waters of Egypt and frogs came up and covered the land of Egypt. **3** But the magicians did the same by means of their spells and brought up frogs upon the land of Egypt. **4** Then Pharaoh summoned Moses and Aaron and said, Pray to Yahweh and have him remove the frogs from me and my people and I will let the people go to sacrifice to Yahweh. **5** Moses said to Pharaoh, Do me the honour of specifying when I shall pray for thee and thy servants and thy people to have the frogs cut off from thee and thy houses and be left only in the Nile. **6** He said, Tomorrow. It shall be according to thy word, said [Moses], in order that thou mayest learn that there is none like Yahweh, our god. **7** The frogs shall depart from thee and thy houses and from thy servants and thy people; only in the Nile shall they be left. **8** Moses and Aaron then left Pharaoh's presence and Moses cried unto Yahweh about the frogs which he had appointed for Pharaoh. **9** And Yahweh did according to the word of Moses: the frogs perished from the houses, courtyards and fields. **10** And they piled them up in heaps and the land stank. **11** When Pharaoh saw that relief had come, he hardened[1] his heart and did not listen to them, just as Yahweh had said.

3. *The Lice*

8: 12 Then Yahweh said to Moses, Say to Aaron, Stretch out thy staff and strike the dust of the earth and it shall become lice throughout the whole land of Egypt. **13** They did so: Aaron stretched out his hand with his staff and struck the dust of the earth and there were lice on man and beast. All the dust of the earth was lice throughout the whole land of Egypt. **14** The magicians likewise tried to produce lice by means of their spells but could not, and there were lice on man and beast. **15** The magicians said to Pharaoh, It is the finger of God. But the heart of Pharaoh became stubborn and he did not listen to them, just as Yahweh had said.

4. *The Swarm of Insects*

8: 16 Then Yahweh said to Moses, Get up early in the morning and station thyself in front of Pharaoh when he goes forth to the water and say to him, Thus saith Yahweh, Let my people go that

[1] Reading *wa-yakbēd* with the Sam. VS.

they may worship me. **17** For if thou dost not let my people go, I am going to send a swarm of insects on thee, thy servants, thy people and thy houses. The houses of Egypt will be full of insects as well as the ground on which they are. **18** But on that day I will set apart the land of Goshen on which my people are staying so that there will be no insects there in order that thou mayest learn that I am Yahweh in the midst of the earth. **19** And I will make a distinction between my people and thine. This sign shall take place tomorrow. **20** Yahweh did so; a dense swarm of insects entered the house of Pharaoh and the house of his servants and the whole land of Egypt, the land being ruined by reason of the insects. **21** Then Pharaoh summoned Moses and Aaron and said, Go and sacrifice to your god in the land. **22** But Moses said, It would not be proper to do so, for we sacrifice to Yahweh, our god, what is abhorrent to the Egyptians. If we were to sacrifice what is abhorrent to the Egyptians before their eyes, would they not stone us? **23** We would go a three days' journey into the desert and sacrifice to Yahweh, our god, as he said to us. **24** Pharaoh said, Of course I will let you go and sacrifice to Yahweh, your god, in the desert; only you must not go very far away. Pray for me. **25** Moses said, When I leave thy presence I am going to pray to Yahweh and the insects shall depart from Pharaoh, his servants, and his people tomorrow. Only let not Pharaoh again play false by not letting the people go to sacrifice to Yahweh. **26** Moses then left the presence of Pharaoh and prayed to Yahweh. **27** And Yahweh did according to the word of Moses: he removed the insects from Pharaoh, his servants, and his people so that not one was left. **28** But Pharaoh hardened his heart this time also and did not let the people go.

5. *The Pestilence*

9: 1 Then Yahweh said to Moses, Go in to Pharaoh and say to him, Thus saith Yahweh, the god of the Hebrews, Let my people go that they may worship me. **2** For if thou refusest to let them go and dost continue to restrain them, **3** the hand of Yahweh is going to be on thy livestock [*miqneh*] which is in the field, on the horses, asses, camels, cattle, and sheep [in the form of] a very grievous pestilence. **4** But Yahweh will make a distinction between the livestock of Israel and the livestock of Egypt so that nothing of all that belongs to the Israelites shall die. **5** Then Yahweh set a time, saying, Tomorrow Yahweh will do this thing in the land. **6** Yahweh did this thing on the morrow; and all the livestock of the Egyptians died, but of the livestock of the Israelites not one died. **7** Pharaoh sent [to inquire] and lo, there had not died of the livestock of Israel so much as one. And the heart of Pharaoh became hard and he did not let the people go.

6. *Boils*

9:8 Then Yahweh said to Moses and Aaron, Take two handfuls of soot from a kiln and Moses shall toss it up in the air in the sight of Pharaoh, **9** and it shall become a dust over all the land of Egypt which shall cause boils discharging pus on man and beast throughout the whole land of Egypt. **10** So they took the soot from a kiln and stood before Pharaoh, and Moses tossed it up in the air and it caused boils discharging pus on man and beast. **11** The magicians were unable to stand before Moses because of the boils, for the boils were on the magicians and on all the Egyptians. **12** But Yahweh made the heart of Pharaoh stubborn and he did not listen to them, just as Yahweh had said to Moses.

7. *The Hail*

9:13 Then Yahweh said to Moses, Get up early in the morning and station thyself before Pharaoh and say to him, Thus saith Yahweh, the god of the Hebrews, Let my people go that they may worship me; **14** for on this occasion I am going to send all my plagues on thy person and on thy servants and on thy people in order that thou mayest learn that there is none like me in the whole earth. **15** Verily by now I could have put out my hand and smitten thee and thy people with pestilence so that thou wouldst have been effaced from the earth. **16** But I have preserved thee for this reason: in order to show thee my power and in order to spread my fame throughout the whole earth. **17** Since thou art still setting thyself against my people by not letting them go, **18** about this time tomorrow I am going to rain down a very heavy hail, the like of which has never been in Egypt from the day of its foundation until now. **19** Send, therefore, and bring thy livestock under shelter and everything that thou hast in the field, for the hail shall come down upon every man and beast that is found in the field and has not been gathered indoors and they shall die. **20** Those of Pharaoh's servants who feared the word of Yahweh had their servants and livestock hasten indoors, **21** while those who paid no attention to the word of Yahweh left their servants and livestock out in the fields. **22** Then Yahweh said to Moses, Stretch out thy hand towards the sky that there may be hail throughout the whole land of Egypt, on man and beast and on all the vegetation in the fields in the land of Egypt. **23** So Moses stretched out his staff towards the sky and Yahweh caused thunder and hail, while fire travelled earthwards and Yahweh rained hail upon the land of Egypt. **24** There was hail with fire darting about in the midst of the very heavy hail, the like of which had never been in all the land of Egypt since it became a nation. **25** The hail struck down everything in the fields throughout the whole land of Egypt, both man and beast; the hail struck down all the vegetation of the fields and shattered every tree in the fields. **26** Only in the land of Goshen, where the Israelites were, was there no hail. **27** Then Pharaoh sent and summoned Moses and Aaron and said to them, I have sinned this time. Yahweh is in the right, while I and my people are the wrongdoers. **28** Pray to Yahweh, for this terrific thunder and hail is intolerable, and I will let you go and you need stay no longer. **29** Moses said to him, As soon as I leave the city I shall spread out my hands to Yahweh; the thunder shall cease and the hail shall be no more in order that thou mayest learn that the earth is Yahweh's. **30** But as for thee and thy servants, I know that you do not yet fear the face of Yahweh God [*YHWH 'elohim*]. **31** The flax and barley were smitten, for the barley was in ear and the flax in bud; **32** but the wheat and spelt were not smitten because they had not yet sprouted. **33** When Moses departed from Pharaoh's presence to the outside of the city and spread out his hands to Yahweh, the thunder and hail ceased and the rain was no longer poured earthwards. **34** When Pharaoh saw that the rain and hail and thunder had ceased, he sinned again and hardened his heart, he and his servants. **35** And the heart of Pharaoh became stubborn and he did not let the Israelites go, just as Yahweh had said through Moses.

8. *The Locusts*

10:1 Then Yahweh said to Moses, Go in to Pharaoh, for I have hardened his heart and the heart of his servants in order to place these signs of mine in his midst, 2 and in order that thou mayest relate in the hearing of thy son and thy grandson the way I amused myself with the Egyptians and the signs that I put among them, and you shall learn that I am Yahweh. 3 So Moses and Aaron went in to Pharaoh and said to him, Thus saith Yahweh, the god of the Hebrews, How long wilt thou refuse to humble thyself before me? Let my people go that they may worship me. 4 For if thou refusest to let my people go, I am going to bring a swarm of locusts into thy territory tomorrow. 5 They shall cover the circuit of the land so that one will not be able to see the land; and they shall eat up any remnant that escaped, anything that was left to you by the hail, and they shall eat up all the trees that you have sprouting up in the fields. 6 And thy houses and the houses of all thy servants and the houses of all the Egyptians will be full of them, something that neither thy fathers nor thy grandfathers have witnessed from the time of their arrival on earth unto this day. Then he turned and went out from Pharaoh's presence. 7 And Pharaoh's servants said to him, How long is this fellow going to be a snare to us? Let the men go and worship their god, Yahweh. Dost thou not yet realize that Egypt is ruined? 8 So Moses and Aaron were brought back to Pharaoh and he said to them, Go and worship Yahweh, your god. Who all are going? 9 Moses said, We would go with our young and our old, with our sons and our daughters; we would go with our flocks and our herds; for we are holding a festival to Yahweh. 10 He said to them, So be it. Yahweh be with you, since I am letting you and your little ones go. But look here! It may be that you are up to some mischief. 11 No! You adults go and worship Yahweh, for that is what you are requesting. And they were driven out from Pharaoh's presence. 12 Then Yahweh said to Moses, Stretch out thy hand over the land of Egypt for the locusts to come up upon the land of Egypt and eat up all the vegetation of the land, everything that the hail left. 13 So Moses stretched out his staff over the land of Egypt, and Yahweh directed an east wind onto the land all that day and all night. When morning came, the east wind brought the locusts. 14 The locusts came up upon the whole land of Egypt and settled in dense masses throughout all the territory of Egypt. There had never been such locusts before and there will never be such again. 15 They covered the whole circuit of the land so that the land was darkened, and they ate up all the vegetation of the land and any fruit that the hail had left on the trees. Not a leaf was left on the trees and plants of the field throughout the whole land of Egypt. **16** Then Pharaoh hurriedly summoned Moses and Aaron and said, I have sinned against Yahweh, your god, and against you. **17** Now forgive my sin just this once and pray to Yahweh to remove at least this deadly menace from me. **18** So he went forth from Pharaoh's presence and prayed to Yahweh, **19** and Yahweh changed [the wind] into a very strong sea wind which lifted up the locusts and hurled them into the Red Sea [*yam sûph*], not a single locust being left in all the territory of Egypt. **20** And Yahweh made the heart of Pharaoh stubborn and he did not let the Israelites go.

9. *Darkness*

10: 21 Then Yahweh said unto Moses, Stretch out thy hand towards the sky that there may be darkness upon the land of Egypt, a darkness that one can feel. **22** So Moses stretched out his hand towards the sky and it became as dark as pitch throughout the whole land of Egypt for three days. **23** Men could not see one another, and no one stirred from his place for three days. But all the Israelites had light in their abodes. **24** Then Pharaoh summoned Moses and said, Go and serve Yahweh; your flocks and your herds will alone be detained; your little ones, however, may go with you. **25** Moses said, Thou thyself must place at our disposal sacrifices and burnt-offerings to make to Yahweh, our god. **26** Moreover, our livestock must go with us; not a hoof must be left behind; for we may use some of them in the worship of Yahweh, our god, and we ourselves do not know how we shall worship Yahweh until we arrive there. **27** But Yahweh made the heart of Pharaoh stubborn and he was not willing to let them go.[1]

10. *The Slaughter of the First-Born*

11: 1 Then Yahweh said to Moses, One more plague will I bring upon Pharaoh and upon Egypt; after that he will let you go from here. When he finally lets you go, he will drive you out of here. **2** Speak in the hearing of the people and have each man borrow

---

[1]Verses 28f. will be found between 11: 8*a* and 8*b*. The justification for this will be found on pp. 7, 11f.

Original Form of the Mosaic Tradition 185

from his neighbour and each woman from her neighbour articles of silver and gold. **3** Yahweh granted the people favour in the eyes of the Egyptians; moreover, the man Moses was very great in the land of Egypt, in the eyes of Pharaoh's servants and in the eyes of the people. **4** Moses said [to Pharaoh], Thus saith Yahweh, About midnight I am going forth among the Egyptians, **5** and all the first-born in the land of Egypt shall die, from the first-born of Pharaoh sitting on the throne to the first-born of the slave-girl behind the mill, and all the first-born of animals. **6** And there shall be a great cry throughout the whole land of Egypt, the like of which has never been and the like of which will never be again. **7** But as for the Israelites, both man and beast, not a dog of them shall utter a sound in order that you may learn that Yahweh makes a distinction between Egypt and Israel. **8a** Then shall all these servants of thine come down to me and prostrate themselves to me, saying, Depart, thou and all the people that are in thy following. After that I shall depart. **10: 28** Pharaoh said to him, Leave my presence! Take care not to see my face again, for on the day thou seest my face thou shalt die! **29** And Moses said, Be it as thou hast said. I will not [ask to] see thy face again. **11: 8b** And he departed from Pharaoh's presence in a rage.

THE EXODUS

12: 29 At midnight Yahweh smote all the first-born in the land of Egypt, from the first-born of Pharaoh sitting upon the throne to the first-born of the captive in the dungeon, and all the first-born of animals. **30** And Pharaoh arose by night, he and all his servants and all the Egyptians, and there was a great outcry in Egypt, for there was not a house where someone was not dead. **31** He summoned Moses and Aaron by night and said, Arise, depart from among my people, both you and the Israelites, and go, serve Yahweh as you said. **32** Take both your flocks and your herds as you said and go; and ask a blessing for me also. **33** The Egyptians urged the people to hasten their departure from the land, For, they said, we shall all be dead. **34** So the people picked up their dough which was not yet leavened, placing the bowls, wrapped up in cloaks, upon their shoulders. **35** And the Israelites did according to the word of Moses, borrowing from the Egyptians articles of silver and gold and clothes, **36** while Yahweh granted the people such favour in the eyes of the Egyptians that they loaned these things to them, and so they despoiled the Egyptians. **37** The Israelites journeyed from Rameses to Succoth, about six hundred thousand on foot, adults, apart from children. **38** A crowd of mixed origin also went up with them, as well as a very considerable possession in the way of flocks and herds. **39** And they baked unleavened cakes out of the dough which they had brought from Egypt; it was not leavened because they were driven out of Egypt and could not tarry; nor had they prepared any provisions for themselves.[1]

THE FIRST MURMURING: AT THE CROSSING OF THE SEA

13:17 Now when Pharaoh let the people go, God did not lead them by the road to the land of the Philistines, although it was near at hand, Lest, said God, the people change their mind when they experience war and return to Egypt. **18** So God had the people take a roundabout way by the desert road to the Red Sea [*yam sûph*]. The Israelites went up from the land of Egypt in battle array. **19** Moses took the bones of Joseph with him, for [Joseph] had solemnly adjured the Israelites, saying, God will certainly visit you, and then you must take up my bones from here with you. **20** They journeyed from Succoth and encamped at Etham on the edge of the desert. **21** Now Yahweh went in front of them in a pillar of cloud by day to lead them along the road, and in a pillar of fire by night to give them light so that they might travel day and night; **22** the pillar of cloud by day and the pillar of fire by night never left the front of the people.

14:1 Then Yahweh spoke unto Moses, saying, **2a** Speak to the Israelites and have them turn back and encamp in front of Pi-hahiroth....[2] **3** Pharaoh will say of the Israelites, They are trapped in the land; the desert has shut them out. **4** I will make the heart of Pharaoh stubborn so that he will pursue after them and I will gain glory through Pharaoh and all his army, and the Egyptians shall learn that I am Yahweh. And so they did. **5** When the king of Egypt was told that the people had fled, the attitude of Pharaoh

---

[1]Verses 40-51 and 13:1f. are the work of P, but 13:3-16 was added in the reign of Hezekiah; see pp. 157-61.

[2]Omitting "between Migdol and the sea, in front of Baal-zephon."

Original Form of the Mosaic Tradition 187

and his servants towards the people changed and they said, Whatever have we done to let Israel go from our service? **6** So he harnessed up his chariots and took his people with him; **7** he took six hundred choice chariots and all the [other] chariots of Egypt with charioteers [?] upon each of them. **8** Yahweh made the heart of Pharaoh, the king of Egypt, stubborn so that he pursued the Israelites, since the Israelites were leaving in triumph. **9** The Egyptians pursued them and overtook them camping by the sea . . .[1] beside Pi-hahiroth . . . .[2] **10** As Pharaoh drew near, the Israelites looked up and there were the Egyptians coming after them and they were very much afraid. And the Israelites [murmured against Moses[3]] **11** and they said to Moses, Was it because there are no graves in Egypt that thou hast taken us into the desert to die? Why treat us in this way by bringing us out of Egypt? **12** Is not this the very thing we told thee in Egypt would happen, when we said, Leave us alone and let us serve the Egyptians, for it were better for us to serve the Egyptians than to die in the desert? **13** But Moses said to the people, Do not be afraid. Stand still and see the salvation which Yahweh will accomplish for you today, for the Egyptians you see today you will never see again forever. **14** Yahweh will fight for you, while you shall keep still. **15** Then Moses cried out unto Yahweh[4] but Yahweh said to Moses, Why criest thou unto me? Speak to the Israelites and have them move on. **16** Do thou raise thy staff and stretch out thy hand over the sea and cleave it, that the Israelites may enter into the sea on dry land. **17** Of course, I am going to make the heart of the Egyptians stubborn so that they will go in after them and thus I will gain glory through Pharaoh and his army, his chariots and his horsemen, **18** and the Egyptians shall learn that I am Yahweh when I have gained glory through Pharaoh, his chariots, and horsemen. **19b** Then the pillar of cloud moved from in front of them and stood behind them, **20** and came between the camp of Egypt and the camp of Israel. There was both the cloud and the dark-

---

[1] Omitting "all the horses of the chariots of Pharaoh and his horsemen and his army."

[2] Omitting "in front of Baal-zephon."

[3] Reasons for believing that this was the original reading are given on pp. 153f. The Hebrew reads, "cried out unto Yahweh."

[4] Inserting this phrase with the Syr. VS.

ness . . .¹ so that they did not come near each other all night. **21** Then Moses stretched out his hand over the sea, and Yahweh moved the sea away by a strong east wind all night long and turned the sea into a dry waste. The waters were cleft **22** so that the Israelites entered into the midst of the sea on dry land, the waters forming a wall to right and left of them. **23** The pursuing Egyptians—all the horses and chariots and horsemen of Pharaoh—followed them right into the midst of the sea. **24** At the morning watch Yahweh looked down at the camp of the Egyptians from his pillar of fire and cloud and threw the Egyptian host into a panic. **25** He clogged the wheels of their chariots and made them drive with difficulty. Then Egypt said, Let me flee from Israel, for Yahweh is fighting for them against Egypt. **26** Then Yahweh said to Moses, Stretch out thy hand over the sea that the waters may return upon the Egyptians, upon their chariots and their horsemen. **27** So Moses stretched out his hand over the sea and the sea swept back, at the turn of the morning, to its natural state. The Egyptians were fleeing towards it, and Yahweh hurled the Egyptians into the midst of the sea. **28** The waters returned and covered the chariots and the horsemen of the whole army of Pharaoh which had entered into the sea after them, not even one of them being left. **29** But the Israelites had walked on dry ground through the midst of the sea, the waters forming a wall to right and left of them. **30** Yahweh saved Israel that day from the hand of the Egyptians, and Israel saw the Egyptians dead upon the shore of the sea. **31** When Israel witnessed the great assistance which Yahweh rendered against Egypt, the people feared Yahweh and believed in Yahweh and in his servant, Moses. **15:1** Then Moses and the Israelites sang this song to Yahweh and said,

> I will sing to Yahweh, for he is highly exalted;
> The horse and its rider he has cast into the sea.

THE SECOND MURMURING: AT MARAH

15:22 [The Israelites journeyed from the sea]² and went out into the desert of Shur; they travelled in the desert for three days

---

¹Omitting the phrase "and it [he] illumined the night."

²The Hebrew reads, "Then Moses caused the Israelites to journey from the *yam sûph*." Reasons for the above reading are presented on pp. 85, 87.

Original Form of the Mosaic Tradition 189

without finding water. **23** Then they came to Marah, but they could not drink any water from Marah because it was bitter [*mar*]. That is why it was called Marah. **24** So the people murmured against Moses, saying, What shall we drink? **25** He cried to Yahweh, and Yahweh pointed out to him a tree, and when he threw it into the water, the water became sweet. There he appointed for them rules and regulations, and there he tested [*nissah*] them. **26** He said, If thou wilt listen carefully to the voice of Yahweh, thy god, and do what is right in his eyes and heed his commandments and observe all his statutes, I will not put on thee any of the diseases which I have put on the Egyptians, but I will be Yahweh, thy physician.

27 Then they came to Eloth[1] where there were twelve springs of water and seventy palm trees, and they encamped there beside the water.

THE THIRD MURMURING: IN THE DESERT OF SIN

16: 1 Then they journeyed from Eloth[1] and ...[2] came to the desert of Sin, which is between Eloth[1] and Horeb[3]....[4] **2** And ...[5] the Israelites murmured against Moses and Aaron in the desert. **3** And the Israelites said to them, Would that we had died by the hand of Yahweh in the land of Egypt when we sat by pots of flesh and ate our fill of food, for you have brought us out to this desert to kill this whole assembly [*qāhāl*] with famine. **4** Then Yahweh said to Moses, Behold I am going to rain food for you from the sky. The people shall go out and collect one day's supply at a time in order that I may test [*nissah*] them [to see] whether they will walk in my law or not. **13b** In the morning there was a layer of dew around the camp, **14** and when the layer of dew evaporated, there, on the face of the desert was a fine scaly substance, as fine as hoarfrost on the ground. **15** When the Israelites saw it, they said to one another, What [*man*] is it?—for they did not know what it was. Moses said to them, It is the food which Yahweh has given you to

---

[1]For the reading *Eloth* instead of *Elim*, see pp. 89f.
[2]Omitting "all the '*edah* of the Israelites," a P phrase.
[3]For the reading *Horeb* instead of *Sinai*, see p. 91.
[4]Omitting P's chronological note "on the fifteenth day of the second month of their exodus from the land of Egypt."
[5]Omitting "all the '*edah* of."

eat. **21** So they collected it morning after morning, each according to his eating capacity; and when the sun grew hot it melted. **31** The house of Israel called it manna [*man*]; it was as white as coriander seed, and its taste was like that of wafers made with honey.

The Fourth Murmuring: at Taberah

17: 1a Then . . .[1] the Israelites journeyed from the desert of Sin [and encamped at Taberah].[2] **Nu. 11: 1** And the people [murmured against Moses],[3] and when Yahweh heard it he became angry and the fire of Yahweh burned among them and consumed some of the outskirts of the camp. **2** The people cried to Moses, and Moses prayed to Yahweh, whereupon the fire abated. **3** That place was called Taberah because the fire of Yahweh burned [*ba'arah*] among them.

The Fifth Murmuring: at Rephidim

Ex. 17: 1b [Then the Israelites journeyed from Taberah][4] and encamped at Rephidim; but there was no water for the people to drink. **2** So the people disputed with Moses and said, Give us water to drink. Moses said to them, Why do you dispute with me? Why do you put Yahweh to the test? **3** The people thirsted there for water, and the people murmured against Moses and said, Why didst thou ever bring us up from Egypt to have me and my sons and my livestock die of thirst? **4** Moses cried unto Yahweh, saying, What shall I do for this people? A little more and they will stone me. **5** Yahweh said to Moses, Pass on ahead of the people, and take with thee some of the elders of Israel, and take in thy hand the staff with which thou didst smite the Nile, and go. **6** I am going to stand before thee there upon the rock [*ṣûr*] in Horeb, and thou shalt strike the rock, and water shall come forth from it, so that the people may drink. And Moses did so in the sight of the elders of Israel. **7** And he called the place Massah [place of testing] and Meribah [place of disputing] because of the disputing

---

[1] Omitting "all the '*edah* of."

[2] For this reading, see pp. 93, 131-3.

[3] The Hebrew reads, "Now the people were complaining of misfortune in the hearing of Yahweh." For the above reading, see p. 133.

[4] For this insertion, see pp. 93, 131-3.

Original Form of the Mosaic Tradition

of the Israelites and because of their putting Yahweh to the test by saying, Is Yahweh in our midst or not?

THE BATTLE WITH THE AMALEKITES

17:8 Then Amalek came and fought with Israel at Rephidim. **9** And Moses said to Joshua, Pick out some men for us, and go and fight with Amalek; tomorrow I am going to stand on the top of the hill with the sacred staff in my hand. **10** Joshua did as Moses told him about fighting with Amalek, while Moses, Aaron, and Hur went up to the top of the hill. **11** And whenever Moses raised his hand, Israel prevailed; and whenever he lowered his hand, Amalek prevailed. **12** Since Moses' hands became heavy, they took a stone and placed it under him and he sat on it, while Aaron and Hur supported his hands, one on one side and the other on the other, and his hands remained steady until the going down of the sun. **13** And Joshua reaped Amalek and his people with the edge of the sword. **14** Yahweh said to Moses, Write this as a reminder in the book, and put it in the ears of Joshua, that I will completely erase the memory of Amalek from under the heavens. **15** Moses built an altar and named it *Yahweh-nissi*. **16** He said, [I swear] by a hand placed upon the throne of Yahweh, Yahweh will have war with Amalek from generation to generation.

THE REVELATION OF THE LAW

19:2 Then they journeyed from Rephidim and came to [the sacred mountain, Horeb,][1] and Israel encamped there before the mountain, **3a** while Moses went up to the Deity. **9a** And Yahweh said to Moses, I am going to come to thee in a mass of cloud in order that the people may hear me speaking with thee, and also that they may have faith in thee forever. **10** . . .[2] Go to the people and purify them today and tomorrow. They shall wash their clothes, **11** and be ready for the third day; for on the third day Yahweh will descend in the sight of all the people upon the mountain. . . .[3] **12** Thou shalt set bounds for the people, saying,

---

[1]The Hebrew reads, "to the desert of Sinai and encamped in the desert." For the above reading, see p. 92.
[2]Omitting "And Yahweh said to Moses."
[3]For the omission of the word "Sinai," see pp. 73f.

Be careful about ascending the mountain or touching its edge; whoever touches the mountain must be put to death. **13** No hand shall touch him; he must be stoned or shot; whether beast or man he shall not live. When the ram's horn sounds, they may ascend the mountain. **14** So Moses went down from the mountain unto the people and purified the people and they washed their clothes. **15** He said to the people, Be ready for three days; do not approach a woman. **16** And on the third day, when it was morning, there was thundering and lightning and a dense cloud over the mountain and a very loud trumpet blast, so that all the people who were in the camp trembled. **17** Then Moses brought the people forth from the camp to meet the Deity and they stationed themselves in the lower part of the mountain. **18** The whole mountain smoked because Yahweh had descended upon it in fire; its smoke ascended like the smoke from a kiln and the whole mountain trembled greatly. **19** As the sound of the trumpet grew louder, Moses was speaking and the Deity was answering him with a voice.[1] **20: 1** And God spoke all these words, saying:

I. **20: 23** Thou shalt not make me into a god of silver or gold.[2]

II. **20: 24** Thou shalt make me an altar of earth and sacrifice upon it thy burnt-offerings [*'ôlôth*] and thy thank-offerings [*shelamîm*], thy sheep and thy cattle; at every place where I record my name, I will come to thee and bless thee. **25** If, however, thou makest me an altar out of stones, thou shalt not build it of hewn stones; for if thou wieldest thy blade upon it, thou wilt defile it. **26** And thou shalt not ascend by steps to my altar upon which thy nakedness should not be exposed.

III. **23: 10** For six years thou shalt sow thy land and gather in its increase, **11** but during the seventh year thou shalt leave it untouched and let it lie fallow, so that the poor of thy people may eat, and what they leave the wild animals may eat. Thou shalt do the same with thy vineyard and olive grove.

IV. **12** For six days thou shalt do thy work, but on the seventh day thou shalt abstain, in order that thy ox and thy ass may rest, and that thy slave and the stranger may refresh themselves.

[1] Reasons for regarding 20: 23-6; 23: 10-19 as the original Mosaic Decalogue and for believing that it once stood after 19: 19 will be found on pp. 33-7.

[2] For this translation, see W. A. Irwin, "Images of Yahweh," *Crozer Quarterly* (Oct., 1942), pp. 300f.

Original Form of the Mosaic Tradition 193

V. **13** Be careful about everything that I have said to you. Thou shalt not mention the name of another god; it shall not be heard upon thy mouth.

VI. **14** On three occasions in the year thou shalt celebrate a feast to me: **15** the feast of unleavened bread [*maṣṣôth*] thou shalt keep, eating unleavened bread for seven days, as I commanded thee, at the appointed time of the month of Abib, for in it thou camest forth from Egypt, and my face shall not be seen unless thou bringest a gift[1]; **16** the feast of harvest [*qaṣîr*], the first-fruits of thy produce which thou sowest in the field; and the feast of ingathering [*'asîph*] at the end of the year, when thou gatherest in thy produce from the field. **17** Three times in the year all thy males shall present themselves to the face of the Lord Yahweh.

VII. **18a** Thou shalt not offer the blood of my sacrifice with anything leavened.

VIII. **18b** And the fat of my feast shall not be left overnight until morning.

IX. **19a** The earliest of the first-fruits of thy soil thou shalt bring to the house of Yahweh, thy god.

X. **19b** Thou shalt not boil a kid in its mother's milk.

20: 18 All the people were witnessing the thundering and lightning, the sound of the trumpet, and the mountain smoking; and when the people saw it they trembled and stood at a distance. **19** And they said to Moses, Do thou speak with us and we will listen, but let not God speak with us lest we die. **20** Do not be afraid, Moses said to the people, because it is merely for the purpose of testing you that the Deity has come and in order that his fear may be upon your faces that you may not sin. **21** But the people stood at a distance while Moses approached the dense darkness where the Deity was.

24:1 And he said to Moses, Come up to Yahweh, thou and Aaron, Nadab and Abihu, and seventy of the elders of Israel, and prostrate yourselves at a distance. **2** Moses alone is to approach Yahweh; they are not to approach, nor are the people to come up with him. **9** So Moses and Aaron, Nadab and Abihu, and seventy of the elders went up. **10** And they saw the god of Israel, and under his feet there was a sort of sapphire tile work, as clear as the substance of the sky. **11** He did not lay a hand on the leaders

[1]Literally, "empty-handed."

of the Israelites, but they beheld the Deity and ate and drank. **12** And Yahweh said to Moses, Ascend the mountain to me and remain there that I may give thee the stone tablets . . .[1] which I have written for their instruction. **13** So Moses arose with his attendant, Joshua, and Moses went up the sacred mountain. **14** He had said to the elders, Wait here for us until we return to you. Aaron and Hur are with you; whoever has a dispute can go to them. **15** So Moses went up the mountain and the cloud covered the mountain. **18b** And Moses was on the mountain for forty days and forty nights. **31:18** As soon as [Yahweh] had finished speaking with him . . .[2] he gave Moses . . .[3] two . . .[4] stone tablets, inscribed by the finger of God.

THE ORDER TO DEPART FROM HOREB

33:1 Then Yahweh said to Moses, Go on up from here, thou and the people whom thou didst bring up from the land of Egypt, unto the land concerning which I swore to Abraham, Isaac, and Jacob, saying, To thy descendants I will give it.

THE TENT OF MEETING

33:7 Moses used to take a tent and pitch it outside the camp, at a distance from the camp. It was called "the Tent of Meeting" [*'ohel mô'edh*]. Anyone wanting to consult Yahweh would go to the Tent of Meeting which was outside the camp. **8** Whenever Moses went out to the tent, the people would all rise and stand, each at the entrance of his tent, and gaze after Moses until he had entered the tent. **9** As soon as Moses entered the tent, the pillar of cloud would descend and remain at the entrance of the tent, and he would speak with Moses. **10** When all the people would see the pillar of cloud standing at the entrance of the tent, all the people would rise and prostrate themselves, each at the entrance of his tent. **11** And Yahweh would speak to Moses face to face, just as one man speaks to another. Then he would return to the camp; but his youthful attendant, Joshua the son of Nun, would not depart from inside the tent.

[1]Omitting "and the law and the commandment."
[2]Omitting "on Mount Sinai."
[3]Omitting "the."
[4]Omitting "tablets of the testimony."

THE VISIT OF JETHRO TO THE ISRAELITE CAMP[1]

Ex. 18: 1 Now Jethro, the priest of Midian, the father-in-law of Moses, heard of all that God had done for Moses and for Israel, his people, how Yahweh had brought Israel out of Egypt. **2** So Jethro, the father-in-law of Moses, took Zipporah, Moses' wife . . .[2] **3** and her two sons, the name of one being Gershom (Because, he said, I was a stranger [*ger*] in a foreign land), **4** and the name of the other Eliezer (Because my father's god is my help [*'ezer*] and has delivered me from the sword of Pharaoh). **5** Jethro, the father-in-law of Moses, came with the sons and wife of Moses to the desert where he was camping at the sacred mountain. **6** He sent Moses word, saying,[3] I, thy father-in-law, Jethro, am on my way to thee, with thy wife, accompanied by her two sons. **7** Then Moses went out to meet his father-in-law and prostrated himself and kissed him and they asked after each other's health. Then they entered the tent, **8** where Moses related to his father-in-law everything that Yahweh had done to Pharaoh and the Egyptians for Israel's sake, all the hardships that had befallen them on the way and how Yahweh had delivered them. **9** Jethro rejoiced at all the good which Yahweh had done to Israel, especially that he had delivered them from the hand of the Egyptians. **10** Blessed be Yahweh, said Jethro, who has delivered you from the hand of the Egyptians and from the hand of Pharaoh, who has delivered the people from the hand of the Egyptians. **11** Now I know that Yahweh is greater than all the gods, for in ruin[4] are those who acted presumptuously against them. **12** Jethro, the father-in-law of Moses, then took a burnt-offering and sacrifices for God, while Aaron and all the elders of Israel came to eat food with Moses' father-in-law before the Deity. **13** On the morrow Moses sat to judge the people, and the people stood about Moses from morning till evening. **14** When Moses' father-in-law saw all that he was doing for the people, he said, What is this thing that thou art doing for the people? Why dost thou sit by thyself, with all the people standing about thee from morning until evening? **15** Moses said to his father-in-law, Because the people come to me to inquire of God. **16** Whenever they have a dispute, they come to me, that I

---

[1] For evidence that this was the original position of the chapter, see pp. 61f.
[2] Omitting "after she had been sent [home]."
[3] Literally, "And he said to Moses."
[4] Heb. *dābār*; cf. Ar. *dabār*, "ruin."

may judge between one man and another, and make known the divine statutes and laws. **17** Moses' father-in-law said to him, What thou art doing is not good. **18** Thou wilt completely wear out both thyself and this people that are with thee, for the task is too heavy for thee; thou art not able to do it alone. **19** Now listen to my suggestion; let me give thee some advice, and may God be with thee! Be thou the people's advocate with the Deity and bring the matters to the Deity. **20** Warn them about the statutes and laws and make known to them the way in which they must walk and what they must do. **21** Do thou thyself select from all the people men of ability who reverence God, men of integrity who hate dishonest gain, and set them over them as captains [*sarîm*] of thousands, hundreds, fifties, and tens. **22** They shall judge the people on every occasion; all important matters they shall bring to thee but all lesser matters they shall judge themselves. And so make it easier for thyself, since they will share the burden with thee. **23** If thou doest this thing—and God so commands thee—thou wilt be able to carry on and all these people will arrive safely at their destination as well. **24** Moses heeded the suggestion of his father-in-law and did all that he said. **25** Moses chose men of ability from all Israel and appointed them as heads over the people, as captains of thousands, hundreds, fifties, and tens. **26** They judged the people on every occasion; any difficult matter they brought to Moses but any lesser matter they themselves judged.[1]

Nu. 10:29 Moses said to [Jethro, his father-in-law],[2] We are setting out for the place concerning which Yahweh said, I will give it to you. Come along with us and we will do well by thee, for Yahweh has spoken favourably concerning Israel. **30** I will not go anywhere, he said, except to my own land and kindred. **31** Pray, do not leave us, said [Moses], since thou knowest the camping-places for us in the desert and thou couldst act as eyes for us. **32** If thou wilt accompany us, we will let thee share in the good which Yahweh will bestow on us. . . .[3] **Ex. 18:27** So Moses let his father-in-law depart, and he betook himself to his own land.

[1]Verse 27 will be found after Nu. 10:32, at the end of the next paragraph. The justification for placing it there will be found on p. 62.

[2]The Hebrew reads, "Hobab, the son of Reuel, the Midianite, the father-in-law of Moses." For the above reading, see pp. 62f.

[3]Jethro's reply, reiterating his refusal to accompany the Israelites, has been omitted by P. See p. 63.

Original Form of the Mosaic Tradition

THE SIXTH MURMURING: AT KIBROTH-HATTAAVAH

[The Israelites journeyed from the sacred mountain and encamped at Kibroth-hattaavah where the people again murmured against Moses,][1] **Nu. 11: 4b**$^\beta$ and said, O that we had meat to eat! **5** We remember the fish that we used to eat for nothing in Egypt, the cucumbers, the melons, the leeks, the onions, and the garlic. **6** But now we are famished, and there is not a thing, except that the manna is still with us. **11** Moses said to Yahweh ... **13** Where can I get meat to give all these people? For they weep upon me, saying, Give us meat to eat. **16** And Yahweh said to Moses ... **18** Say to the people, Purify yourselves for tomorrow, and you shall eat meat; for you have wept in the hearing of Yahweh, saying, O that we had meat to eat, for we were well off in Egypt! Yahweh will give you meat and you shall eat. **19** You shall eat it, not for one day, nor two days, nor five days, nor ten days, nor twenty days, **20** but for a whole month, until it comes out of your very nostrils and becomes loathsome to you—because you have spurned Yahweh who is in your midst, and have wept before him, saying, Why did we ever leave Egypt? **21** Moses said, The people among whom I am are six hundred thousand men on foot, and thou sayest, I will give them meat to eat for a whole month! **22** Can enough sheep and cattle be slaughtered to suffice them? Or if all the fish of the sea were collected for them, would it suffice them? **23** Yahweh said to Moses, Has the power of Yahweh diminished? Thou shalt now see whether my word will come to pass for thee or not. **24a** Moses went out and told the people the words of Yahweh.

31 Then there proceeded a wind from Yahweh's presence which brought quails across from the sea and dropped them upon the camp, about a day's journey in each direction round about the camp and about two cubits deep upon the surface of the earth. **32** The people were up all that day and all that night and all the next day gathering the quails; he who got the least gathered ten homers; then they spread them out all around the camp. **33** While the meat was still between their teeth, before it was all gone, Yahweh became angry with the people, and Yahweh smote the people very severely. **34** That place was called Kibroth-hattaavah

---

[1]Reasons for believing that the introduction to the story of the Sixth Murmuring has been omitted by P are given on p. 94.

[the Graves of Craving] because it was there they buried the people who craved.

Moses' Marriage to the Daughter of Hobab, the Kenite

11:35 From Kibroth-hattaavah the people journeyed to Hazeroth, and they stayed at Hazeroth. [Here Moses married the daughter of Hobab, sheikh of the Kenites, and this led to a violent quarrel with Aaron and particularly with Miriam.][1]

The Story of the Spies

12:16 Afterwards the people journeyed from Hazeroth and encamped [at Kadesh][2] in the desert of Paran. **20:1b** There Miriam died and there she was buried.[3]

[Moses proposed an attack on the Promised Land and appointed spies to reconnoitre its southern border.][4]

13:17b He said to them, Go up this way into the Negeb...[5] **18** and see what the land is like, and whether the people who inhabit it are strong or weak, few or many. **22a** So they went up into the Negeb...[6] **23** and penetrated as far as the Valley of Eshcol where they cut off a branch with a single cluster of grapes which required two of them to carry on a pole, along with some pomegranates and some figs. **26** They travelled about and then came to Moses and Aaron...[7] at Kadesh, in the desert of Paran, and brought them...[8] back word and showed them the fruit of the land. **27** They gave him a report, saying, We reached the land to which thou didst send us and it is indeed flowing with milk and honey, and this is its fruit. **28** However, the people who inhabit the land are strong and the cities fortified and very large....[9]

---

[1] Nu. 12:1-15 represents a P expansion and recasting of the original tradition. See pp. 67-9.

[2] Reasons for this insertion will be found on p. 105.

[3] For the insertion of 20:1b at this point, see p. 105.

[4] P has replaced the original introduction to the Story of the Spies by his own composition, 13:1-17a; see pp. 95, 137.

[5] Omitting "and go up to the highland."

[6] Omitting "and he penetrated as far as Hebron, where Ahiman, Sheshai, and Talmai, the offspring of the Anak, were. (Now Hebron was built seven years before Zoan in Egypt.)"

[7] Omitting "and unto all the *'edah* of the Israelites."

[8] Omitting "and all the *'edah*."

[9] Omitting "moreover, we saw there the offspring of the Anak."

Original Form of the Mosaic Tradition

30 But Caleb broke through the people to Moses and said, We ought to go up and take possession of it, for we are quite able to do so. **31** But the men who went up with him said, We are not able to go up against the people for they are stronger than we. **33** And we saw ...[1] giants [*bene 'Anaq*] ...[2] there who made us feel like grasshoppers and we must have appeared as such to them.

THE SEVENTH MURMURING: AT KADESH

14:2 Then all the Israelites murmured against Moses and Aaron and ...[3] said to them, Would that we had died in the land of Egypt! Or would that we had died in this desert! **3** And why is Yahweh bringing us into this land, only to fall by the sword? Our wives and our little ones will become a prey. Would it not be better for us to return to Egypt? **4** Let us appoint a leader, they said to one another, and return to Egypt. [Then Yahweh became angry and swore, saying, None of these men][4] **23a** shall see the land which I swore to their fathers ....[5] **24** But because my servant Caleb has manifested a different spirit and followed me completely, I shall let him enter the land which he penetrated and his descendants shall possess it. ...[6] **14:31** And your little ones who you said would become a prey, I shall bring in and they shall know the land which you have despised. **25b** Tomorrow, turn around and journey into the desert by the Red Sea [*yam sûph*] road.[7]

THE ABORTIVE ATTACK ON SOUTHERN CANAAN

14:39 When Moses spoke these words to all the Israelites, the people mourned greatly. **40** Early in the morning they went up to the top of the highland, saying, Here we are, ready to go up to the place of which Yahweh spoke, for we have sinned. **41** Moses said, Why is it that you keep on violating the command of Yahweh,

---

[1] Omitting "the Nephilim."
[2] Omitting "of the Nephilim."
[3] Omitting "all the *'edah*."
[4] Some such statement must be supplied; cf. Dt. 1:34.
[5] Omitting "and none of those who despised me shall see it."
[6] The original tradition seems to have contained at this point a statement specifically including Moses in the group condemned not to see the Promised Land but excluding Joshua. Cf. p. 139 and Dt. 1:37f.
[7] The justification for placing v. 25b after v. 31 is given on pp. 140, 142.

when that cannot succeed? **42** Do not go up, for Yahweh is not among you; then you will not be smitten before your enemies. **43** For the Amalekites and Canaanites are there in front of you, and you will fall by the sword; Yahweh will not be with you since you have turned back from following Yahweh. **44** But they went up, without heeding, to the top of the highland, although . . .[1] Moses did not depart from the midst of the camp. **45** Then the Amalekites and Canaanites who inhabited that highland came down and attacked them and harried them as far as Hormah.

THE EIGHTH MURMURING: AT KADESH

16: 12 Moses sent for Dathan and Abiram, the sons of Eliab, but they said, We will not come. **13** Is it such a trifling matter that thou hast brought us up from a land flowing with milk and honey to kill us in the desert that thou dost play the prince over us as well? **14** Certainly, it is to no land flowing with milk and honey that thou hast brought us, and it is no heritage of fields and vineyards that thou hast given us! Art thou trying to blind the eyes of those men? We will not come! **15** Moses was very angry and he said to Yahweh, Take no notice of their offering. Not a single ass have I taken from them, nor done wrong to any of them. **25** Then Moses arose and went to Dathan and Abiram, and the elders of Israel followed him, **27b** while Dathan and Abiram came forth and stood at the entrance of their tents, along with their wives and children and little ones. **28** Moses said, Hereby shall you know that Yahweh has sent me to do all these deeds, [and] that I have not done them of my own accord: **29** If these men die as all men die and suffer the usual human fate, Yahweh has not sent me. **30** But if Yahweh does something new, and the ground opens its mouth and swallows them up, with all that belongs to them, and they descend alive into Sheol, then you shall know that these men have despised Yahweh. **31** Just as he had finished uttering these words, the ground under them split open; **32** the earth opened its mouth and swallowed up them and their households . . .[2] and all their possessions. **33** So they and all who belonged to them descended alive into Sheol; the earth closed upon them and they vanished from the midst of the community. **34** And all the Israel-

---
[1]Omitting "the ark of the covenant of Yahweh and"; cf. p. 59.
[2]Omitting "and all the men who belonged to Korah."

ites who were in the vicinity fled at their cry; Lest, they said, the earth swallow us up.

THE INSTITUTION OF A PRIESTHOOD

[Aaron and his sons were appointed to the priesthood and the other members of the tribe of Levi to the position of priestly assistants.][1]

THE NINTH MURMURING: AT KADESH

16: 1a Now Korah, the son of Izhar, the son of Kohath, the son of Levi, **2a** along with two hundred and fifty of the Israelites, stood before Moses. **3** And they [murmured[2]] against Moses and Aaron and said to them, We have had enough of you!...[3] Why do you exalt yourselves above the assembly of Yahweh? **4** When Moses heard this, he fell on his face. **16** And Moses said to Korah...[4] Thou and they and Aaron are to appear before Yahweh tomorrow. **17** Each of you is to take his fire-pan and place incense on it and present his fire-pan before Yahweh....[5] **18** So each of them took his fire-pan and put fire on it and placed incense on it and then stood at the entrance of the Tent of Meeting, along with Moses and Aaron. **35** And fire came forth from Yahweh and consumed the two hundred and fifty men offering the incense.

THE ATTEMPT TO CROSS EDOM

20: 14 Then Moses sent messengers from Kadesh to the king of Edom: Thus saith thy brother Israel, Thou knowest all the hardships that have befallen us, **15** how our fathers went down to Egypt, and we remained in Egypt for a long time. The Egyptians treated us and our fathers badly, **16** so we cried unto Yahweh and he heeded our cry and sent a messenger [*mal'akh*] and brought

---

[1]Evidence that the original tradition regarding the institution of the priesthood once stood at this point in the narrative but has been omitted by P will be found on pp. 146-8.

[2]The Hebrew reads "were assembled"; for the above reading, see pp. 148, 153.

[3]Omitting "for all the *'edah* are holy, every one of them, since Yahweh is in their midst."

[4]Omitting "thou and all thy *'edah*."

[5]Omitting "two hundred and fifty fire-pans; thou also, and Aaron, each with his fire-pan."

us forth from Egypt. And here we are at Kadesh, a city ['îr] on the edge of thy territory. 17 Pray, let us pass through thy land; we will not pass through field or vineyard, nor drink the water of a well; we will go only by the king's highway, turning neither to the right nor to the left, until we have crossed thy territory. 18 But Edom said to him, Thou mayest not pass through me or else I will come out to meet thee with the sword. 19 The Israelites said to him, We will go only by the highway, and if I and my livestock drink any of thy water, I will pay for it. Merely—it is nothing—let me pass through on foot. 20 But he said, Thou shalt not pass. And Edom came out to meet them with many people and with a display of force. 21 Edom refused to allow Israel to pass through his territory, so Israel turned away from him.

The Death of Aaron and the Appointment of his Successor

20:22 Then they journeyed from Kadesh, and the Israelites...[1] came to Mt. Hor. **23** And Yahweh said to Moses and Aaron at Mt. Hor, near the frontier of the land of Edom, as follows, **24a** Aaron is to be gathered unto his people, for he shall not enter the land which I have given to the Israelites....[2]

The Tenth Murmuring: on the Journey around Edom

21:4 Then they journeyed from Mt. Hor by the Red Sea [*yam sûph*] road to go around the land of Edom, and the people grew impatient over the journey. **5** And the people [murmured[3]] against...[4] Moses, [saying,] Why have you brought us up from Egypt to die in the desert? For there is neither food nor water, and our souls loathe this miserable food. **6** Then Yahweh sent *saraph*-snakes among the people, and they bit the people so that many people of Israel died. **7** So the people came to Moses and said, We have sinned, for we have [murmured[5]] against Yahweh and against thee; pray to Yahweh and have him remove the snakes

[1]Omitting "all the *'edah*."
[2]Here followed an account of Aaron's death on Mt. Hor and of the appointment of his successor, in all probability his eldest son, Nadab. Verses 24b-29 represent a P corruption of the original tradition; see p. 108.
[3]The Hebrew reads "spoke"; for the above reading, see p. 153.
[4]Omitting "God and against."
[5]The Hebrew reads "spoken"; cf. n. 3.

Original Form of the Mosaic Tradition

from us. So Moses prayed on behalf of the people. 8 And Yahweh said to Moses, Make thyself a *saraph* and mount it on a standard; then whenever anyone is bitten and sees it, he will live. 9 So Moses made a bronze snake and mounted it on a standard, and whenever a snake bit a man, he looked at the bronze snake and lived.

The Journey to Pisgah

21: 10 Then the Israelites journeyed and encamped at Oboth.

11 Then they journeyed from Oboth and encamped at Ije-abarim in the desert which confronts Moab on the side where the sun rises.

12 From there they journeyed and encamped in the valley of the Zered.

13a From there they journeyed and encamped on the other side of the Arnon, which is in the desert that extends out from the frontier of the Amorites.

16a And from there to a well.

18b And from the desert [-well] to Mattanah.

19a And from Mattanah to Nahaliel.

19b And from Nahaliel to Bamoth.

20 And from Bamoth to the valley which is in the country of Moab, at the peak of Pisgah which overlooks Jeshimon.

The Conquest of the Amorite Kingdoms of Heshbon and Bashan

21: 21 Then Israel sent messengers to Sihon, king of the Amorites, saying, **22** Let me pass through thy land. We will not turn aside into field or vineyard; we will not drink the water from a well; we will go only by the king's highway until we pass through thy territory. **23** But Sihon would not allow Israel to pass through his territory; Sihon collected all his people and came out to meet Israel in the desert. Arriving at Jahaz, he fought against Israel, **24** but Israel smote him with the sword and took possession of his land from the Arnon to the Jabbok, as far as the Ammonites, but the frontier of the Ammonites was strong [?]. **25** Israel took all these cities, and Israel settled in all the cities of the Amorites, in Heshbon and in all its villages. **26** For Heshbon was the capital of Sihon, king of the Amorites; he had fought against the former king of Moab and had taken from him all his land as far as the Arnon. **31** So Israel settled in the land of the Amorites. **32** Then Moses sent [men] to reconnoitre Jazer and they captured its villages and evicted the Amorites that were there.

33 Then they turned and proceeded up the road to Bashan. Og, the king of Bashan, came out to meet them with all his people for a battle at Edrei. **34** But Yahweh said to Moses, Do not be afraid of him; for I have given him and all his people and his land into thy hand, and thou shalt do to him as thou didst to Sihon, king of the Amorites, who resided in Heshbon. **35** So they smote him and his sons and all his people until not a survivor was left to him, and took possession of his land.

The Promulgation of a Supplementary Code[1]

Ex. 22:20 (EV 21) Thou shalt not ill-treat a stranger [*ger*], nor oppress him, for you were strangers in the land of Egypt. **21 (22)** You shall not wrong any widow or orphan. **22 (23)** If thou dost wrong them [it will be bad for you], for if they cry out to me, I will certainly hear their cry, **23 (24)** and my anger will be aroused and I will slay you with the sword so that your wives will become widows and your children orphans.

24 (25) If thou lendest money to my people, the poor who are with thee, thou shalt not act like a creditor towards him; you shall not charge him interest. **25 (26)** If thou dost ever take another's cloak in pledge, thou shalt return it to him by sunset, **26 (27)** for that is his only covering; it is his cloak for his skin. In what else shall he lie down? If he should cry to me, I would hear [him], for I am compassionate.

27 (28) Thou shalt not curse God, nor revile a ruler of thy people.

28 (29) Thou shalt not hold back the fruit and wine [of thy vineyard]. The first-born of thy sons thou shalt give me. **29 (30)** Thou shalt do the same with thine ox and thy sheep; for seven days it shall remain with its mother; on the eighth day thou shalt give it to me.

---

[1] For the transfer of the Supplementary Code to this position, see pp. 40, 115. The original introduction has been omitted by P.

30 (31) Since you are men holy to me, you shall not eat any flesh that has been mangled in the field; you shall throw it to the dogs.

23:1 Thou shalt not repeat a false rumour. Do not join hands with a wicked person to be an accessory to crime. **2** Thou shalt not follow a crowd to evil. Thou shalt not give evidence concerning a dispute by turning aside with the crowd so as to pervert [justice]. **3** Thou shalt not favour a poor man in his dispute.

4 When thou comest upon thine enemy's ox or ass astray, thou must return it to him. **5** When thou seest the ass of one who hates thee lying down under its load, thou shalt refrain from chastising[1] it; thou shalt be very good-natured[2] with it.

6 Thou shalt not pervert the justice due the poor man in his dispute. **7** Avoid anything false. Do not slay an innocent, righteous person, for I will not exonerate a wrongdoer. **8** Thou shalt not take a bribe; for a bribe blinds those who can see and perverts the words of the righteous.

9 Thou shalt not oppress a stranger, for you yourselves know the feelings of a stranger since you were strangers in the land of Egypt.

THE COMMAND TO INSCRIBE THE SUPPLEMENTARY CODE ON THE ALTAR ON MT. GERIZIM[3]

Dt. 27:1 Then Moses and the elders of Israel commanded the people, as follows, Observe the whole command that I am enjoining on you today. **2** On the day that you cross the Jordan to the land which Yahweh, thy god, is giving thee, thou shalt set up some large stones and coat them with plaster. **3** Then thou shalt write upon them all the words of this law, when you have crossed over, in order that thou mayest enter the land which Yahweh, thy god, is giving thee, a land flowing with milk and honey, just as Yahweh, the god of thy fathers, promised thee. **4** When you cross the Jordan, you shall set up these stones, concerning which I am commanding you today, on Mt. [Gerizim,[4]] and thou shalt coat them with plaster.

[1]Cf. Ar. *'ad̲d̲aba*, "to chastise, torment."
[2]Cf. Ar. *'ad̲uba*, "to be sweet, pleasant."
[3]The following account represents a D recasting of the original tradition; see p. 40.
[4]Heb. "Mt. Ebal." For this reading, see p. 40, n. 2.

5 And thou shalt build there an altar to Yahweh, thy god, an altar of stones on which thou shalt not employ any iron [tool]. **6** Out of undressed stones thou shalt build the altar of Yahweh, thy god, and thou shalt offer up upon it burnt-offerings ['ôlôth] to Yahweh, thy god, **7** and sacrifice peace-offerings [shelamîm] and eat [them] there with joy before Yahweh, thy god. **8** And thou shalt write upon the stones all the words of this law very distinctly.

The Appointment of Joshua as Moses' Successor

Dt. 31:14 Then Yahweh said to Moses, The time for thee to die has drawn nigh. Call Joshua and present yourselves at the Tent of Meeting that I may commission him. So Moses and Joshua went and presented themselves at the Tent of Meeting. **15** Thereupon Yahweh appeared at the tent in a pillar of cloud, and the pillar of cloud stood at the entrance to the tent. **23** And he commissioned Joshua, the son of Nun, and said, Be strong! be firm! for it is thou who wilt bring the Israelites into the land which I swore to give them. I will be with thee.

The Death of Moses

Dt. 34:1 Then Moses went up . . .[1] to the top of Pisgah . . .[2] and Yahweh showed him the whole land . . . .[3] **4** And Yahweh said to him, This is the land concerning which I swore to Abraham, Isaac, and Jacob, saying, To thy descendants I will give it; I have let thee see it with thine eyes but thou shalt not pass over thither. **5** So Moses, the servant of Yahweh, died there in the land of Moab . . .[4] **6b**[5] but to this day no one knows his burial-place.

---

[1]Omitting "from the steppes of Moab to Mt. Nebo."
[2]Omitting "which confronts Jericho."
[3]Omitting "Gilead to Dan."
[4]Omitting "at the command of Yahweh."
[5]Omitting "And he was buried in the valley in the land of Moab in front of Beth-peor."

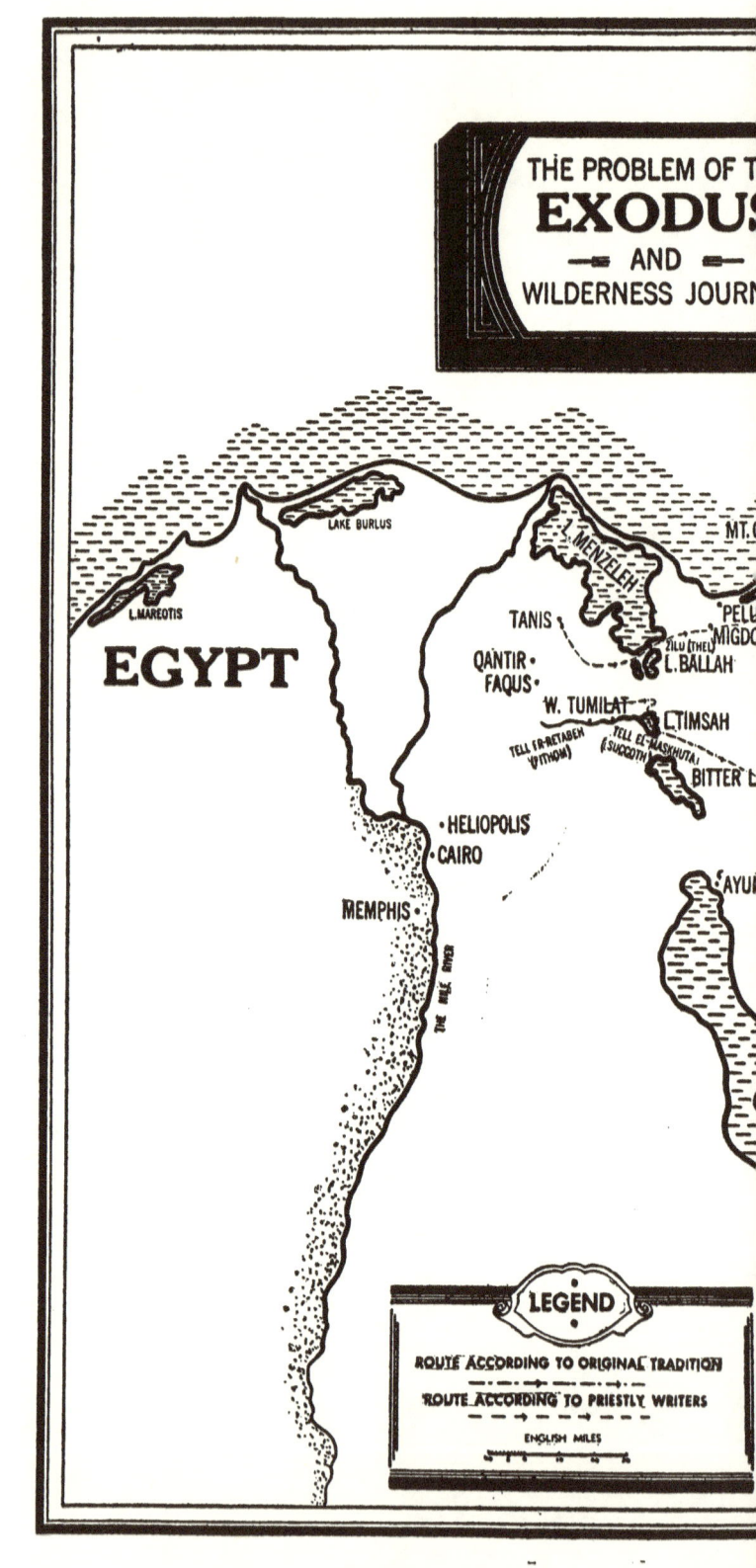

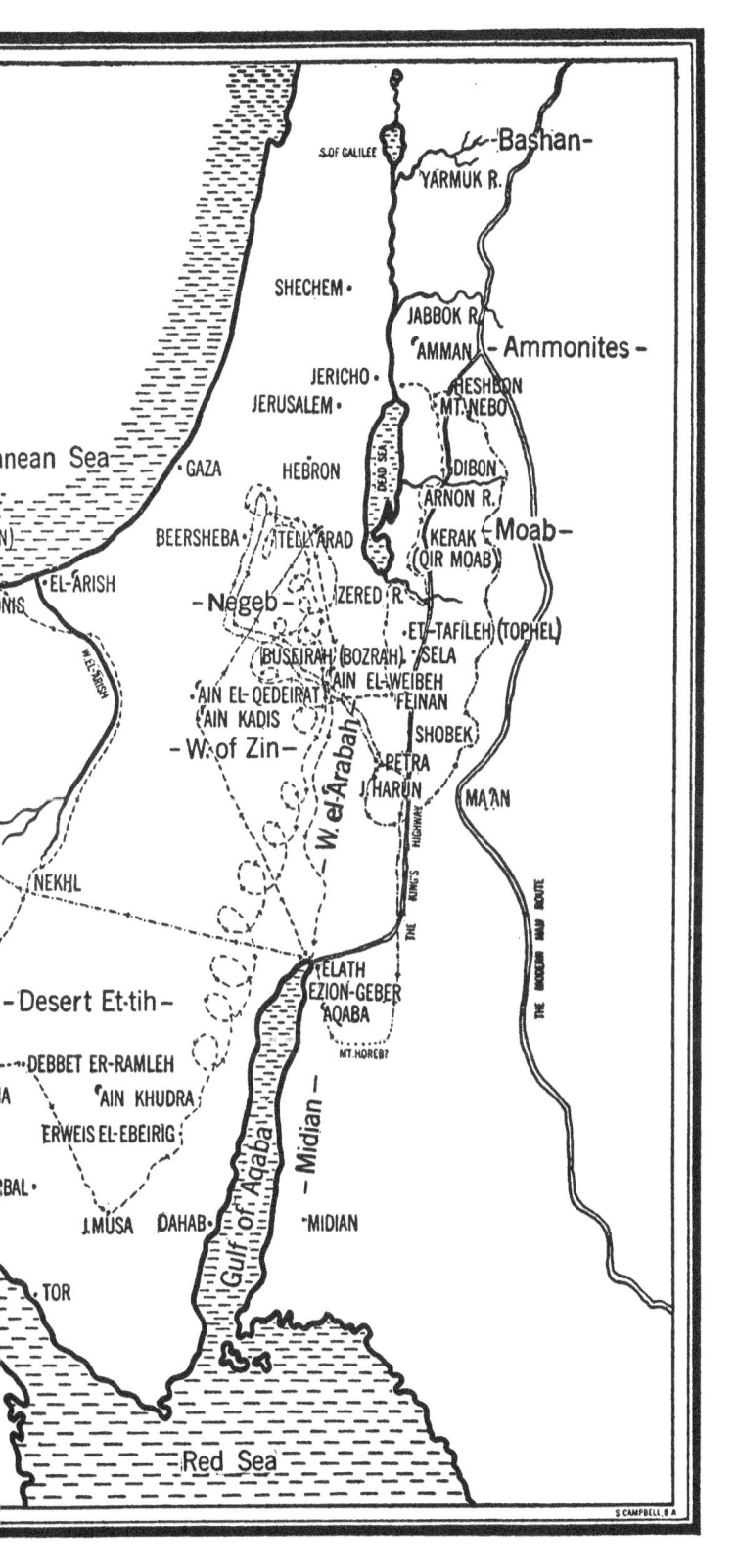

Index of Subjects

Aaron, 4-6, 9f., 22, 26f., 29, 32f., 43, 68, 74, 79, 95, 101, 105f., 108, 111, 117-19, 121, 127, 129, 132, 136, 142f., 144-7, 150, 152f., 165, 167, 170
'abar, Hiph'il, 158f.
'Abarîm, mts. of, 114
Abel-shittim, 115
Abihu, 43
Abiram, 142-6, 170
Abraham, 28, 116
Abronah, 98
'adam, 11
'adh 'anah, 139
Ahaz, 101f., 159
'aḥôr, plur., 60
Aila, 89, 99
'Ain Hawwārah, 88f.
'Ain Hudherah, *see* 'Ain Khuḍrā
'Ain Kadeis, 96
'Ain Kadîs, 96-8, 100, 103-6, 111, 117, 149-51, 164
'Ain Khuḍrā, 94
'Ain Mūsā, 100
'Ain el-Qedeirat, 96f.
'Ain el-Weiba, 112
Almon-diblathaim, 113f.
'al-pî, 91
altar-law, 38, 53
Alush, 91
'amah, 18
Amalekites, 91f., 97, 99, 104, 132, 141, 169
Amaziah, 102
Amorites, 113f., 120, 141, 150f., 162, 170
Anakites, 110, 137f.
'anan, 133, 153
angel, guiding, 23f., 46, 57f.

'anî, 60
'Aqan, 75
'Aqabah, Gulf of, 72, 85f., 88-91, 94, 98, 101, 106f., 119
'Aqrabbim, 150f.
Ar, 114
'Arabah, 95, 100, 107, 113, 119, 164
Arabs, 64f., 99
'Arad, 104, 108f., 111f., 119
el-'Arîsh, 84; *see* Wady
ark, 48, 52, 59, 74, 93, 140, 147
Arnon, 113f., 117
'aṣal, 136
'athar, *'atharîm*, 108, 111
'Ayūn Mūsā, 88

Baal-berith, 41
Baal of Peor, 115
Baal-zephon, 81-4, 124
ba'ar, Hiph'il, 158
Balaam, oracles of, 115
Ballah, Lake, 78
Bamoth, 113f., 117
Bardawil, Lake, 83
Barnea, 104
Basemath, 65
Bashan, 40, 114, 120, 170
Beersheba, 81, 95, 98
behemah, 138
bekôr, 157f.
Beth-jeshimoth, 115
Beth-peor, 114-16
Book of Life, 49
Book of the Covenant, 44, 46
Book of the laws of God, 38
Book of the laws of Moses, 38
Book of the Wars of Yahweh, 114
Bozrah, Buseirah, 102

Index of Subjects

Cain, 65
Caleb, Calebites, 108-10, 137-40, 142
calendar, Hebrew, 31
Calf, Golden, 45, 48-51, 54, 57f., 122, 131-3, 146f., 150, 153, 161f., 171
Canaan, 112, 115, 120, 137, 139, 141f., 150, 170; pre-Israelite inhabitants of, 20, 58, 65, 138, 141, 162f.
Canaanites, 108f., 111, 141, 162
Casius, Mt., 83
centralization of worship, 54, 158, 160
Code of the Covenant, 30, 32-4
Code, Miscellaneous, 30, 34, 37
Code, Supplementary, 37-42, 44-7, 51, 55, 115, 118, 156-8, 166, 168, 170
Code, the Deuteronomic, 47, 118, 168
Crossing, sea of the, 81f., 84-7, 117, 121-5, 169
Cush, Cushan, Cushites, 64-6
Cushite woman, 64, 66, 68

Darb es-Sulṭān, 105, 107
Dathan, 142-6, 170
Debbet er-Ramleh, 90
Debir, 110
Decalogue, 22, 34, 37, 41f., 57, 169; Moral, 30, 32-5, 42, 44, 46f., 51-6, 73, 118, 168; Ritual, 30-2, 34-8, 42, 44-7, 51-6, 60, 73, 118, 156-9, 164, 168
desert, the great and terrible, 131, 164; speed of travel in, 78
Deuteronomic age, 161
"Deuteronomic" compositions by P, 46, 56, 162-6
Deuteronomy, Book of, 42f., 47, 55, 115, 118f., 163, 168, 171; secondary additions to, 164, 166
Dhībān, see Dibon-gad
$dibber\ b^e$, 68, 152
Dibon-gad, 113
divine names in Exodus, 20-4
Dophkah, 91
dramatic style, 79f., 122, 124

Ebal, Mt., 40f., 93
$'\bar{e}dah$, 90f., 95, 105, 116, 127, 136, 138

Edom, Edomites, 65, 72, 74-6, 98, 100-2, 105-10, 112f., 117, 120, 122, 150f., 165, 170
El-berith, 41
El-paran, 97
El Shaddai, 26
Elath, 89-91, 99, 102, 107
Eldad, 135f.
elders, the seventy, 22, 43; the seventy prophetic, 68, 134-6
Eleazar, son of Aaron, 74, 118f.
Eliezer, son of Moses, 60
Elijah, 43, 60, 73
Elim, 87-90, 117
$Elohim,\ ha\text{-}'elohim$, 20-4
Eloth, see Elath
$'emeq$, 141f.
En-mishpat, 97, 126, 151
En-rimmon, 98
ephod, 59
Erweis el-Ebeirig, 94
Esau, 65, 107
Eshcol, 142
Etham, 76, 80f., 88, 117
Ezekiel, 136, 165f.
Ezer, 75
Ezion-geber, 98, 107
Ezra, 171

Feinān, 112
festivals, the three annual, 35-7, 54, 158f.; Unleavened Bread, 80, 156f., 159f., 167, 171; Harvest, 31, 159; Ingathering, 31, 159f.
firstlings, 157-61, 171

Gad, 115
$gai',\ g\hat{e},\ g\hat{e}'a$, 103
Gerizim, Mt., 40-2, 93, 118, 160, 170
Gershom, 60
el-Gī, 101, 103
giants, 137, 142
Girgashites, 162
Glory of Yahweh, 57; see $keb\hat{o}d\ Yahweh$
Gog, 136
Goshen, 18, 77, 79, 81, 86
ha-Gudgod, 75, 98, 119

Index of Subjects

Hagar, 99
ḥagg ha-'asîph, 31
ḥagg ha-qaṣîr, 31
ḥagg shabû'ôth, 31
ḥakamîm, 10
Hamdan, 65
har, 142
harṭummîm, 10
Hashmonah, 98
Hazeroth, 66-8, 94f., 97, 105, 117
Hebron, 109-11, 137
Hermon, Mt., 112
Heshbon, Ḥesbān, 40, 114, 120, 170
Heshmon, 98
Hezekiah, 35, 50, 56, 159-62, 167-70
Hobab, 23, 62-8, 109, 170
ḥoq û-mishpaṭ, 38, 125
Hor, Mt., 105f., 108, 111f., 117-20, 151, 153, 170
Hor ha-Gidgad, 119
Horeb, 22, 37f., 46f., 60f., 69f., 72-6, 88, 91f., 97f., 104, 106, 117f., 126, 130f., 133-5, 147, 149f., 164f., 169
Hormah, 107, 111f., 165
Hoshea, 26
Hur, 43, 132

Ije-abarim, 112f., 117
incense, 145
inconsistencies of the tradition, 18, 77, 79f.
'îr, 67, 100, 149
Isaac, 116
'îsh, 11
Ishmael, Ishmaelite, 66, 99
Israel, 163, 167

Jacob, 116; house of, 163
Jebel el-Aqra', 83
Jebel Hārūn, 105f.
Jebel Mūsa, 72f., 76, 91, 94
Jebel Nebā, 114, 117
Jebel Serbal, 72f., 76, 91
Jericho, 113f., 116f.
Jeroboam I, 49f.
Jerusalem, 33, 41f., 47, 55, 118, 157, 160f., 167f.

Jeshimon, 113f.
Jeshurun, 26
Jethro, 22, 27, 60-4, 66, 69, 140, 165, 169
Joel, 136
Joktheel, 102
Joshua, 6, 38f., 41, 43, 47f., 59, 108-10, 116, 132, 138, 140, 142, 146, 166f., 170; laws of, 38f., 47
Josiah, 156, 161, 168, 171
Jotbah, see Yotbah
Judah, Judaeans, 95, 98, 101, 104, 109f., 114, 151
Judges, Book of, 3, 150
Jupiter Casius, 83

K Document, 19, 30, 93
Kadesh, 66f., 69f., 94-106, 111f., 117-21, 126f., 131, 137, 142, 144-6, 148-50, 153, 164f., 170; see 'Ain Kadīs
Kadesh-barnea, 97, 103f., 117, 119, 151, 164
Kain, 65
kalah, Pi 'el, 58
kebôd Yahweh, 23, 43, 60, 139
Kedesh-Naphtali, 104
Kenaz, 109f.
Kenite, Kenites, 63-9, 104, 108f., 120, 170
Kenizzite, 109f.
kethûbhîm, 135
Kh. Deleilat, 114
Kibroth-hattaavah, 92-4, 117, 121, 128, 131, 133f., 153, 169
kipper, 49
Korah, 143-8, 150f., 170

L Document, 19
law-book, revision of, 160-2, 168
lemas'êhem, 91
Levi, Levites, 45, 48, 59, 144-50
levite, levites, 144f., 147
Leviticus, Book of, 58
Libnah, 98
liphenê, 41
literary pattern, of the itinerary, 116f., 128, 134; of the laws, 34-6, 39; of

Index of Subjects

the Mosaic Tradition, 166; of the murmuring stories, 152f.; of the plague stories, 3-10, 12f.
locusts, 123
lûn, 125-7, 129f., 133f., 136, 148, 152f.

Magog, 136
malak, 24
man, 129
Manasseh, 115
manna, 90, 126-30, 133, 136
Manzaleh, Lake, 86
Ma'on, 99
Marah, 87-9, 117, 121, 125-7, 129, 169
el-Markha, 90
masa' ḥen, 60
Massah, 70, 93, 121, 125f., 130-3, 149, 153
massebôth, 44f.
Mattanah, 113f., 117
Medad, 135f.
mekashshephîm, 10
menûḥah, 93
Meribah, 70, 126, 130-2, 148-50
Midian, Midianites, 17, 27f., 60, 62-6, 68f., 72, 74, 76, 91f., 103, 118f., 164f.
Migdol, 81f.
miqneh, 11, 13
Miriam, 64, 68f., 85, 95, 105, 148
mishpaṭîm, 36, 38f., 44f.
miṣwah, 43
Moab, 40, 107f., 112-17, 120, 168
môphēth, 11, 19
Moserah, 74, 98, 106, 118f.
Moseroth, 119
Moses, birth of, 17, 28; call of, 19, 21f., 25-7, 169; death of, 114-17, 166, 170; rod of, 4, 9f., 19, 27, 123f., 132; second marriage of, 64-9, 170; sin of, 139f., 142, 150; sons of, 19, 60; uniqueness of, as a prophet, 68f.
Muhammad, 66, 144
Murmurings, the Ten, 121-54, 167, 169

Nabataeans, 67, 99f., 102-4
Nadab, 43, 118f.

Nahaliel, 113f., 117
Nahshon ben Amminadab, 109
nasa', 85, 116
Nebaioth, 65, 99
Nebo, Mt., 114, 116f.
Negeb, 91, 95, 98-100, 103-5, 108-12, 119, 137, 141f.
Nekhl, 90
Nephilim, 138
nissah, 125f., 129f., 152

Oboth, 112, 117
'ôlôth, 40f., 44f.
omer, 128
On, son of Peleth, 144
order to depart, 57f., 60f., 169
Othniel, 110

P, anti-foreign spirit of, 61, 63, 109f., 140, 165; editorial habits of, 27f., 62, 68, 85; harmonization of the traditions by, 55, 59, 63, 119, 168, 171; scholarly notes of, 90, 94, 112-14, 116f., 124, 137f.; use of archaisms, 26, 128
P Document, theory of, 168f., 171
Paran, desert of, 70, 93, 95, 98f., 104f., 142, 149
Paran, Mt., 99
Passover, 11, 155-7, 159f., 167, 170
Pelusium, 82, 84
pereḳ, 16
Perez, 98
Perizzites, 162
peṭer reḥem, 158
Petra, 67, 99-106, 112, 120, 150, 164
Philistines, 101, 167; road to the land of, 81f., 84-6, 90
Phinehas, 103
pilgrimages, 71, 104, 149
pillar of cloud and fire, 23, 68
Pi-hahiroth, 81f., 84, 86, 117, 124
Pinon, *see* Punon
Pithom, 79
Pi-Ra'messe, 76f.
Pisgah, 113-17, 170
Plagues, Story of, 3-15, 122-4, 167, 169

Index of Subjects

priesthood, institution of Hebrew, 48, 74f., 144-8, 170; Jerusalemite, 41f., 118, 155f., 160, 168; Samaritan, 41, 118, 162
Punon, 112

qadash, 150, 158
qāhāl, 129
qahal, Niph'al, 145, 147f., 152
qain, 65f.
Qantīr, 77f.
qēn, qēnî, 66
quails, 94, 128, 130, 134, 136

ar-Rafīd, 91
Rameses, 76-9, 84, 117
Rameses II, 77
Rd, theory of an, 51, 155-62
Rechabites, 67
Red Sea, 87, 109, 112, 122, 140, 142; road to, 108, 112
rega', 58
Rephidim, 22, 91f., 130-2, 149f., 153, 169
Reqem, 103
Reuben, Reubenites, 115, 143
Reuel, 27, 62-7
Rezin, 101
rîbh, 130, 148
Rimmon-perez, 98
rod, magic, see Moses

Sabbath, law of, 33, 35, 54
Sabbatical year for the land, 36, 53
Samaria, Samaritans, 40f., 48, 160
Samuel, 47
sanctuaries, plurality of, 157, 159f.
Sanhedrin, 135, 146
Sarai, 26
sarîm, 60, 134
segullah, 163
Seir, 75, 106f., 112, 118, 164
Sela', 67, 101f., 150f.
Serbonis, Lake, 83-7
sĕ'th, 31
shahat, 31
Shaubak, 101
Shechem, Shechemites, 38, 40-2, 55, 160

shelamîm, 40, 44f.
shephelah, 142
Shiloh, 41f.
shiphhah, 18
Shittim, 115
shôfetîm, 3
shôterîm, 134f.
Shur, desert of, 87f.
Simeon, 109
Sin, desert of, 90-2, 117, 121, 127, 169
Sinai, desert of, 92f.; Mt., 32, 43f., 51, 53f., 61, 67, 69-74, 76, 90-3, 103, 115, 117, 119, 126, 129, 135, 147, 164; peninsula of, 71f., 74-6, 91-4, 99, 107f., 112, 119f., 128
singers, guild of, 145
sir'ah, 46
spies, 95, 109, 122, 137-9, 141f., 164f., 170
Succoth, 76, 78, 80, 117
Suez, Gulf of, 86
sur, 150

et-Tāba, 119
Taberah, 92-4, 97, 117, 121, 131-4, 153, 169
Tahpanhes, 83
Talmud, 103, 111, 122
Tanis, 77-9, 81, 84
taph, 140
Targum, 103, 111
Tell el-Maskhuteh, 80
Teman, 99, 101
Tent of Meeting, 6, 48, 52, 57-61, 145f., 169
teqûphath, 31
Thel, see Zilu
theophany, 51, 53, 56, 60, 149, 163
et-Tīh, 90, 99, 164
Timsah, Lake, 78, 80, 86
Tor, 89
tôrah, 43
Transjordan, 99, 103f., 114f., 164
tûr, 93, 137f.

Umm el-Biyāra, 101
Urim and Tummim, see ephod

Wady el-'Arīsh, 90, 95; Feiran, 91; Gharandel, 89f.; el-Ḥesā, 113; Mūsa, 100; Refayid, 91; Tumilat, 79-81, 86; Werdān, 88; Zered, 107, 112f., 117
water-miracle story, 105, 149
weeping of the Israelites, 134, 153
well, desert, 113f., 117
wilderness, *see* desert

Ya'aqan, Bene, 74f., 98, 117-19
Yahweh, 20-6; as guide, 61; mountain of, 93; revelation of the name, 26, 69
Yahwism, origin of, 69
ha-yam, 81, 84f., 87
yam sôph, 86f.

yam sûph, 85-7, 89, 106, 112, 117
Yoqthe'el, 102
Yotbah, 59, 75, 98, 119

zabaḥ, 31
Zalmonah, 112
Zaru, *see* Zilu
zebaḥîm, zebaḥîm shelamîm, 41, 44f.
Zephath, 111
Zeus Casius, 83
Zilu, 78, 81
Zin, desert of, 95, 97, 99, 104f.
Zipporah, 19, 27, 60, 64, 66
Zoan, 77, 79, 84

Index of Authors

Abel, F. M., 77, 82, 101, 103, 112, 119
Addis, W. E., 164ff.
Albright, W. F., 31, 77f., 83, 115
Arnold, W. R., 93
Baentsch, B., 32
Barton, G. A., 69
Berry, G. R., 36
Binns, L. E., 8, 64, 68, 98, 122, 135f., 139, 143f., 148, 151
Bourdon, 82, 88f.
Brightman, E. S., 8
Brugsch, 84
Burkitt, F. C., 100
Burney, C. F., 74
Carpenter, J. E., 121, 163
Chadwick, H. M. and N. K., 167
Charles, R. H., 32, 34
Cook, S. A., 50, 70, 108f., 126, 129, 131, 133, 135, 149
Currelly, C. T., 72
Daressy, 82
Dhorme, É., 83
Driver, S. R., 34, 72, 75, 88f., 116, 125, 127, 141, 161
Eissfeldt, O., 19, 83
Gardiner, A. H., 77ff., 82, 84
Glueck, N., 65, 74, 100ff., 112
Gray, G. B., 68, 94, 99, 113f., 122, 135f., 138, 143f., 151
Green, W. H., 4
Gressmann, H., 18
Hall, H. R., 84
Harford-Battersby, 121, 163
Irwin, W. A., 25, 192
Jarvis, C. S., 84, 87, 96, 128
Josephus, 101, 105, 135, 145
Jülicher, 16
Kittel, R., 8
Kuenen, A., 5, 40, 160
Lawrence, T. E., 96
Lods, A., 26, 30, 34, 79, 126
Lucas, A., 78, 85f., 90, 94
McNeile, A. H., 8, 11, 18f., 34, 68, 72, 74, 85, 88f., 123, 125, 127, 130, 132, 155, 163
Meek, T. J., 30, 69f., 108, 173
Montet, P., 77
Montgomery, J. A., 86f.
Morgenstern, J., 19, 23, 30f., 35ff., 43, 60ff., 69, 83, 93
Musil, A., 72, 74, 78, 89ff., 95f., 99ff., 107
Naville, E., 26
Nielsen, D., 103
Olmstead, A. T., 96
Palmer, E. H., 72, 78, 88f., 91, 94, 96, 99, 108
Peet, T. E., 79, 83f.
Petrie, Flinders, 72, 88f.
Pfeiffer, R. H., 18, 31f., 38, 45, 50, 52, 54, 68, 73, 163
Phythian-Adams, W. J., 72ff., 89, 100, 103
Rad, von, 126
Robertson, E., 34, 39, 42, 47
Robinson, G. L., 96
Robinson, T. H., 45, 69, 108
Rowley, H. H., 108
Rudolph, W., 5f., 8, 16, 18f., 24, 32, 51, 68, 85, 93, 127f., 130, 135, 151
Schaeffer, F. A., 83
Siebens, A., 42
Simpson, C. A., 12, 108, 126
Skinner, J., 99, 159
Smend, 3
Toynbee, A. J., 17
Trumbull, H. C., 78, 84f., 94, 96, 99f., 103, 106, 108, 150, 164
Welch, A. C., 47, 107
Wellhausen, J., 126
Wiener, H. M., 4, 6
Winckler, 72
Wolfe, R. E., 6
Woolley, C. L., 96
Wright, G. E., 86, 88f., 91, 105, 107, 114

Index of Scriptural Passages

Genesis

1 : 22	16		21 : 21	99
2 : 1-3	33		25 : 1-4	64
4	65		25 : 12-18	99
4 : 26	25		25 : 18	88
6 : 8	60		28 : 13	26
10 : 6f.	64		36 : 4, 10, 13, 17	65-7
10 : 21-31	28		36 : 11	109
12	64		36 : 27	75
14	97		36 : 31-9	102
14 : 7	126, 151		36 : 41	112
15 : 19	65		47 : 11	79
15 : 19-21	162		49 : 3f.	143
16 : 14	97		50 : 25	23

Exodus

1-2	18, 20, 27		7 : 22	6, 13
1 : 1-22	16f., 27		7 : 23-5	13
2 : 1-22	17f.		7 : 26f. (EV 8 : 1f.)	4
2 : 16	63		8 : 1, 8, 12, 16f., 21, 26 (EV 8 : 5,	
2 : 18	27, 63		12, 16, 20f., 25, 30)	4f.
2 : 21	19, 64		8 : 11 (EV 8 : 12)	4
2 : 23-5	18f., 26-8		8 : 15 (EV 8 : 19)	6, 23
3 : 1	27, 72, 74		8 : 18 (EV 8 : 22)	77
3 : 1-22	19-21, 24-7, 169		8 : 27 (EV 8 : 31)	126
3 : 8b	155, 162		8 : 28 (EV 8 : 32)	7
3 : 17	58, 155, 162		9 : 1-3	4
3 : 18	5, 27, 126		9 : 6	4, 11, 13
3 : 20-2	27, 77, 80		9 : 7	7
4 : 1-18	19, 26-8, 169		9 : 8	4
4 : 13-16	6		9 : 9	11
4 : 19f.	18f., 21, 26-8		9 : 10	4, 11
4 : 21-3	11, 19, 28, 122		9 : 12	7
4 : 24-6	19, 27		9 : 13f.	4
4 : 27-31	6, 19, 21, 27f., 169		9 : 13-35	10
5 : 1—6 : 1	169		9 : 18	128
5	28f., 79		9 : 19-25	4, 11, 13f.
5 : 1-4	5, 28f., 126		9 : 26	77
5 : 9, 13	128		9 : 27	5
5 : 20	29		9 : 28, 30	23
6 : 1—7 : 13	29		9 : 31f.	14
6 : 3	25, 69		9 : 33	5
6 : 16ff.	144		9 : 34	13
7 : 1-13	10		9 : 35	7, 13
7 : 7	18		10 : 1-6	4, 5, 155
7 : 8—11 : 10	5		10 : 12f.	4, 123
7 : 9	11		10 : 16, 18	5
7 : 14—11 : 8b	169		10 : 19	86
7 : 14-22	4, 9		10 : 20	7

Index of Scriptural Passages

10 : 21f.	4
10 : 23	77
10 : 27-9	7, 11f.
11 : 1	4
11 : 1-10	11f.
11 : 2f.	77
11 : 8	80
11 : 10	7, 122
12 : 1-14	155
12 : 1-20	11, 170
12 : 13, 15-20	157
12 : 21-8	12, 77, 155f., 159-61, 170
12 : 29-39	12, 169
12 : 33f.	80, 157
12 : 35f.	77, 79f.
12 : 37	76, 85, 92
12 : 39	76, 80
12 : 42-9	157, 159
13 : 2	158
13 : 3-10	157, 171
13 : 3	80, 155
13 : 5	155, 162
13 : 8f., 14-16	80, 155, 160f.
13 : 11-16	157-9, 171
13 : 17	82, 84-6
13 : 17-22	169
13 : 18	23, 80, 85f., 89
13 : 19	23
13 : 20	76, 85, 88, 92
14 : 1-31	123-5, 169
14 : 1, 2, 5, 9	80-5, 124
14 : 10-12	121-3, 153
14 : 16	4, 85
14 : 19	23f.
14 : 21-3	85
14 : 26-30	4, 85
14 : 31	155
15 : 1	85
15 : 2-18	85, 87
15 : 19-21	85
15 : 20	68
15 : 22	85, 87f., 125-7, 169
15 : 23	87f., 122, 125-7, 169
15 : 24	121, 125-7, 138, 153f., 169
15 : 25	129
15 : 26	155
15 : 27	88f.
16	127-30, 169
16 : 1	73, 85, 90, 116, 129
16 : 2-4	121f., 126f., 153
16 : 4	126
16 : 20, 27	122
16 : 23	136
16 : 28	139
17	93, 149f., 169
17 : 1	85, 91, 116
17 : 1-3	149
17 : 1-7	130-2
17 : 2f.	121f., 154
17 : 5	153
17 : 6	92
17 : 7	138
17 : 8-16	132
17 : 9	21
17 : 15f.	138
18	60-3, 69, 134f., 165, 169
18 : 1	21f., 27
18 : 3f.	19
18 : 5	21
18 : 12	22
18 : 15	21
18 : 17	62
18 : 18	135
18 : 19, 21	20-2
18 : 22	135
18 : 23	22
18 : 24, 27	62
19-23	32
19	51, 56, 60, 169
19 : 1	61, 73, 92
19 : 2	22, 61, 73, 85, 92
19 : 3-9	21f., 155, 163f.
19 : 10-13	11, 33, 73f.
19 : 15-17	22
19 : 18	22, 73f.
19 : 19	22, 33, 37, 46f.
19 : 20-5	32f., 73
19 : 20—20 : 17	33, 47
20	73, 169
20 : 1-17	22, 30, 32
20 : 2f.	54
20 : 8-11, 18	33
20 : 18-21	22
20 : 23	35
20 : 23—23 : 19	22, 33f.
20 : 23-6—23 : 10-19	30-2, 34-6, 46f., 50-5
20 : 24	45
20 : 24-6	35, 38
21 : 1	44
21 : 1—23 : 9	30, 34, 36-40, 42, 168
21 : 1—22 : 19 (EV 22 : 20)	38, 47
21 : 6	21
22 : 8	20f.
22 : 8f. (EV 22 : 9f.)	34
22 : 18—23 : 9	34
22 : 20 (EV 22 : 21)—23 : 9	38f., 47, 115, 170
22 : 21f., 24 (EV 22 : 22f., 25)	155
22 : 28f. (EV 22 : 29f.)	157, 171
23 : 9	155
23 : 10-19	35-6, 54, 169
23 : 13	155
23 : 14-17	54, 156

216 Index of Scriptural Passages

Reference	Pages	Reference	Pages
23 : 15	157, 171	33 : 1-6	57f.
23 : 16	31, 159	33 : 1-3	136
23 : 17	54	33 : 1	61, 169
23 : 18	31, 156	33 : 2	155, 162
23 : 20-33	24, 43, 46, 155	33 : 7-11	57-61, 169
23 : 23, 28	162	33 : 12-23	51, 57, 60f.
23 : 31	86	33 : 12f.	136
24	33, 43-7, 52, 169	34	47, 50, 73
24 : 1f	22, 135	34 : 1-13	54, 56, 60, 73, 149
24 : 3	163	34 : 1f., 4	51, 53f., 73f., 155, 171
24 : 9	135	34 : 6f.	139
24 : 10f.	22	34 : 8-18	53
24 : 12f.	21f.	34 : 9	60
24 : 16	73	34 : 10-14	51, 155, 162-4
25-31	48, 52, 59	34 : 14-26	30-2, 35-7, 50-4, 60, 164
31 : 18	24, 44, 52, 73, 169	34 : 19f.	158
32	45, 48, 50	34 : 24f.	155f.
32 : 1-24	48f., 161f., 168, 171	34 : 27f.	46, 50f., 53f., 60f., 155, 171
32 : 7-14	155	34 : 29, 32	50, 53, 73
32 : 10, 12	139	34 : 34f.	60
32 : 16	24	35-40	58f.
32 : 25-9	48f., 146f., 150		
32 : 30-5	57		
33	50		

Leviticus

Reference	Pages	Reference	Pages
8 : 22-30	44	13 : 4	68

Numbers

Reference	Pages	Reference	Pages
1—10 : 28	58	16 : 21	58
10 : 4	109	17	146-8
10 : 11	85	17 : 6, 10	121
10 : 11-13	92f.	17 : 7, 20, 25	153
10 : 29-36	61-3, 67, 85, 93, 164, 169	18	147
11	68, 128f., 133-6, 153, 169	18 : 15-18	158, 171
11 : 1-3	93, 121, 132f., 138, 169	20	100f., 105, 126
		20 : 1	95, 99, 105, 116
11 : 4-34	60, 68, 93, 121f., 128, 133-6, 138	20 : 1-13	148-51
		20 : 2	153
11 : 35	85, 94, 170	20 : 2-5	121
12	64, 66-8	20 : 12	140
12 : 1	152	20 : 13	131
12 : 7f.	116, 152	20 : 14-22	105, 165, 170
12 : 16	85, 95, 105, 148f., 164, 170	20 : 16	24, 67, 100f., 149
		20 : 20f.	113
13	95, 98f., 109, 137f., 141f., 170	20 : 22	85, 105
		20 : 22-4	170
14	136-42, 170	20 : 23:9	108
14 : 1-4	121, 142, 153	21 : 1-3	108-12, 119, 165
14 : 22	121f., 152	21 : 4-9	85f., 106-8, 112-14, 122, 151f., 165, 170
14 : 25	86, 140, 142	21 : 10-13	85
14 : 40ff.	110f.	21 : 10-20	112-14, 116, 170
16	68, 142-8, 170	21 : 21-35	40, 45, 114, 170
16 : 1-3, 12-14	121	22—24	115
16 : 3	153	22 : 1	85, 113-15
16 : 11	121, 153	23 : 7, 10, 21, 23	163
16 : 12-14	121	23 : 13f., 28	115

Index of Scriptural Passages

24 : 5, 17-19	163	33 : 12-14		91
24 : 21f.	66f.	33 : 16-36		97-9, 133
25 : 1-5	115	33 : 32		119
26 : 10	145	33 : 40ff.		111-15, 165
27 : 14	99	34 : 3		99f.
31 : 12	115	34 : 3-5		95
32	115	34 : 4		151
33	71, 94, 117	34 : 7		111
33 : 3	80	35 : 1		115
33 : 8-10	85, 87f.	36 : 13		115

Deuteronomy

1	61, 134f.	9 : 25-9	52, 161
1 : 1-5	164	9 : 28	139
1 : 1—4 : 43	94, 106, 141, 164-6	10	73
1 : 2	72, 97, 164	10 : 1-5	46, 52-4, 73, 75
1 : 5	46	10 : 6f.	52, 59, 74f., 97f., 106, 119, 131, 165
1 : 6	72	10 : 8f.	52, 59, 75, 131, 146f.
1 : 6-8	58, 60	10 : 11	49, 57f.
1 : 7	141	11 : 1f.	161
1 : 9	135	11 : 4	87
1 : 9-18	60	11 : 6	143
1 : 12	135	11 : 13-28	46, 161
1 : 15	40, 134	11 : 29	40
1 : 16-18	165	12-26	40, 42, 168
1 : 19	60, 72, 164	14 : 2	103
1 : 20f.	137, 141f.	15 : 19-23	158
1 : 20-46	137-42	16 : 1-8	156f.
1 : 27	141	16 : 10	31
1 : 40	86	16 : 16	31, 36
1 : 44	164	17 : 9, 18	59
2	106, 113	18 : 1	59
2 : 1	86, 106	18 : 16	72
2 : 1-8	165	20 : 17	141, 162
2 : 8	89, 107	24 : 8	59
2 : 13	107	24 : 9	68
2 : 14	106	26 : 18f.	163
4 : 10, 15	72	27-34	166
4 : 46-9	40, 114f.	27-28	45, 93
4 : 44—26 : 19	168, 171	27 : 1-8	40, 45, 116, 166, 170
5 : 2	72	27 : 14	40
5 : 6-22	33f.	28	46
6 : 7f.	161	28 : 9	163
6 : 16	130	28 : 69 (EV 29 : 1)	73
6 : 20f.	161	29 : 1	45
7	46	31 : 14f., 23	116, 166, 170
7 : 1-6	141, 162-4	32	163
8 : 2f., 16	125, 127f., 152	32 : 10f.	163
9	50	32 : 51	99
9 : 7	122, 152	33 : 2	73f., 76
9 : 8	72	33 : 8	130, 149
9 : 8-29	48f.	33 : 10, 28	163
9 : 12-14	139, 161	34 : 1-6	114, 116, 166, 170
9 : 22-4	130-3	34 : 10	116
9 : 23	104		

Index of Scriptural Passages

Joshua

2:10	87	14:6, 14	109
3:10	162	15:1-4	95, 99f., 151
4:23	87	15:13-19	109
8:30ff.	41, 45	15:13f.	137
8:31	38	15:21-9, 42	98, 100
10:29	98	18:3	139
10:36-9	110	24:6	87
11:17	100	24:11	162
11:21	110	24:25f.	38, 125
12:7	100		

Judges

1:1—2:5	150	4:11	63
1:10-20	109	5:3-5	73f., 76
1:16	63, 104	8:33	41
1:17	111	9:4, 46	41
1:19, 34	142	11:16	86, 89
1:36	150f.	11:17f.	113
2:4	153	21:19	160

I Samuel

1:3, 21	160	15:7	88
2:19	160	25:1	99
10:8	45	27:8	88
15:6	63, 104	30:29	67

I Kings

7:25	60	12:32	160
8:63	45	18:43f.	43
8:65	160	19	60
9:26	86, 89	19:3	43
11:18	99	19:8	73
12:28	49		

II Kings

14:7	101	16:6	89, 101
14:22	89	18:9f., 22	160
16:3	159	23:21	46

Isaiah

29:1	160	33:20	160
32:9ff.	160		

Jeremiah

35:6	67	46:14	82
44:1	82	49:7, 20f.	86

Ezekiel

8:16	60	29:10	82
11:19f.	136	30:6	82
20	139	42:6	136
25:13	99	45:25	160

Hosea

2:13 (EV 2:11)	160	9:10	115
5:2	115	12:10 (EV 12:9)	160

Index of Scriptural Passages

Joel
3 : 1f. (EV 2 : 28f.) 136

Amos
1 : 12 99
5 : 21 160
8 : 10 160

Habakkuk
2 : 14 139
3 : 3 99
3 : 7 65

Zechariah
14 : 16-19 160

Malachi
3 : 22 (EV 4 : 4) 73

Psalms
42-9 145
50 : 20 152
68 : 8, 17 73
72 : 19 139
78 : 12, 43 . . . . . . 79, 84
78 : 19 152
106 : 7 122
106 : 9 87
106 : 19 73
136 : 13, 15 87

Proverbs
7 : 14 45

Job
18 : 18 152

Lamentations
3 : 39 133

I Chronicles
1 : 42 75
1 : 52 112
2 : 55 . . . . 65, 67
4 : 41 136
6 : 54-7 110

II Chronicles
4 : 4 60
5 : 10 73
8 : 17 89
26 : 2 89
28 : 3 . . . . 158f.
28 : 16ff. 101
29-32 159
30 . . . . 156, 159f.
30 : 22 45
33 : 16 45

Ezra
9-10 61

Nehemiah
9 : 9 87
9 : 13 73
12 : 22 136
13 : 23ff. 61

John
4 : 20 42

www.ingramcontent.com/pod-product-compliance
Lightning Source LLC
Chambersburg PA
CBHW020406080526
44584CB00014B/1201